W9-CMT-948

JOHN CONSTANTINE HELLBLAZER

ALL HIS ENGINES

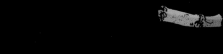

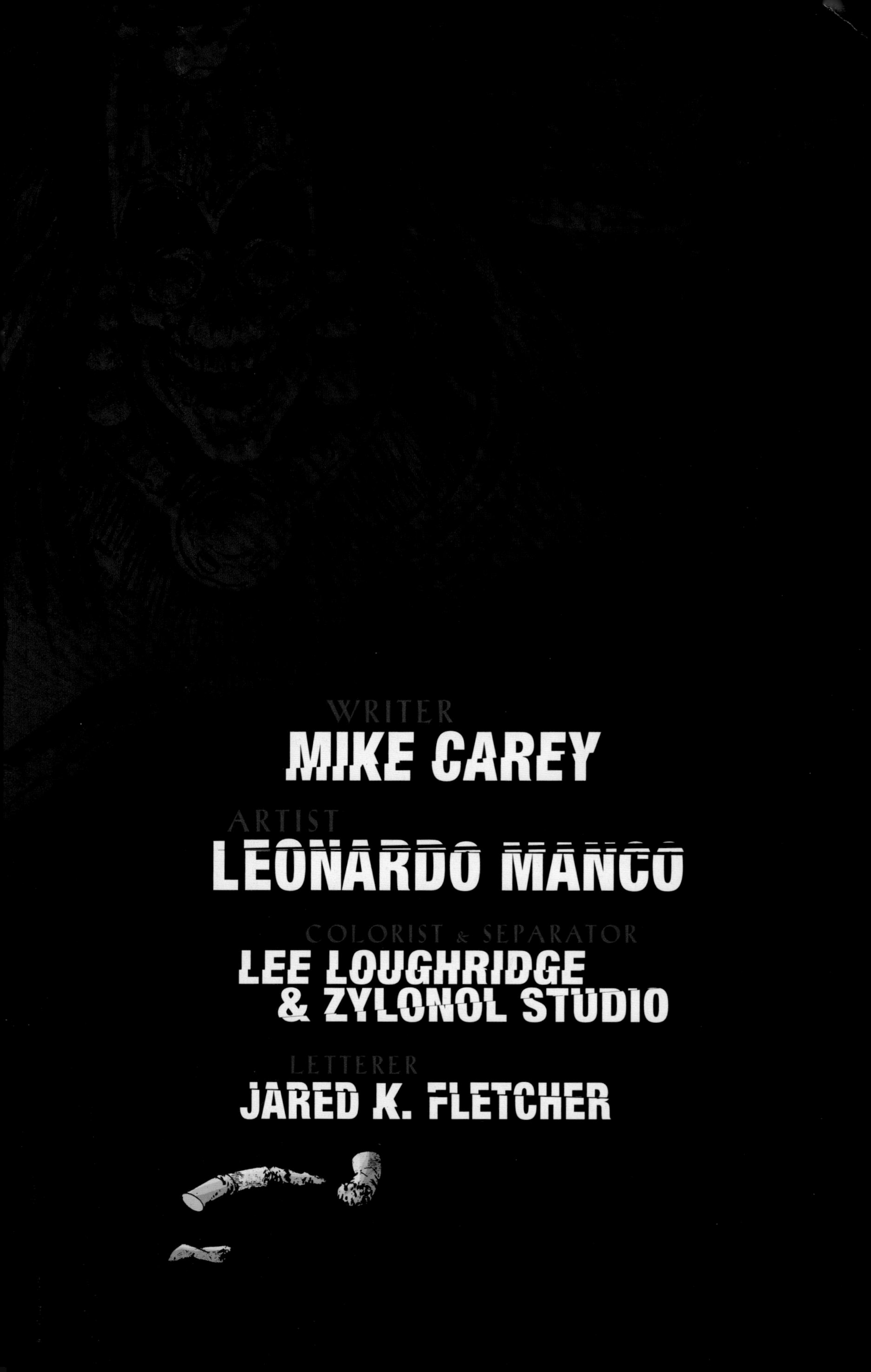

WRITER
MIKE CAREY

ARTIST
LEONARDO MANCO

COLORIST & SEPARATOR
LEE LOUGHRIDGE
& ZYLONOL STUDIO

LETTERER
JARED K. FLETCHER

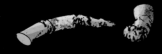

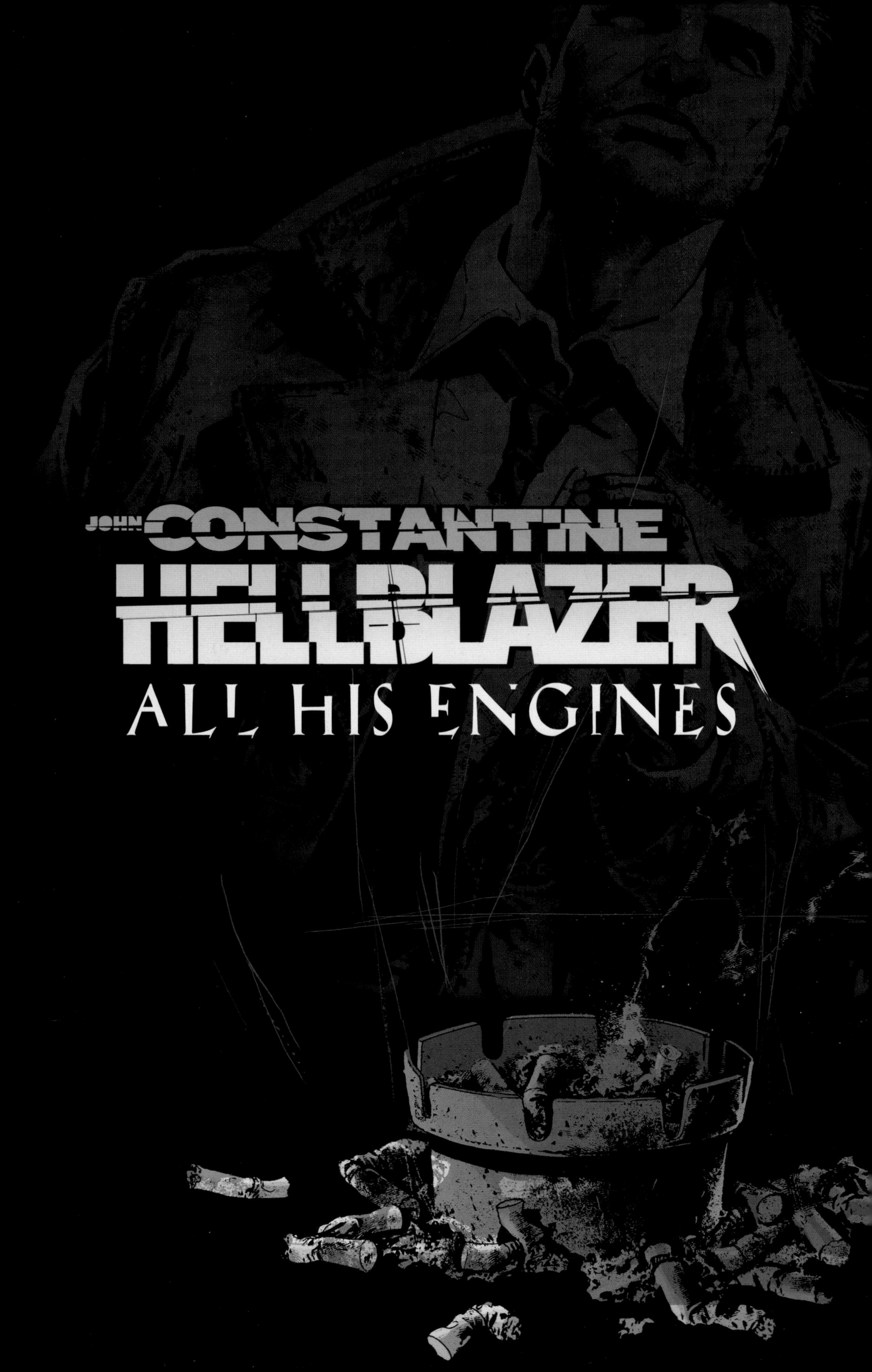
JOHN CONSTANTINE
HELLBLAZER
ALL HIS ENGINES

Karen Berger
VP-EXECUTIVE EDITOR

Will Dennis
EDITOR

Casey Seijas
ASSISTANT EDITOR

Amie Brockway-Metcalf
ART DIRECTOR

Paul Levitz
PRESIDENT & PUBLISHER

Georg Brewer
VP-DESIGN & RETAIL PRODUCT DEVELOPMENT

Richard Bruning
SENIOR VP-CREATIVE DIRECTOR

Patrick Caldon
SENIOR VP-FINANCE & OPERATIONS

Chris Caramalis
VP-FINANCE

Terri Cunningham
VP-MANAGING EDITOR

Dan DiDio
VP-EDITORIAL

Alison Gill
VP-MANUFACTURING

Rich Johnson
VP-BOOK TRADE SALES

Hank Kanalz
VP-GENERAL MANAGER, WILDSTORM

Lillian Laserson
SENIOR VP & GENERAL COUNSEL

Jim Lee
EDITORIAL DIRECTOR-WILDSTORM

David McKillips
VP-ADVERTISING & CUSTOM PUBLISHING

John Nee
VP-BUSINESS DEVELOPMENT

Gregory Noveck
SENIOR VP-CREATIVE AFFAIRS

Cheryl Rubin
SENIOR VP-BRAND MANAGEMENT

Bob Wayne
VP-SALES & MARKETING

DC Comics
1700 Broadway
New York, NY 10019

A Warner Bros. Entertainment Company

Printed in Canada
First Printing

HC ISBN — 1-4012-0316-7
SC ISBN — 1-4012-0317-5

Cover art by LEONARDO MANCO
Cover color by LEE LOUGHRIDGE

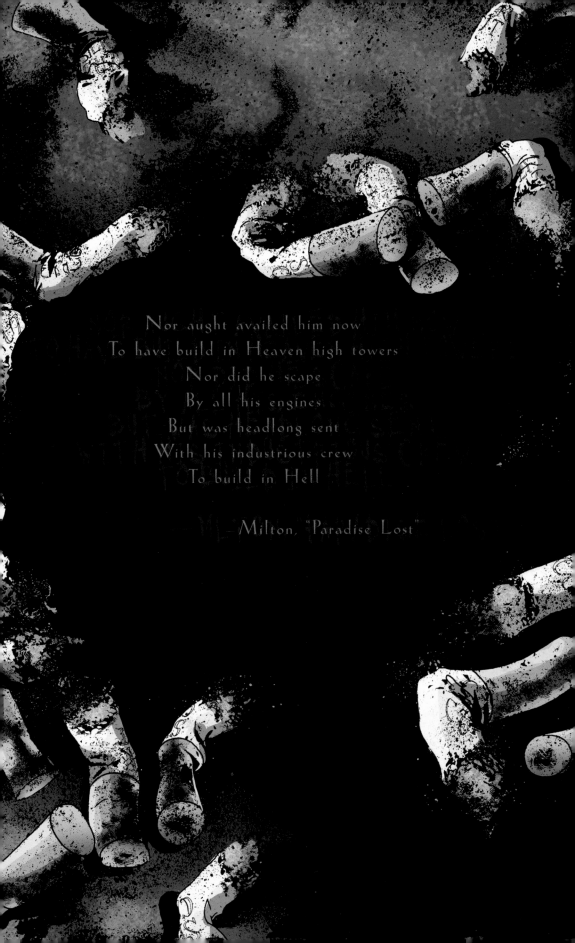

Nor aught availed him now
To have build in Heaven high towers
Nor did he scape
By all his engines
But was headlong sent
With his industrious crew
To build in Hell

—Milton, "Paradise Lost"

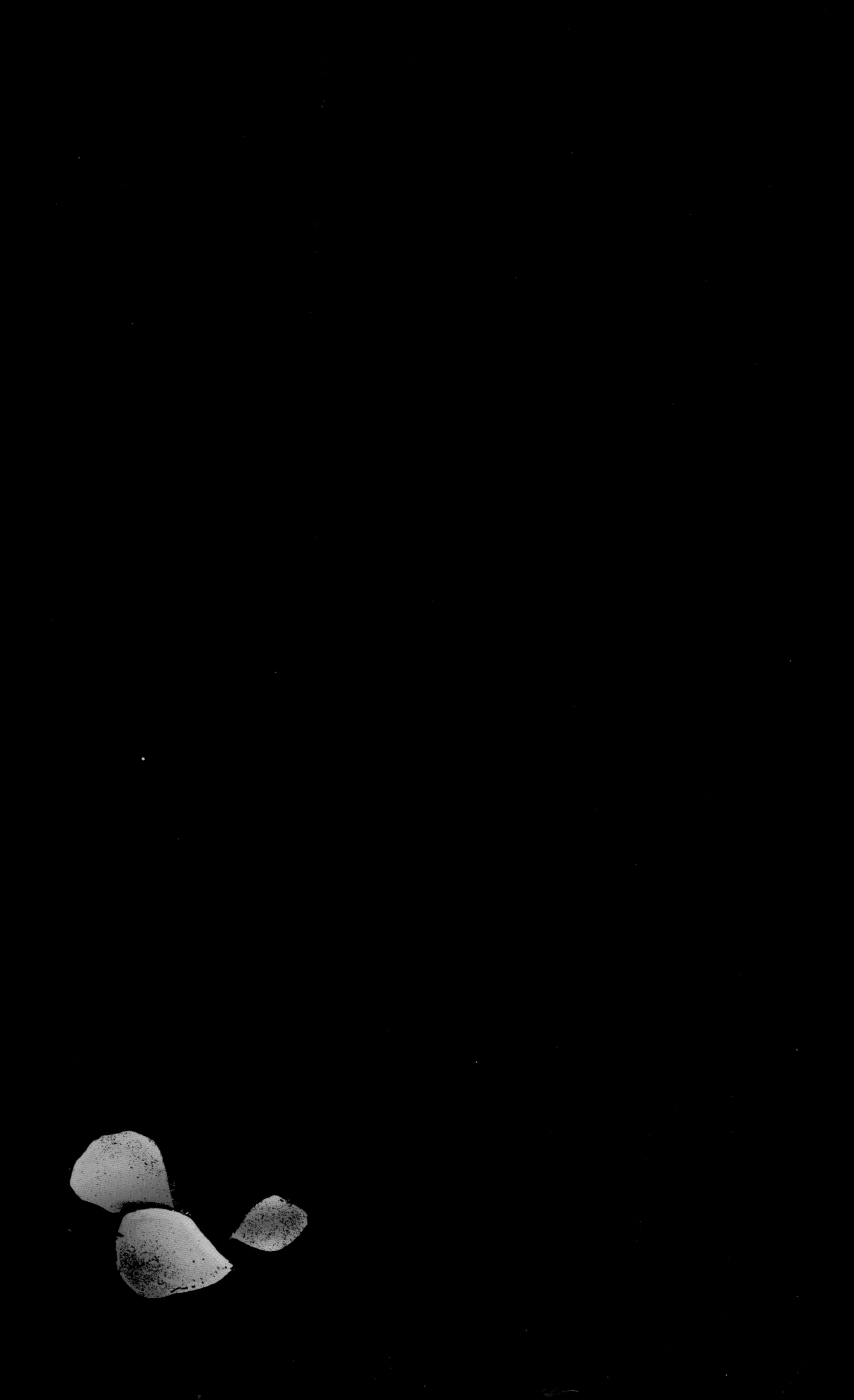

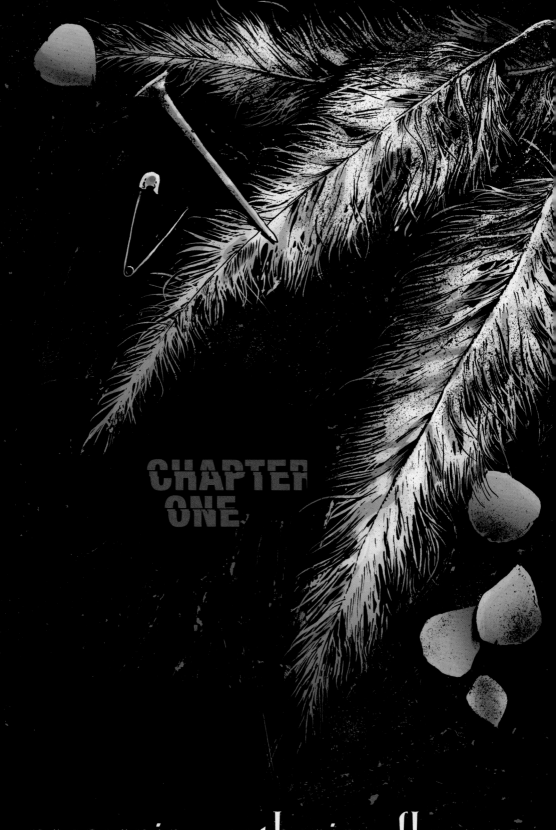

CHAPTER ONE

proserpine gathering flowers

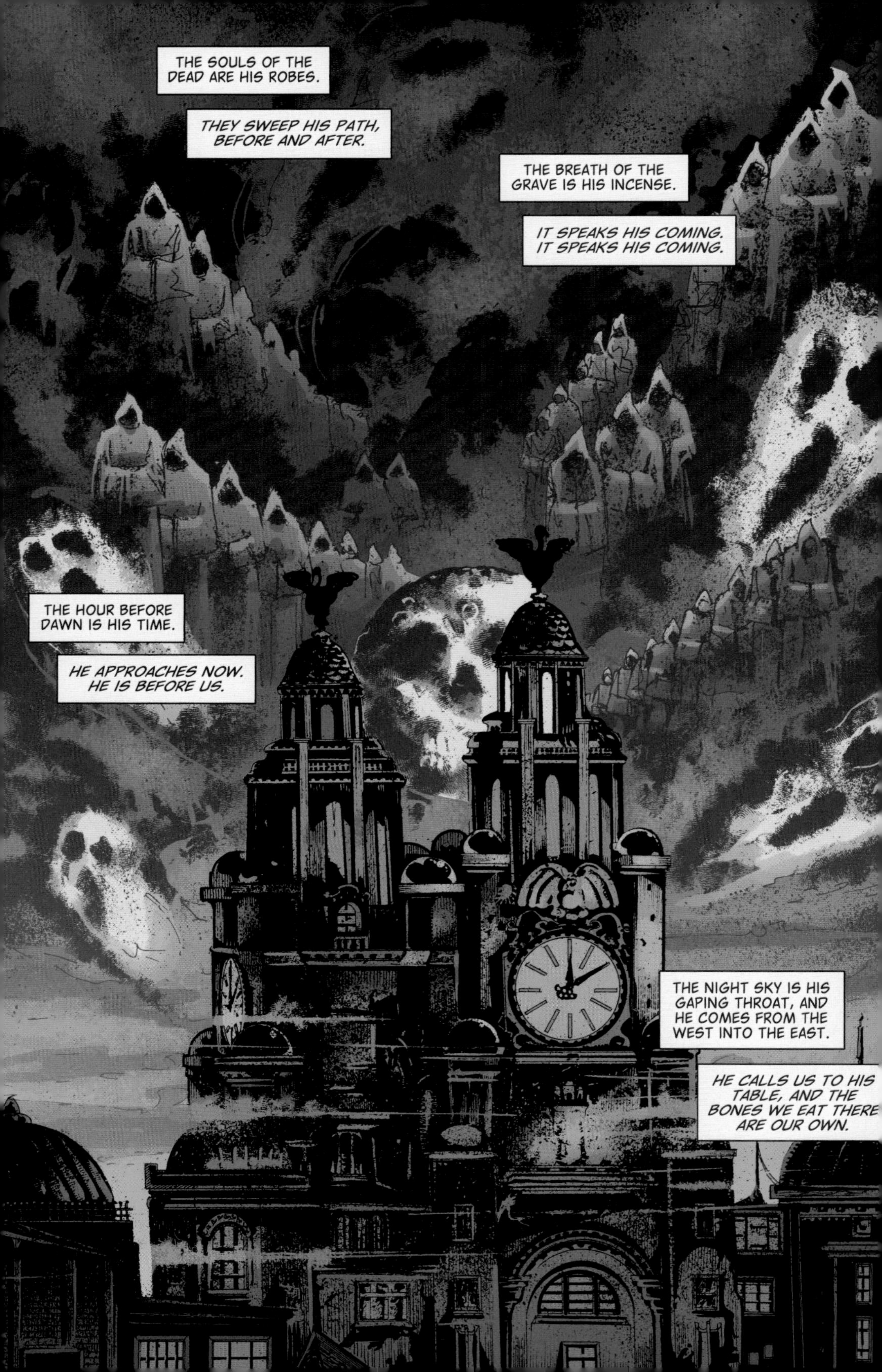
THE SOULS OF THE DEAD ARE HIS ROBES.
THEY SWEEP HIS PATH, BEFORE AND AFTER.
THE BREATH OF THE GRAVE IS HIS INCENSE.
IT SPEAKS HIS COMING. IT SPEAKS HIS COMING.
THE HOUR BEFORE DAWN IS HIS TIME.
HE APPROACHES NOW. HE IS BEFORE US.
THE NIGHT SKY IS HIS GAPING THROAT, AND HE COMES FROM THE WEST INTO THE EAST.
HE CALLS US TO HIS TABLE, AND THE BONES WE EAT THERE ARE OUR OWN.

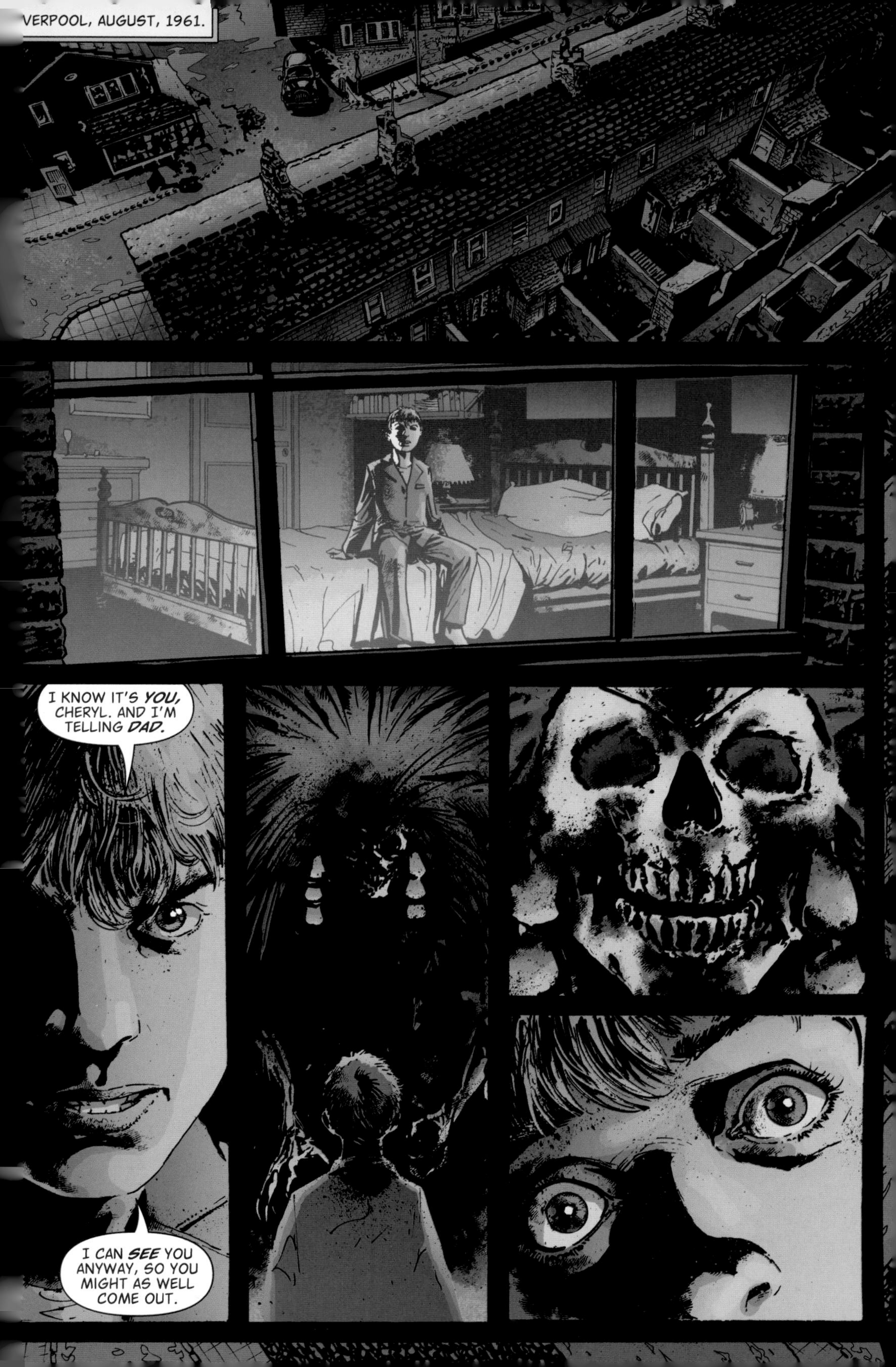
VERPOOL, AUGUST, 1961.
I KNOW IT'S YOU, CHERYL. AND I'M TELLING DAD.
I CAN SEE YOU ANYWAY, SO YOU MIGHT AS WELL COME OUT.

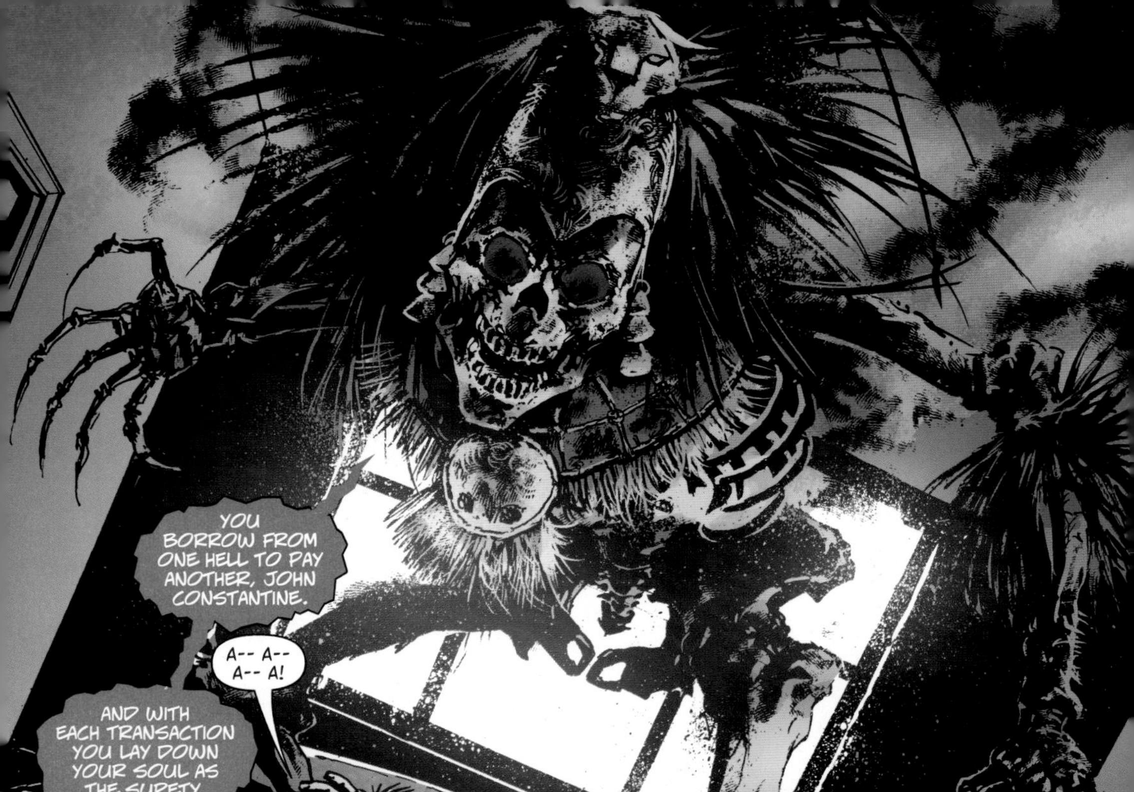
YOU BORROW FROM ONE HELL TO PAY ANOTHER, JOHN CONSTANTINE.
A-- A-- A-- A!
AND WITH EACH TRANSACTION YOU LAY DOWN YOUR SOUL AS THE SURETY.

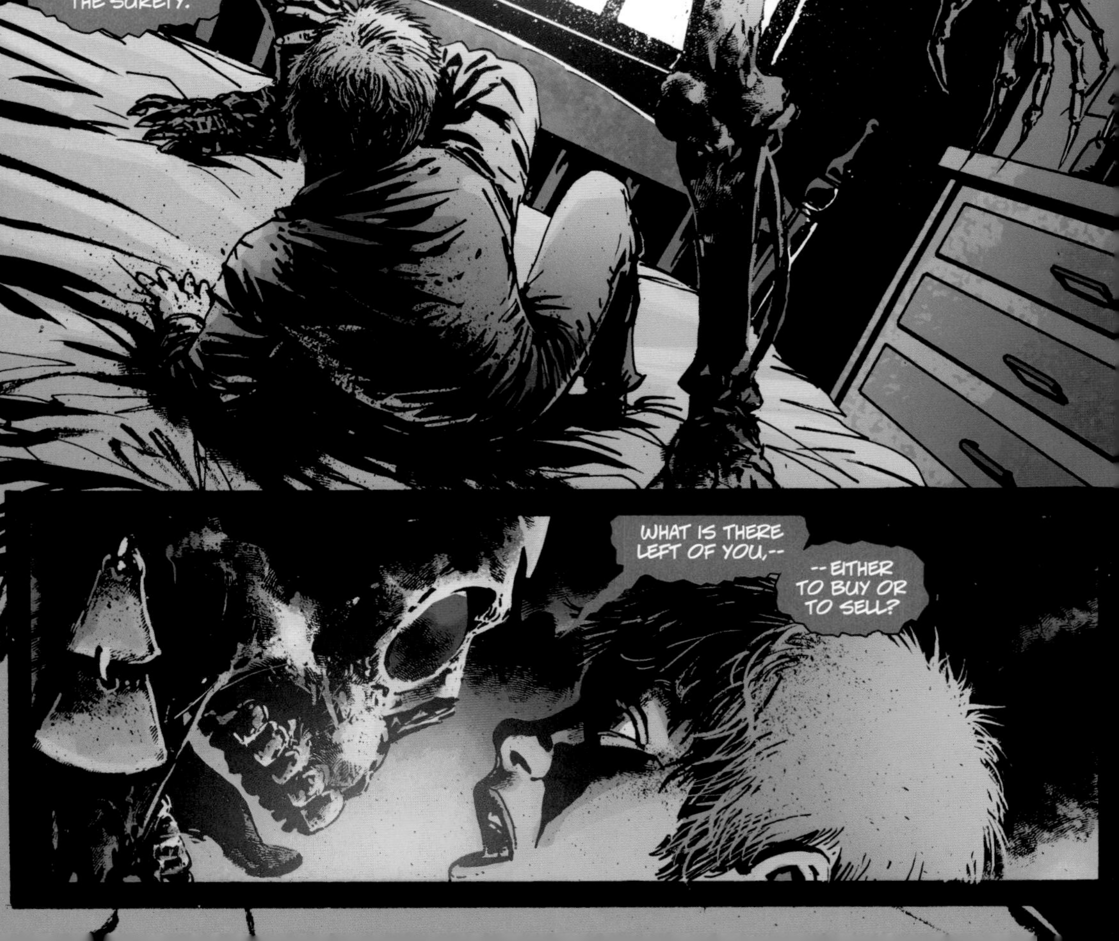
WHAT IS THERE LEFT OF YOU,--
--EITHER TO BUY OR TO SELL?

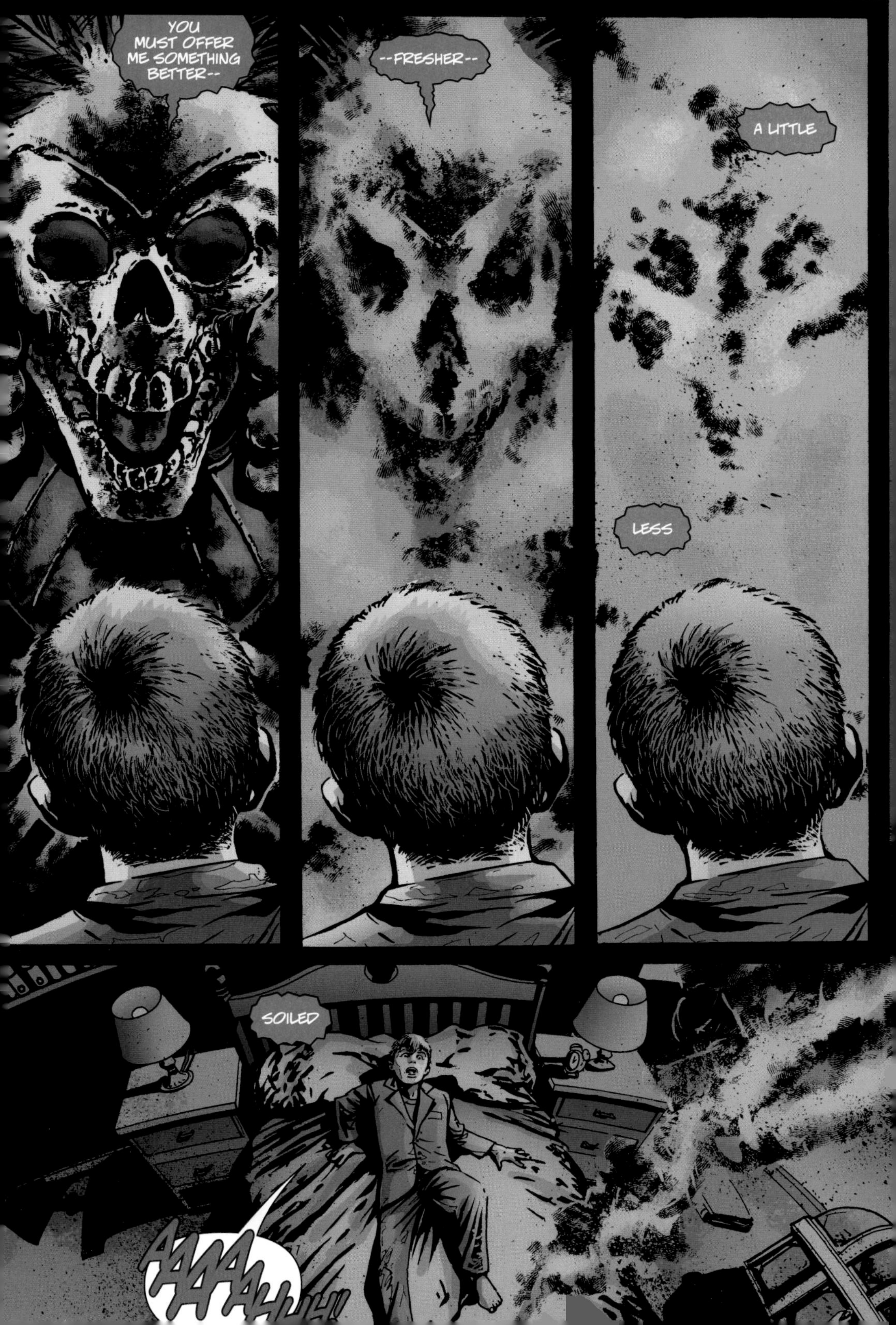
YOU MUST OFFER ME SOMETHING BETTER--
--FRESHER--
A LITTLE
LESS
SOILED
AAAAAAAHHH!!

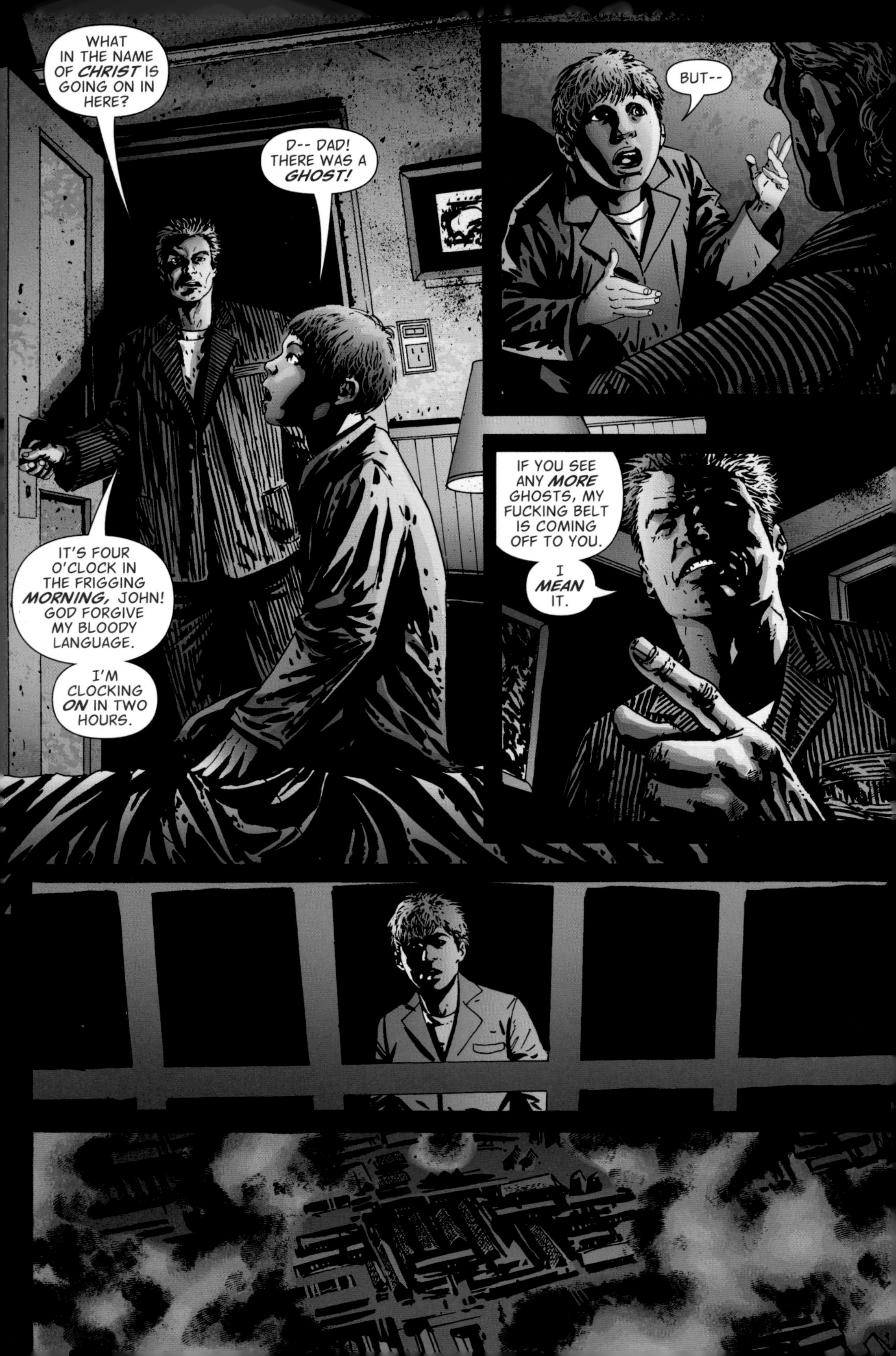
WHAT IN THE NAME OF CHRIST IS GOING ON IN HERE?
D-- DAD! THERE WAS A GHOST!
IT'S FOUR O'CLOCK IN THE FRIGGING MORNING, JOHN! GOD FORGIVE MY BLOODY LANGUAGE.
I'M CLOCKING ON IN TWO HOURS.
BUT--
IF YOU SEE ANY MORE GHOSTS, MY FUCKING BELT IS COMING OFF TO YOU.
I MEAN IT.

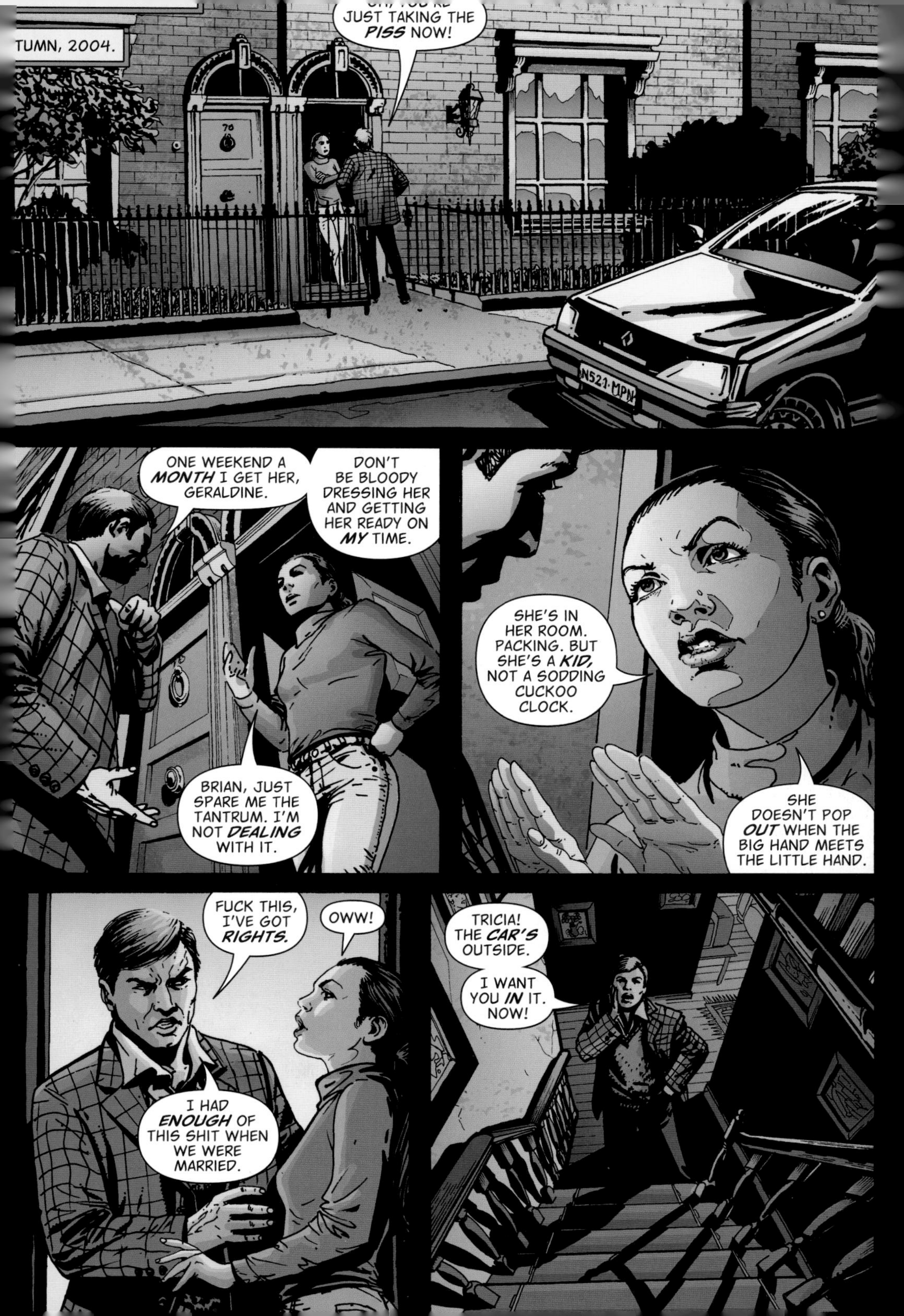
TUMN, 2004.
JUST TAKING THE PISS NOW!
ONE WEEKEND A MONTH I GET HER, GERALDINE.
DON'T BE BLOODY DRESSING HER AND GETTING HER READY ON MY TIME.
BRIAN, JUST SPARE ME THE TANTRUM. I'M NOT DEALING WITH IT.
SHE'S IN HER ROOM. PACKING. BUT SHE'S A KID, NOT A SODDING CUCKOO CLOCK.
SHE DOESN'T POP OUT WHEN THE BIG HAND MEETS THE LITTLE HAND.
FUCK THIS, I'VE GOT RIGHTS.
OWW!
I HAD ENOUGH OF THIS SHIT WHEN WE WERE MARRIED.
TRICIA! THE CAR'S OUTSIDE.
I WANT YOU IN IT. NOW!

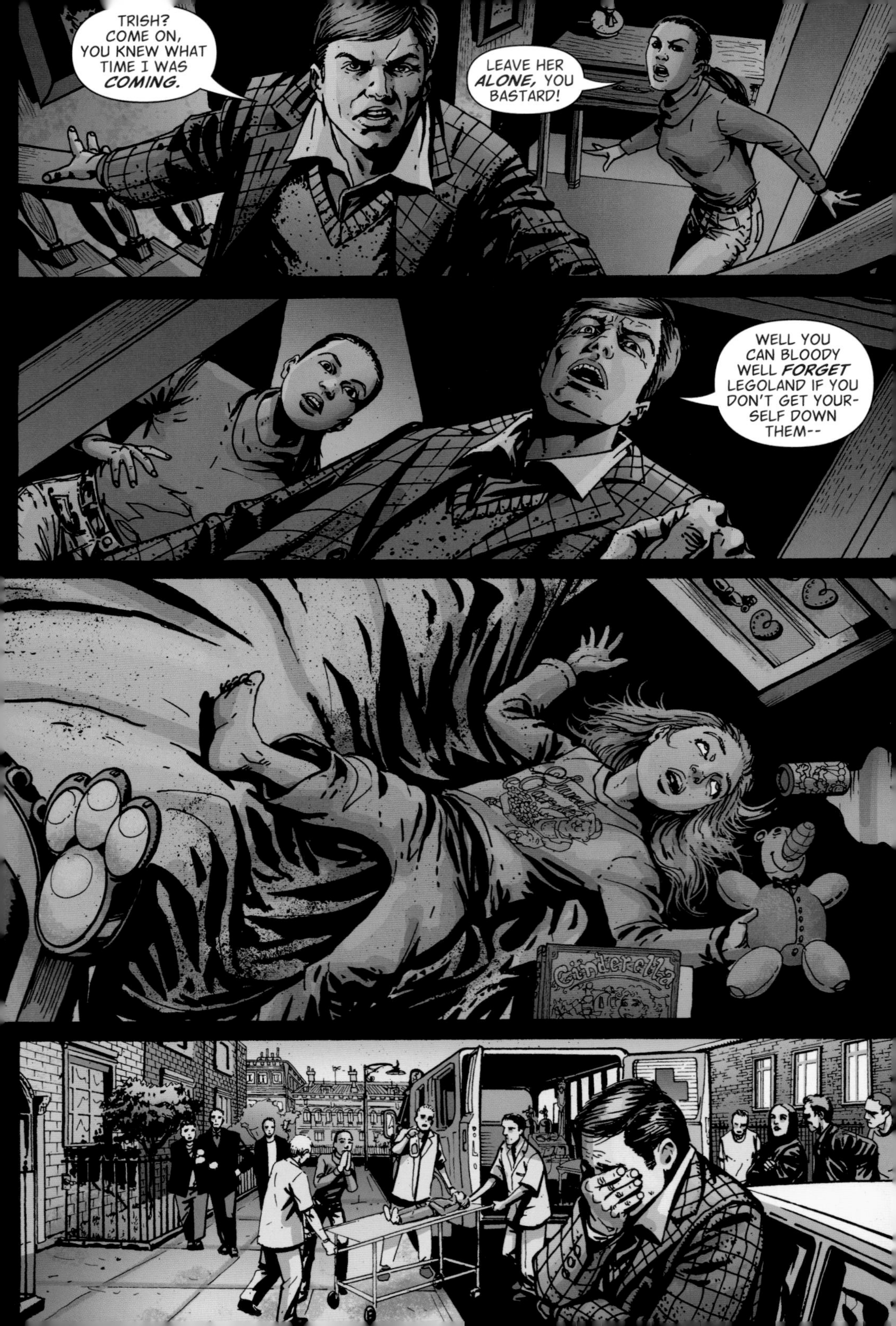
TRISH? COME ON, YOU KNEW WHAT TIME I WAS *COMING.*
LEAVE HER *ALONE,* YOU BASTARD!
WELL YOU CAN BLOODY WELL *FORGET* LEGOLAND IF YOU DON'T GET YOUR-SELF DOWN THEM--
Cinderella

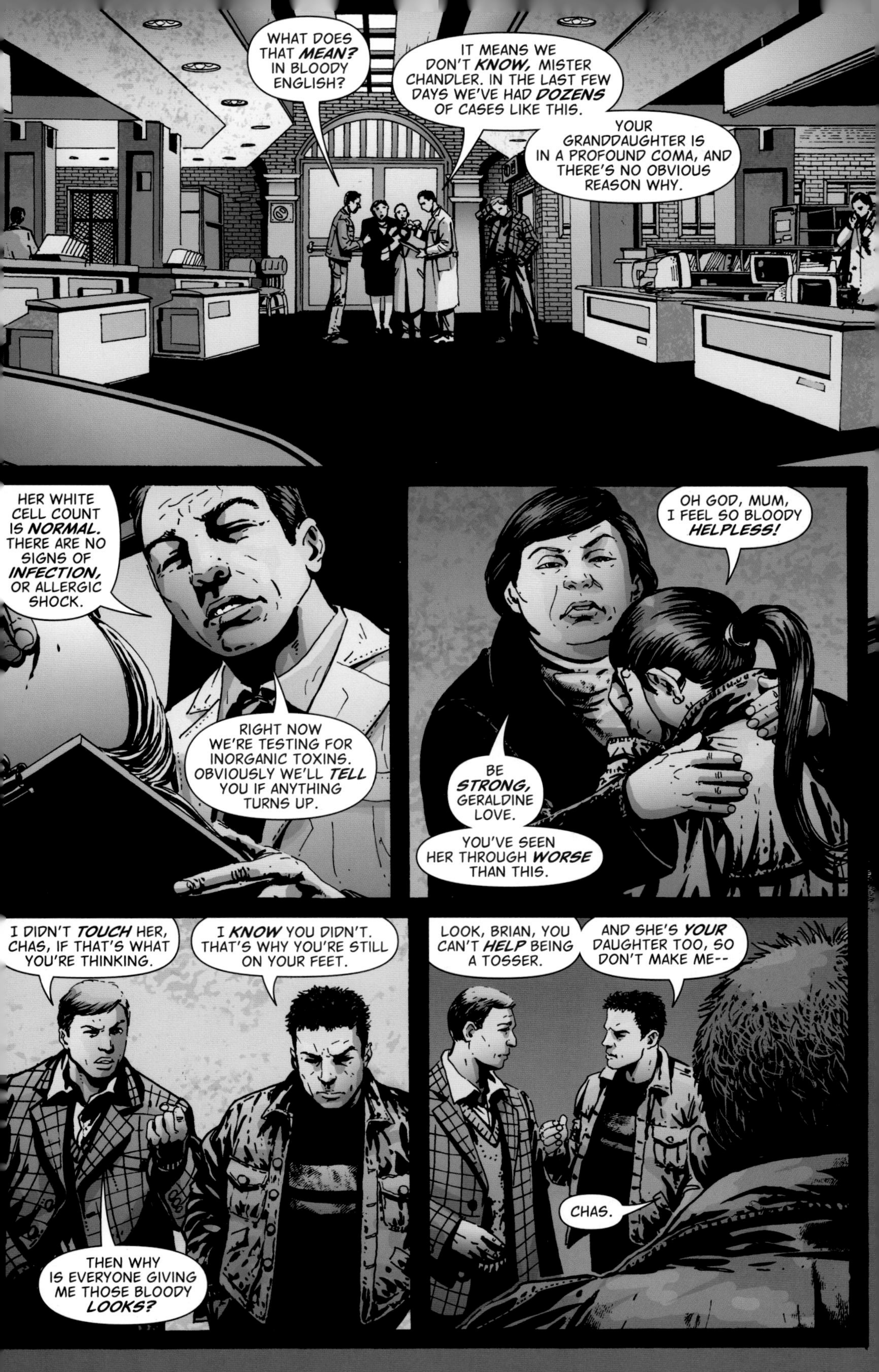
WHAT DOES THAT MEAN? IN BLOODY ENGLISH?
IT MEANS WE DON'T KNOW, MISTER CHANDLER. IN THE LAST FEW DAYS WE'VE HAD DOZENS OF CASES LIKE THIS.
YOUR GRANDDAUGHTER IS IN A PROFOUND COMA, AND THERE'S NO OBVIOUS REASON WHY.
HER WHITE CELL COUNT IS NORMAL. THERE ARE NO SIGNS OF INFECTION, OR ALLERGIC SHOCK.
RIGHT NOW WE'RE TESTING FOR INORGANIC TOXINS. OBVIOUSLY WE'LL TELL YOU IF ANYTHING TURNS UP.
OH GOD, MUM, I FEEL SO BLOODY HELPLESS!
BE STRONG, GERALDINE LOVE.
YOU'VE SEEN HER THROUGH WORSE THAN THIS.
I DIDN'T TOUCH HER, CHAS, IF THAT'S WHAT YOU'RE THINKING.
I KNOW YOU DIDN'T. THAT'S WHY YOU'RE STILL ON YOUR FEET.
THEN WHY IS EVERYONE GIVING ME THOSE BLOODY LOOKS?
LOOK, BRIAN, YOU CAN'T HELP BEING A TOSSER.
AND SHE'S YOUR DAUGHTER TOO, SO DON'T MAKE ME--
CHAS.

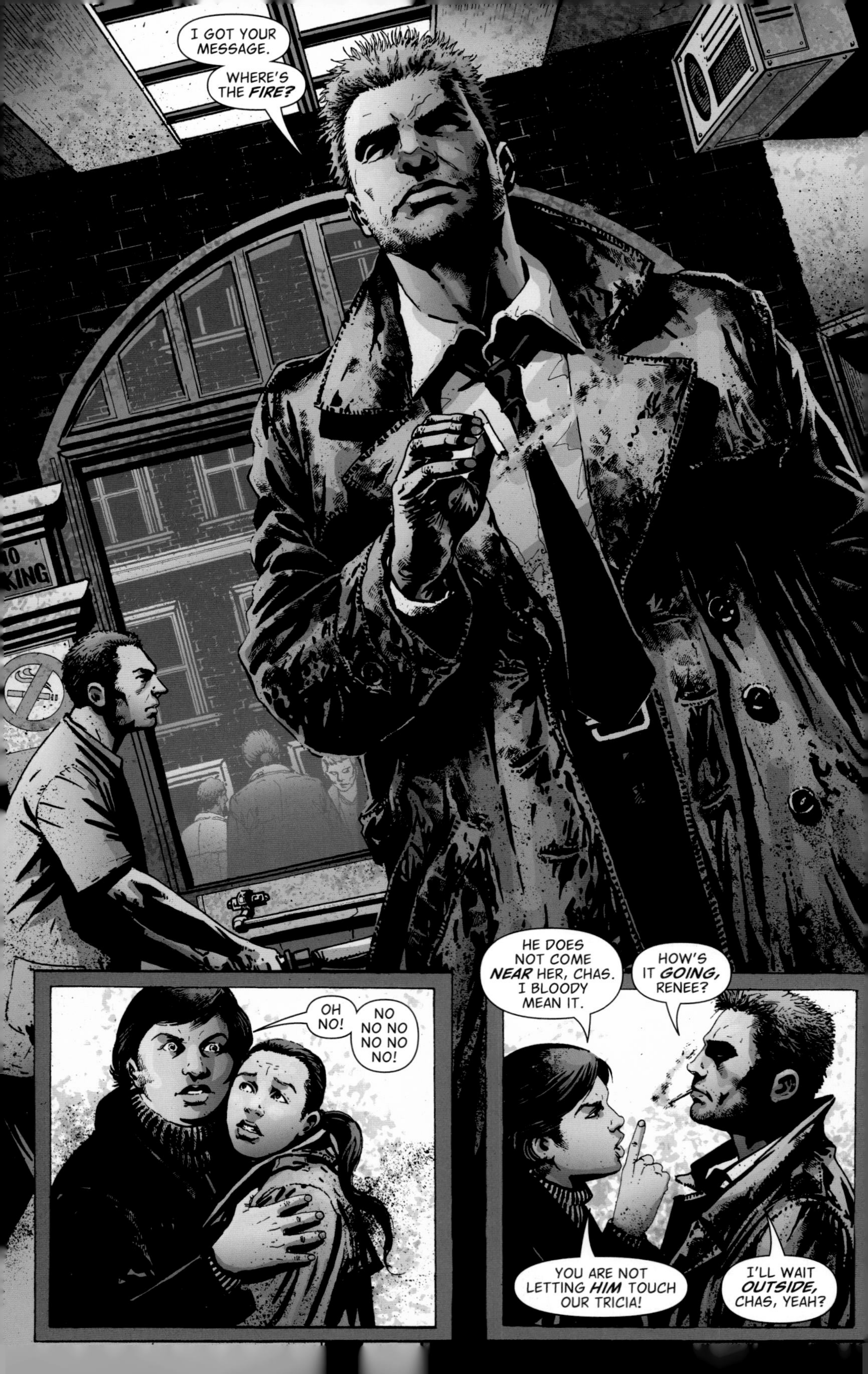
I GOT YOUR MESSAGE.
WHERE'S THE *FIRE?*
OH NO!
NO NO NO NO NO NO!
HE DOES NOT COME *NEAR* HER, CHAS. I BLOODY MEAN IT.
HOW'S IT *GOING,* RENEE?
YOU ARE NOT LETTING *HIM* TOUCH OUR TRICIA!
I'LL WAIT *OUTSIDE,* CHAS, YEAH?

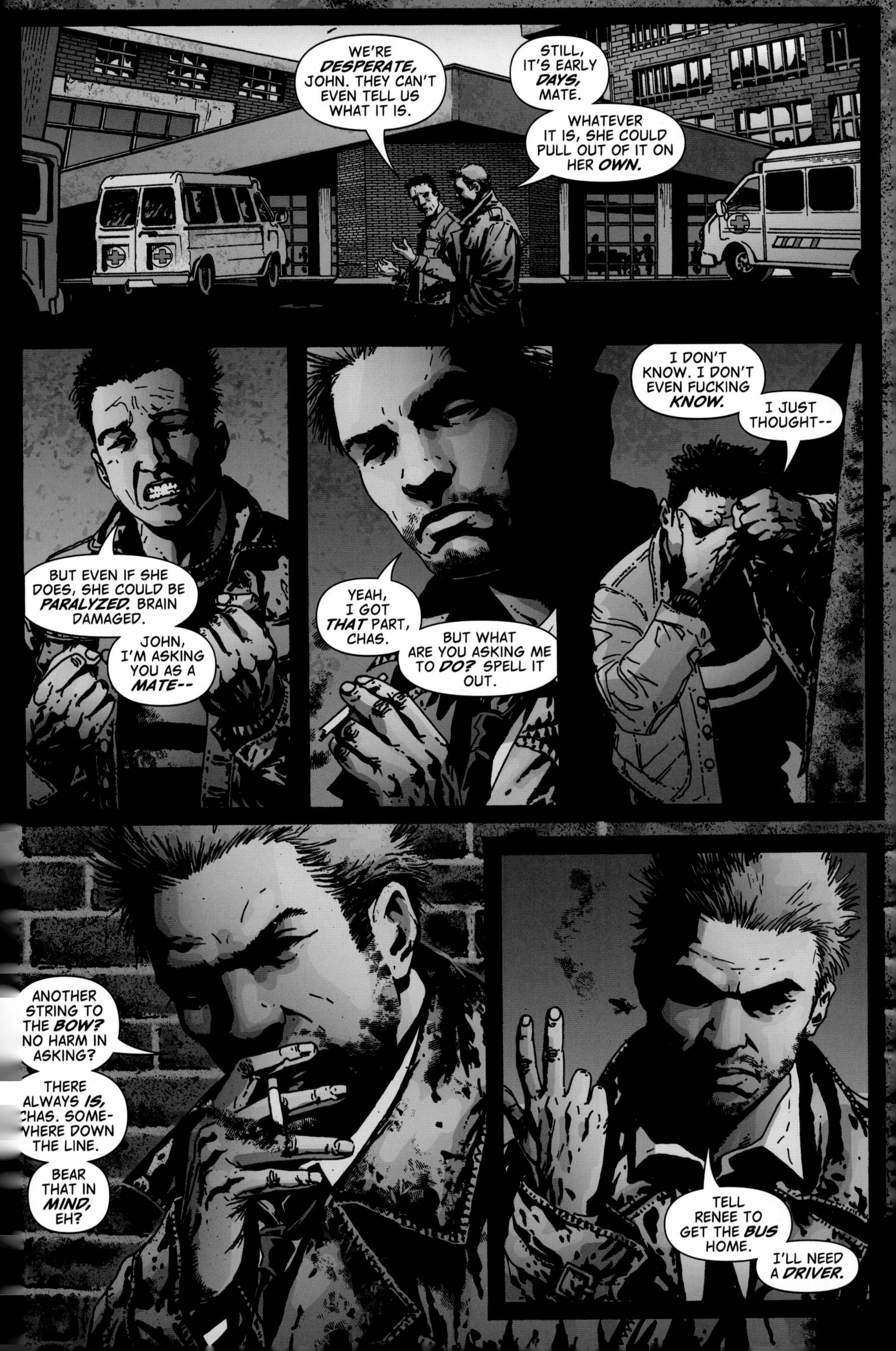
WE'RE DESPERATE, JOHN. THEY CAN'T EVEN TELL US WHAT IT IS.
STILL, IT'S EARLY DAYS, MATE.
WHATEVER IT IS, SHE COULD PULL OUT OF IT ON HER OWN.
BUT EVEN IF SHE DOES, SHE COULD BE PARALYZED. BRAIN DAMAGED.
JOHN, I'M ASKING YOU AS A MATE--
YEAH, I GOT THAT PART, CHAS.
BUT WHAT ARE YOU ASKING ME TO DO? SPELL IT OUT.
I DON'T KNOW. I DON'T EVEN FUCKING KNOW.
I JUST THOUGHT--
ANOTHER STRING TO THE BOW? NO HARM IN ASKING?
THERE ALWAYS IS, CHAS. SOME-WHERE DOWN THE LINE.
BEAR THAT IN MIND, EH?
TELL RENEE TO GET THE BUS HOME.
I'LL NEED A DRIVER.

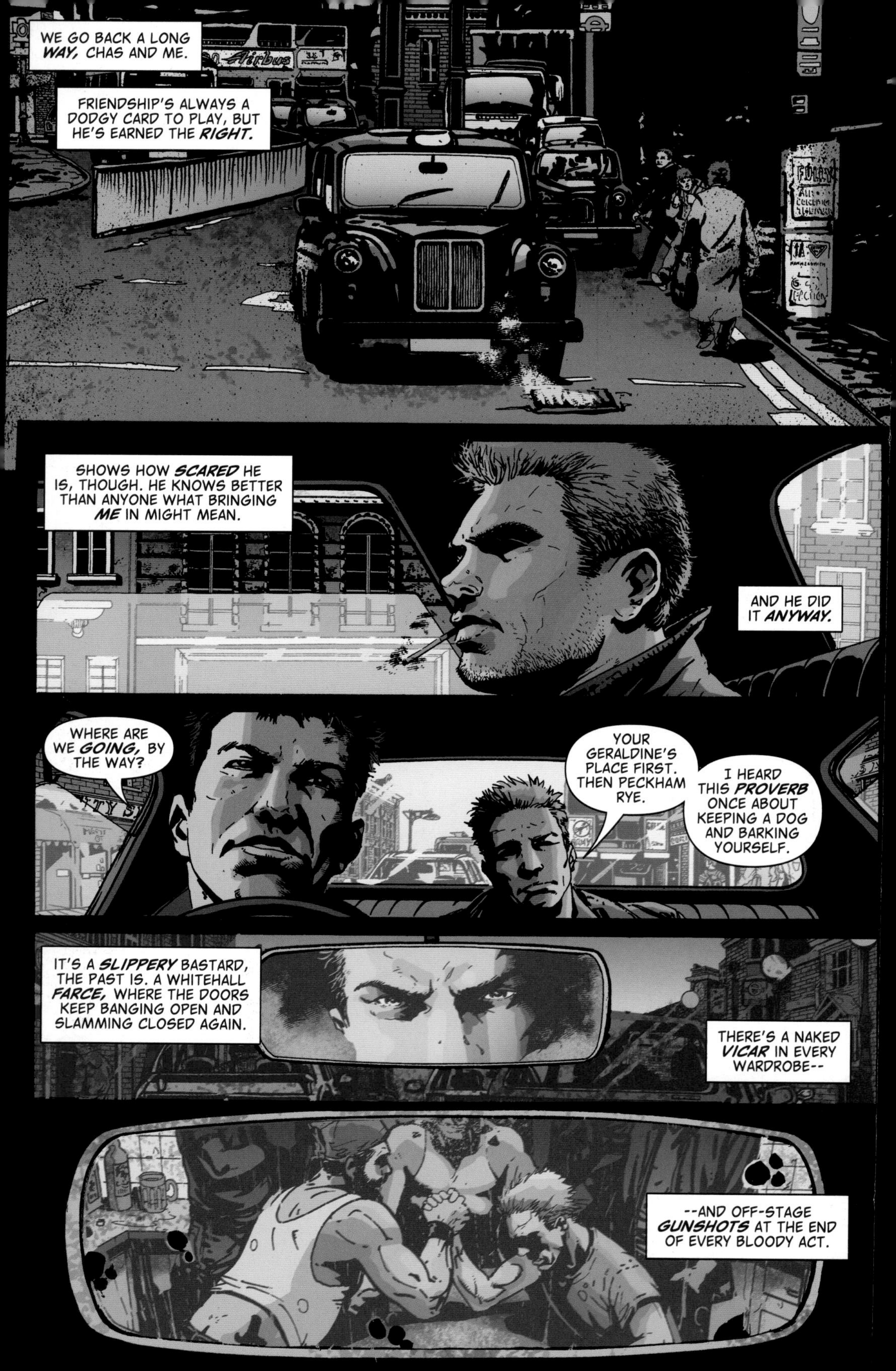

WE GO BACK A LONG WAY, CHAS AND ME.
FRIENDSHIP'S ALWAYS A DODGY CARD TO PLAY, BUT HE'S EARNED THE RIGHT.
SHOWS HOW SCARED HE IS, THOUGH. HE KNOWS BETTER THAN ANYONE WHAT BRINGING ME IN MIGHT MEAN.
AND HE DID IT ANYWAY.
WHERE ARE WE GOING, BY THE WAY?
YOUR GERALDINE'S PLACE FIRST. THEN PECKHAM RYE.
I HEARD THIS PROVERB ONCE ABOUT KEEPING A DOG AND BARKING YOURSELF.
IT'S A SLIPPERY BASTARD, THE PAST IS. A WHITEHALL FARCE, WHERE THE DOORS KEEP BANGING OPEN AND SLAMMING CLOSED AGAIN.
THERE'S A NAKED VICAR IN EVERY WARDROBE--
--AND OFF-STAGE GUNSHOTS AT THE END OF EVERY BLOODY ACT.

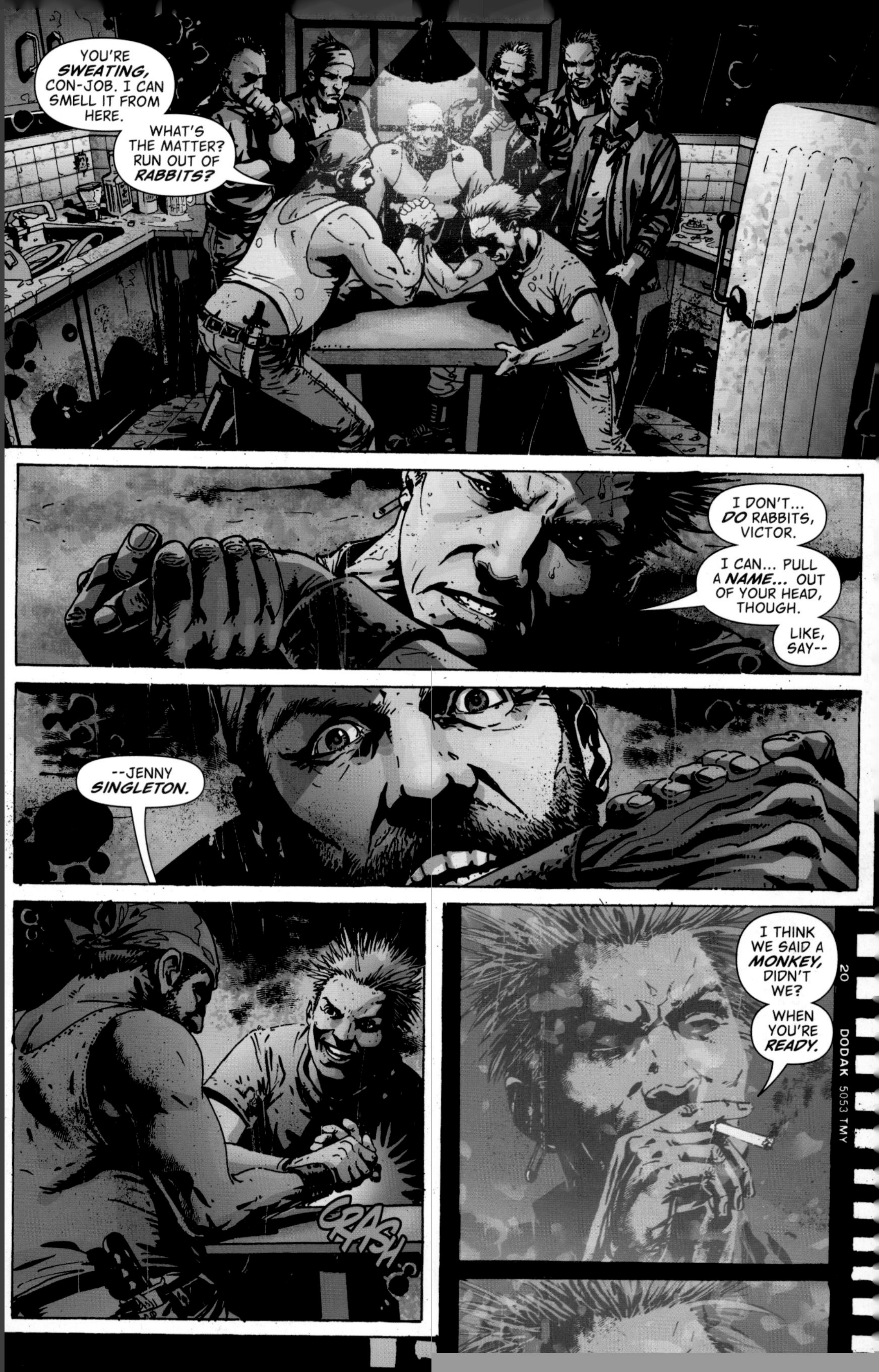
YOU'RE SWEATING, CON-JOB. I CAN SMELL IT FROM HERE.
WHAT'S THE MATTER? RUN OUT OF RABBITS?
I DON'T... DO RABBITS, VICTOR.
I CAN... PULL A NAME... OUT OF YOUR HEAD, THOUGH.
LIKE, SAY--
--JENNY SINGLETON.
CRASH
I THINK WE SAID A MONKEY, DIDN'T WE?
WHEN YOU'RE READY.
20
DODAK 5053 TMY

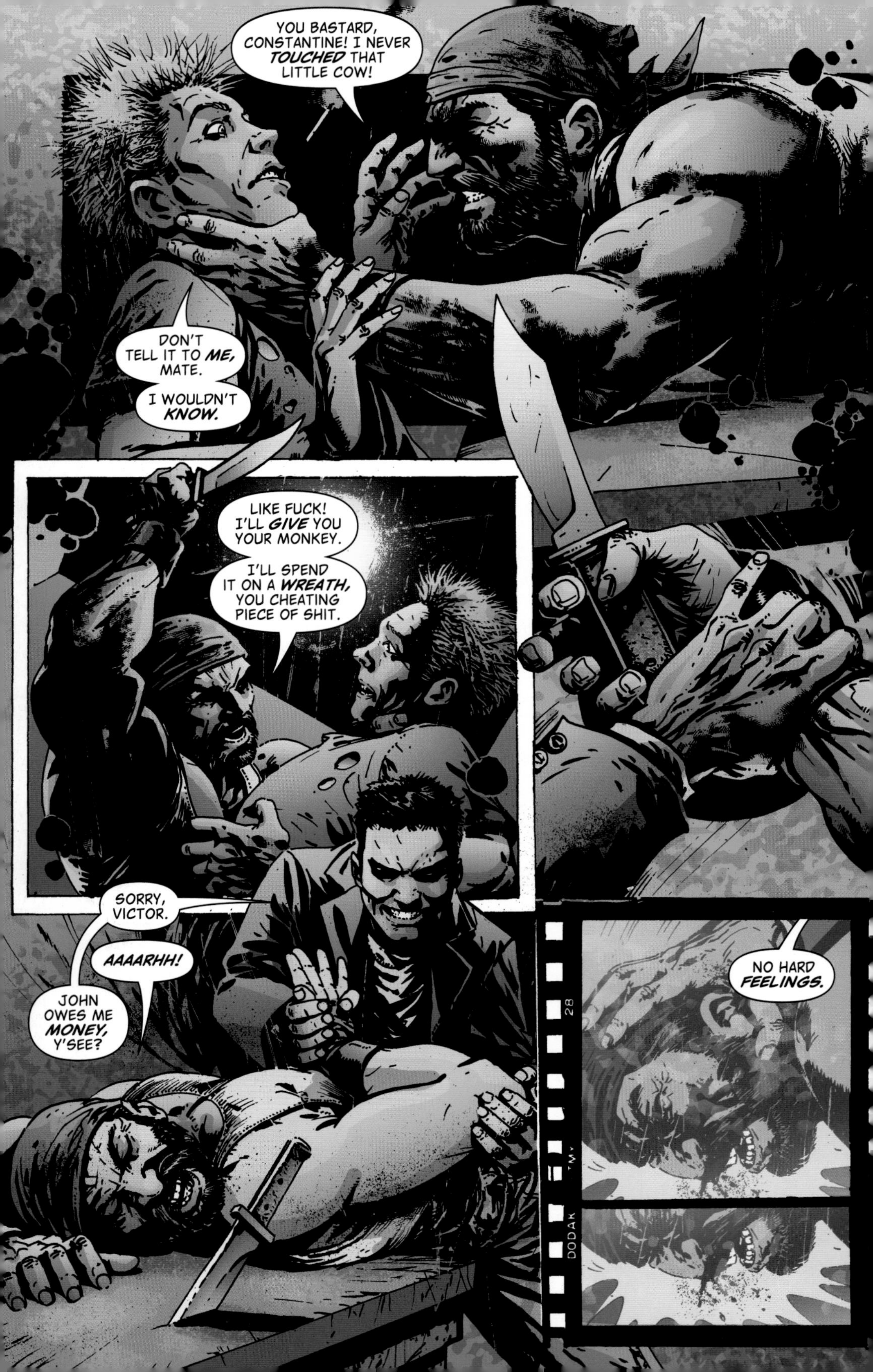
YOU BASTARD, CONSTANTINE! I NEVER *TOUCHED* THAT LITTLE COW!
DON'T TELL IT TO *ME,* MATE.
I WOULDN'T *KNOW.*
LIKE FUCK! I'LL *GIVE* YOU YOUR MONKEY.
I'LL SPEND IT ON A *WREATH,* YOU CHEATING PIECE OF SHIT.
SORRY, VICTOR.
AAAARHH!
JOHN OWES ME *MONEY,* Y'SEE?
NO HARD *FEELINGS.*

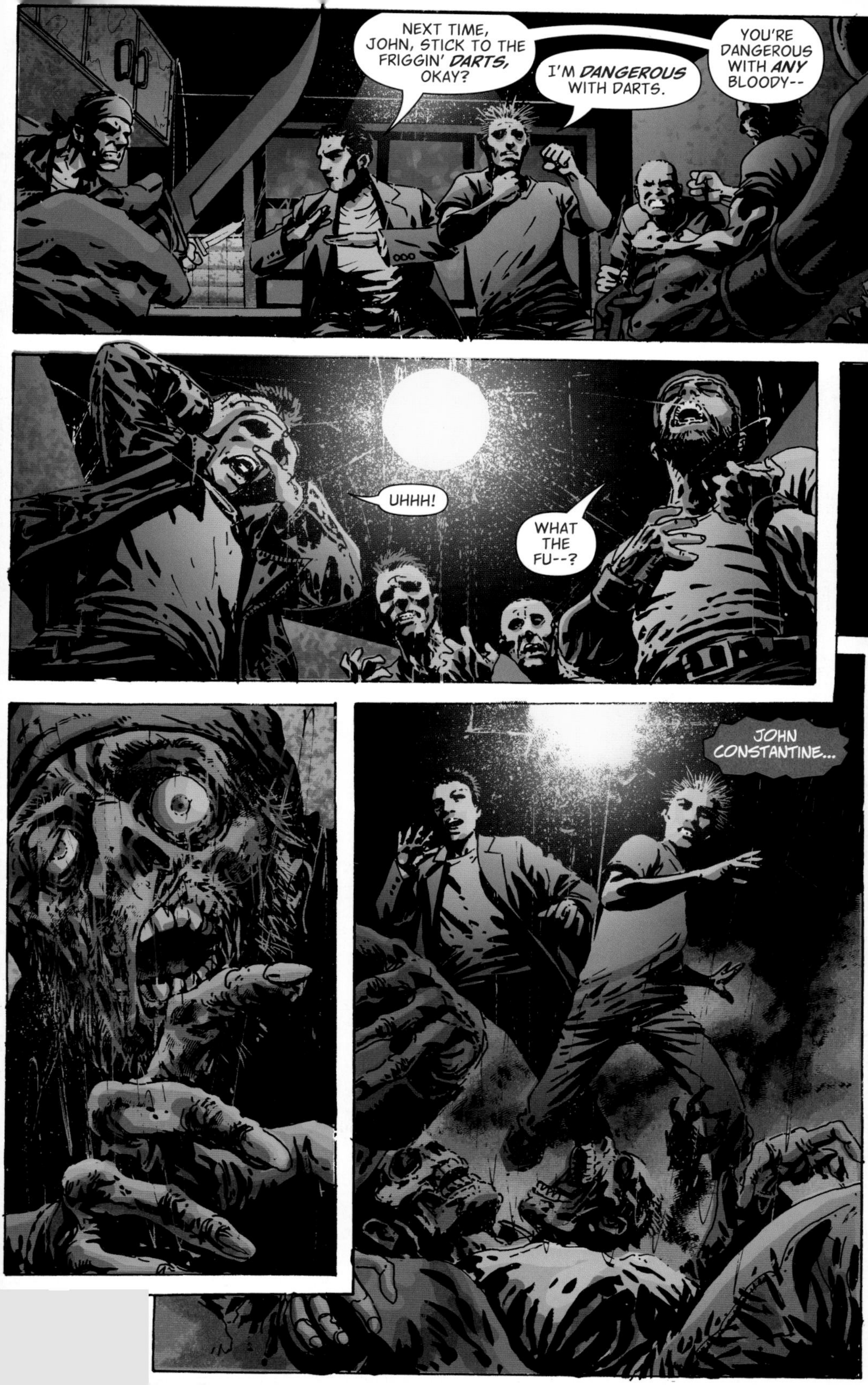
NEXT TIME, JOHN, STICK TO THE FRIGGIN' DARTS, OKAY?
I'M DANGEROUS WITH DARTS.
YOU'RE DANGEROUS WITH ANY BLOODY--
UHHH!
WHAT THE FU--?
JOHN CONSTANTINE...

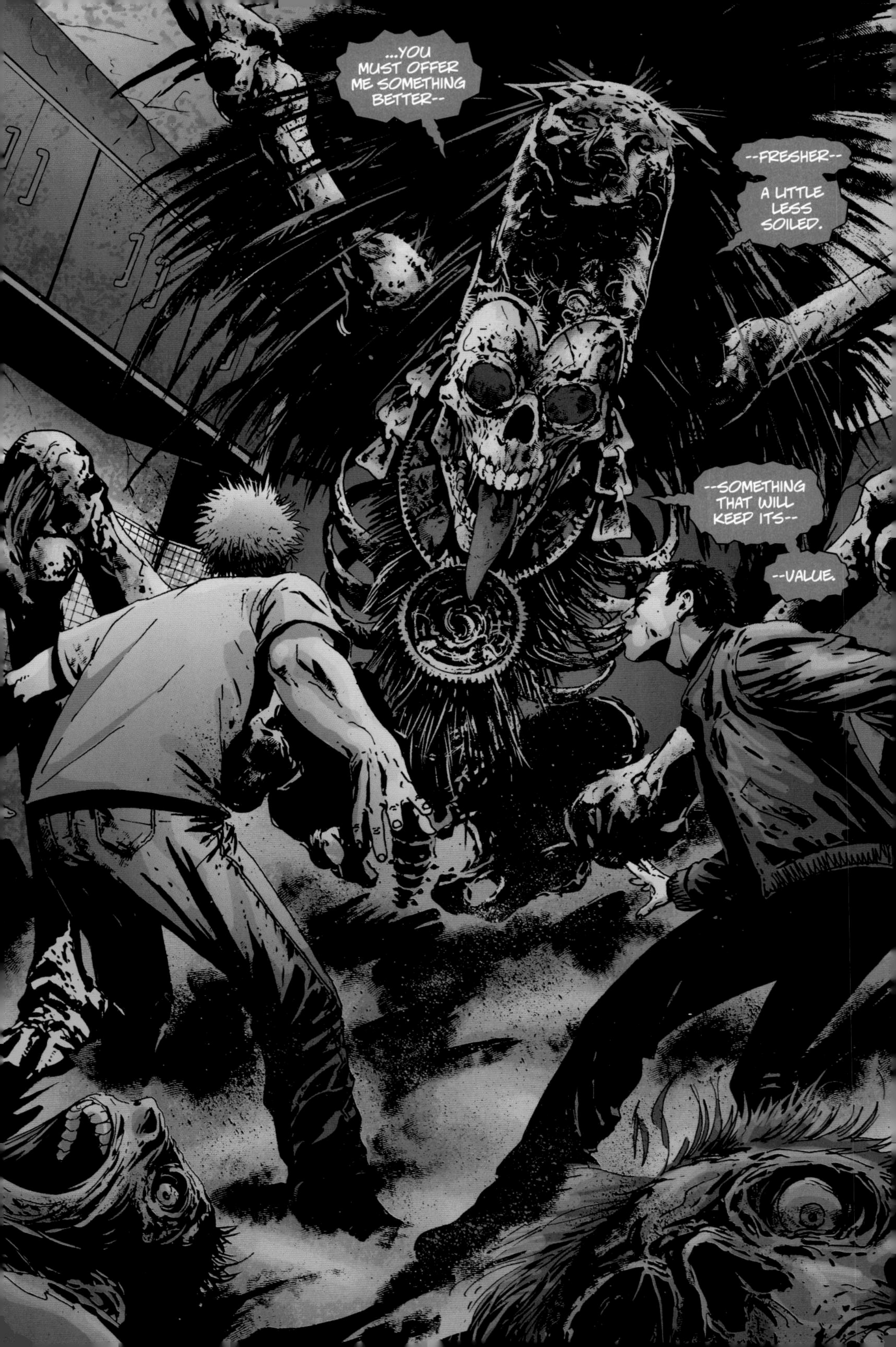
...YOU MUST OFFER ME SOMETHING BETTER--
--FRESHER--
A LITTLE LESS SOILED.
--SOMETHING THAT WILL KEEP ITS--
--VALUE.

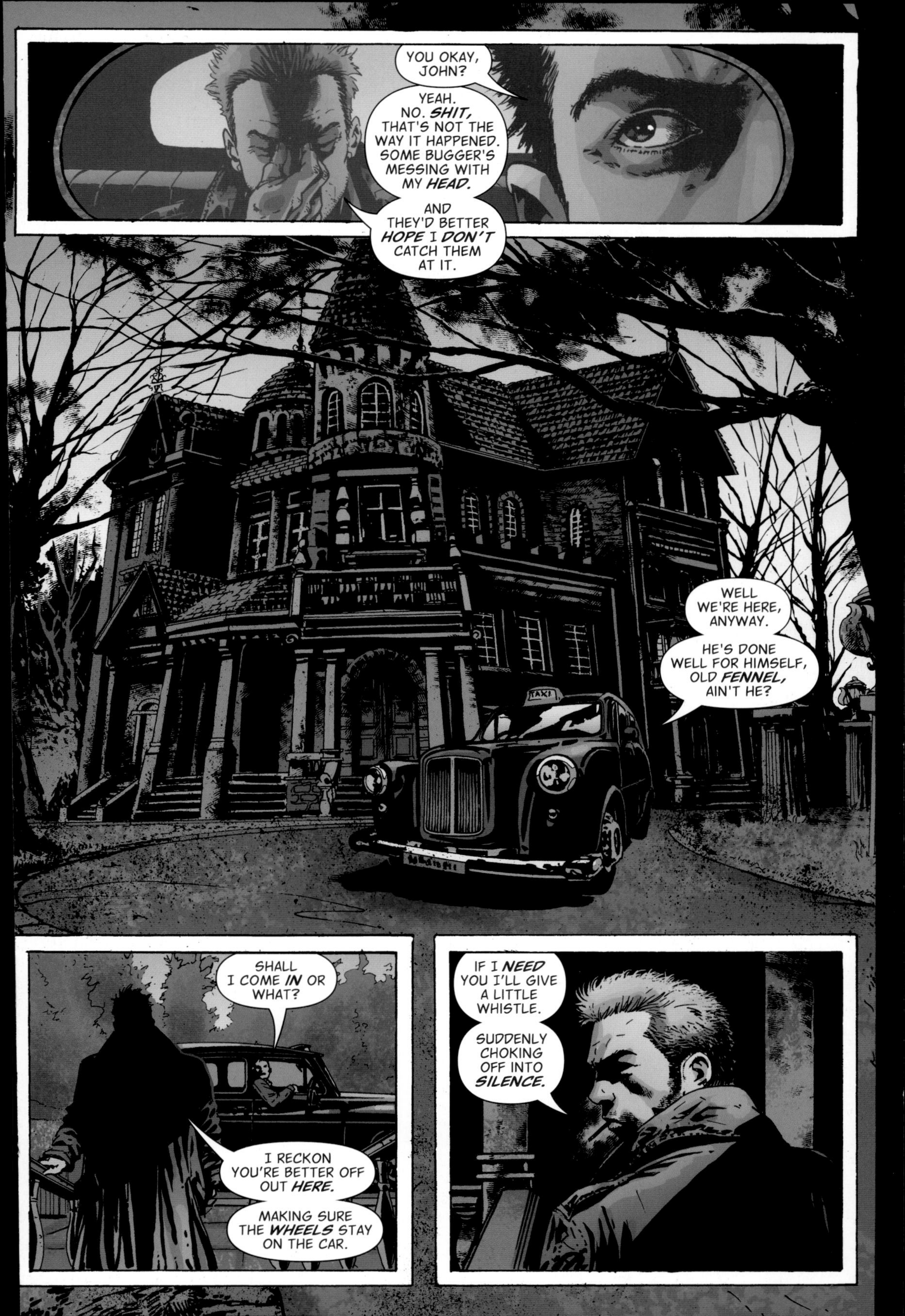

YOU OKAY, JOHN?
YEAH. NO. SHIT, THAT'S NOT THE WAY IT HAPPENED. SOME BUGGER'S MESSING WITH MY HEAD.
AND THEY'D BETTER HOPE I DON'T CATCH THEM AT IT.
TAXI
WELL WE'RE HERE, ANYWAY.
HE'S DONE WELL FOR HIMSELF, OLD FENNEL, AIN'T HE?
SHALL I COME IN OR WHAT?
I RECKON YOU'RE BETTER OFF OUT HERE.
MAKING SURE THE WHEELS STAY ON THE CAR.
IF I NEED YOU I'LL GIVE A LITTLE WHISTLE.
SUDDENLY CHOKING OFF INTO SILENCE.

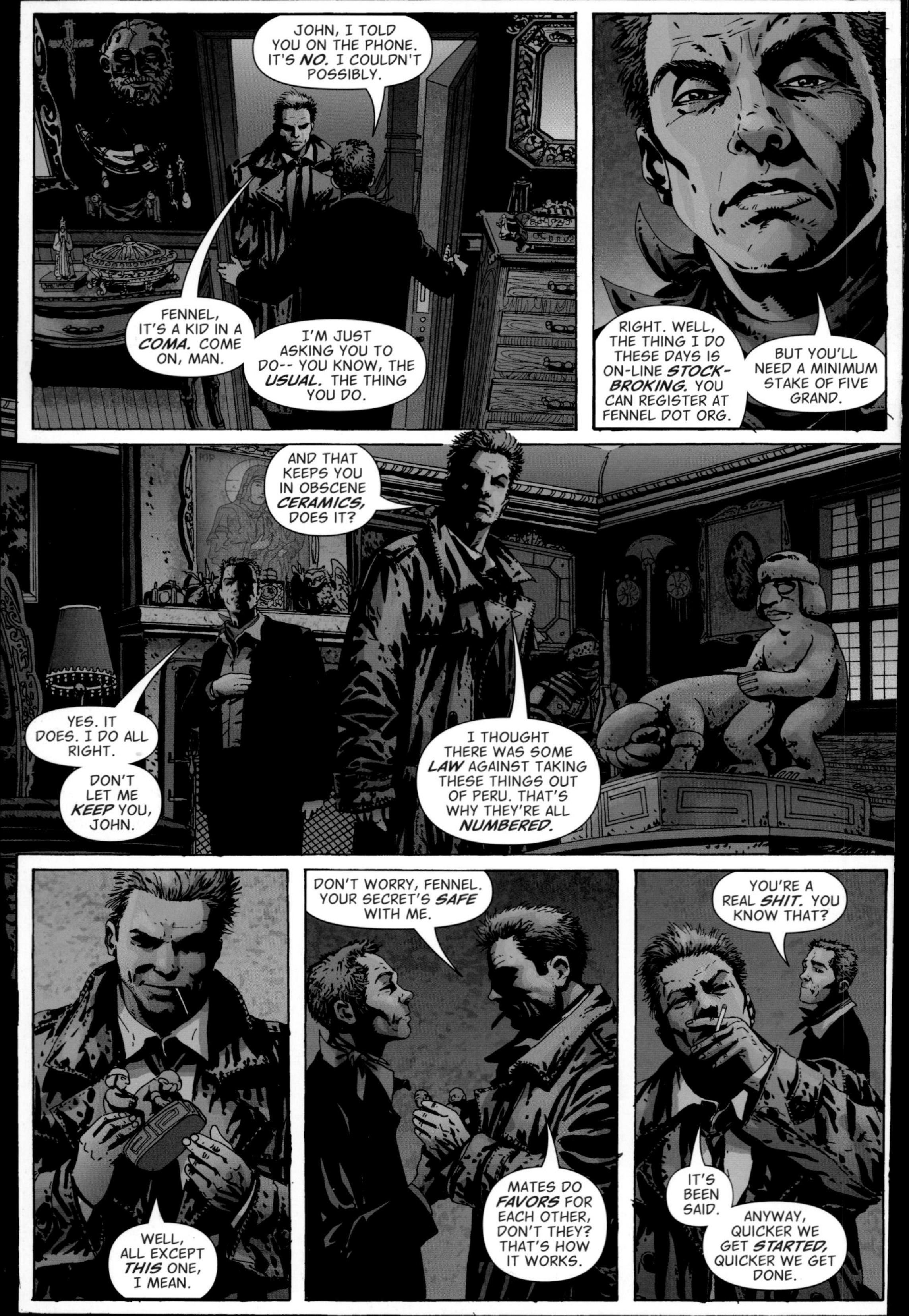
JOHN, I TOLD YOU ON THE PHONE. IT'S NO. I COULDN'T POSSIBLY.
FENNEL, IT'S A KID IN A COMA. COME ON, MAN.
I'M JUST ASKING YOU TO DO-- YOU KNOW, THE USUAL. THE THING YOU DO.
RIGHT. WELL, THE THING I DO THESE DAYS IS ON-LINE STOCK-BROKING. YOU CAN REGISTER AT FENNEL DOT ORG.
BUT YOU'LL NEED A MINIMUM STAKE OF FIVE GRAND.
AND THAT KEEPS YOU IN OBSCENE CERAMICS, DOES IT?
YES. IT DOES. I DO ALL RIGHT.
DON'T LET ME KEEP YOU, JOHN.
I THOUGHT THERE WAS SOME LAW AGAINST TAKING THESE THINGS OUT OF PERU. THAT'S WHY THEY'RE ALL NUMBERED.
WELL, ALL EXCEPT THIS ONE, I MEAN.
DON'T WORRY, FENNEL. YOUR SECRET'S SAFE WITH ME.
MATES DO FAVORS FOR EACH OTHER, DON'T THEY? THAT'S HOW IT WORKS.
YOU'RE A REAL SHIT. YOU KNOW THAT?
IT'S BEEN SAID.
ANYWAY, QUICKER WE GET STARTED, QUICKER WE GET DONE.

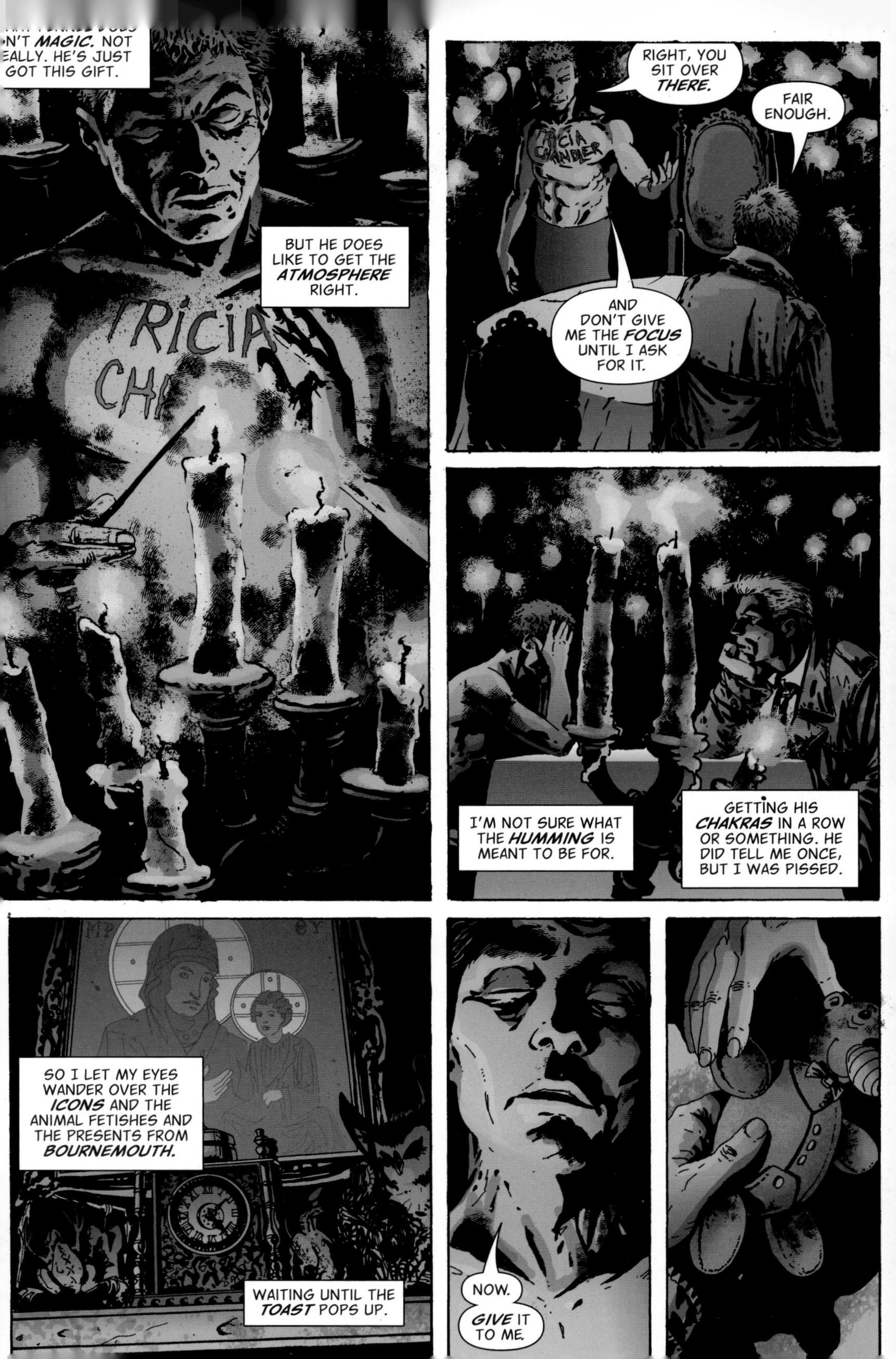

N'T MAGIC. NOT
EALLY. HE'S JUST
GOT THIS GIFT.
BUT HE DOES LIKE TO GET THE ATMOSPHERE RIGHT.
TRICIA CH
RIGHT, YOU SIT OVER THERE.
FAIR ENOUGH.
TRICIA CHANDLER
AND DON'T GIVE ME THE FOCUS UNTIL I ASK FOR IT.
I'M NOT SURE WHAT THE HUMMING IS MEANT TO BE FOR.
GETTING HIS CHAKRAS IN A ROW OR SOMETHING. HE DID TELL ME ONCE, BUT I WAS PISSED.
SO I LET MY EYES WANDER OVER THE ICONS AND THE ANIMAL FETISHES AND THE PRESENTS FROM BOURNEMOUTH.
WAITING UNTIL THE TOAST POPS UP.
NOW.
GIVE IT TO ME.

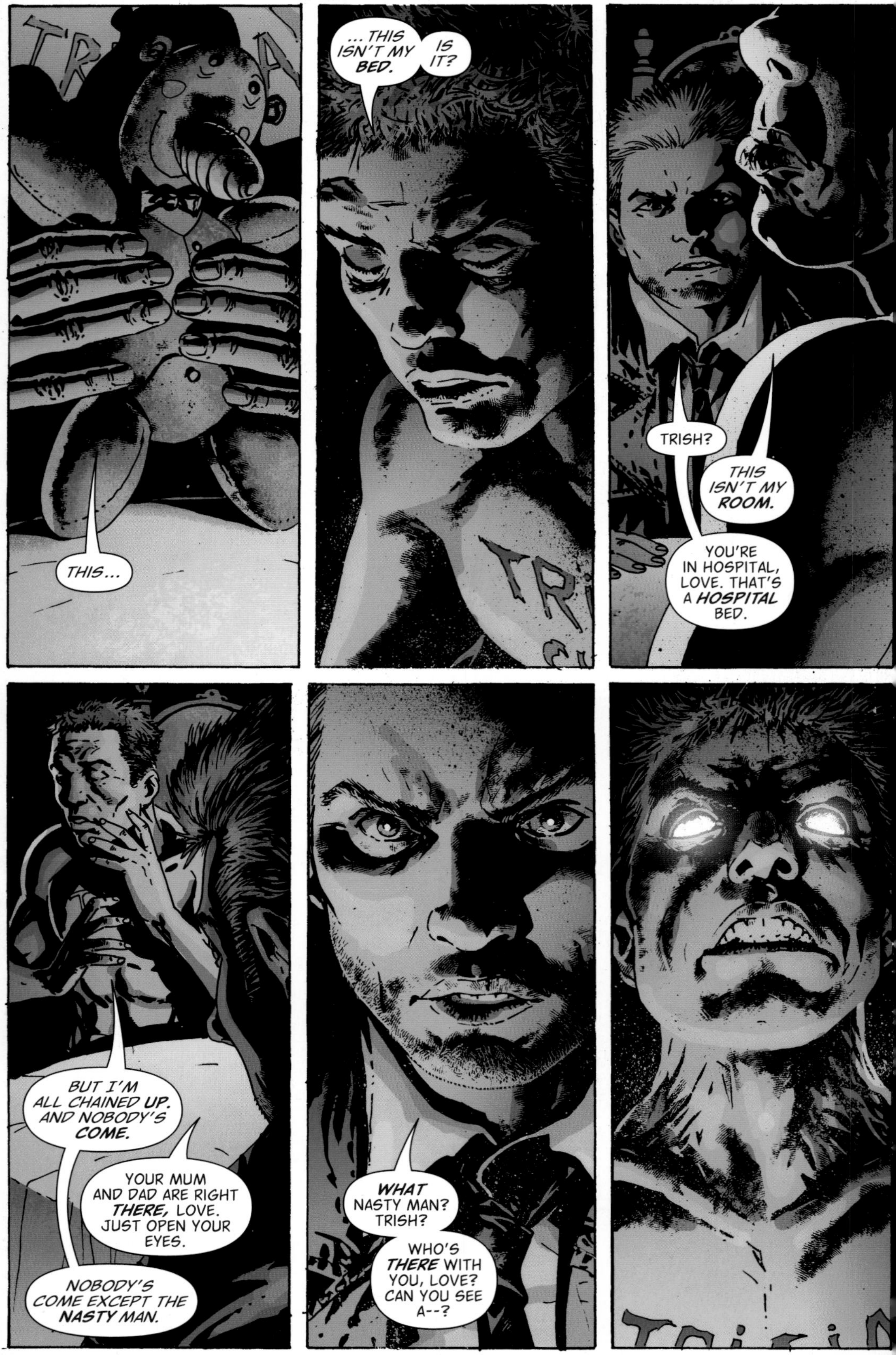

THIS...
...THIS ISN'T MY BED.
IS IT?
TRISH?
THIS ISN'T MY ROOM.
YOU'RE IN HOSPITAL, LOVE. THAT'S A HOSPITAL BED.
BUT I'M ALL CHAINED UP. AND NOBODY'S COME.
YOUR MUM AND DAD ARE RIGHT THERE, LOVE. JUST OPEN YOUR EYES.
NOBODY'S COME EXCEPT THE NASTY MAN.
WHAT NASTY MAN? TRISH?
WHO'S THERE WITH YOU, LOVE? CAN YOU SEE A--?

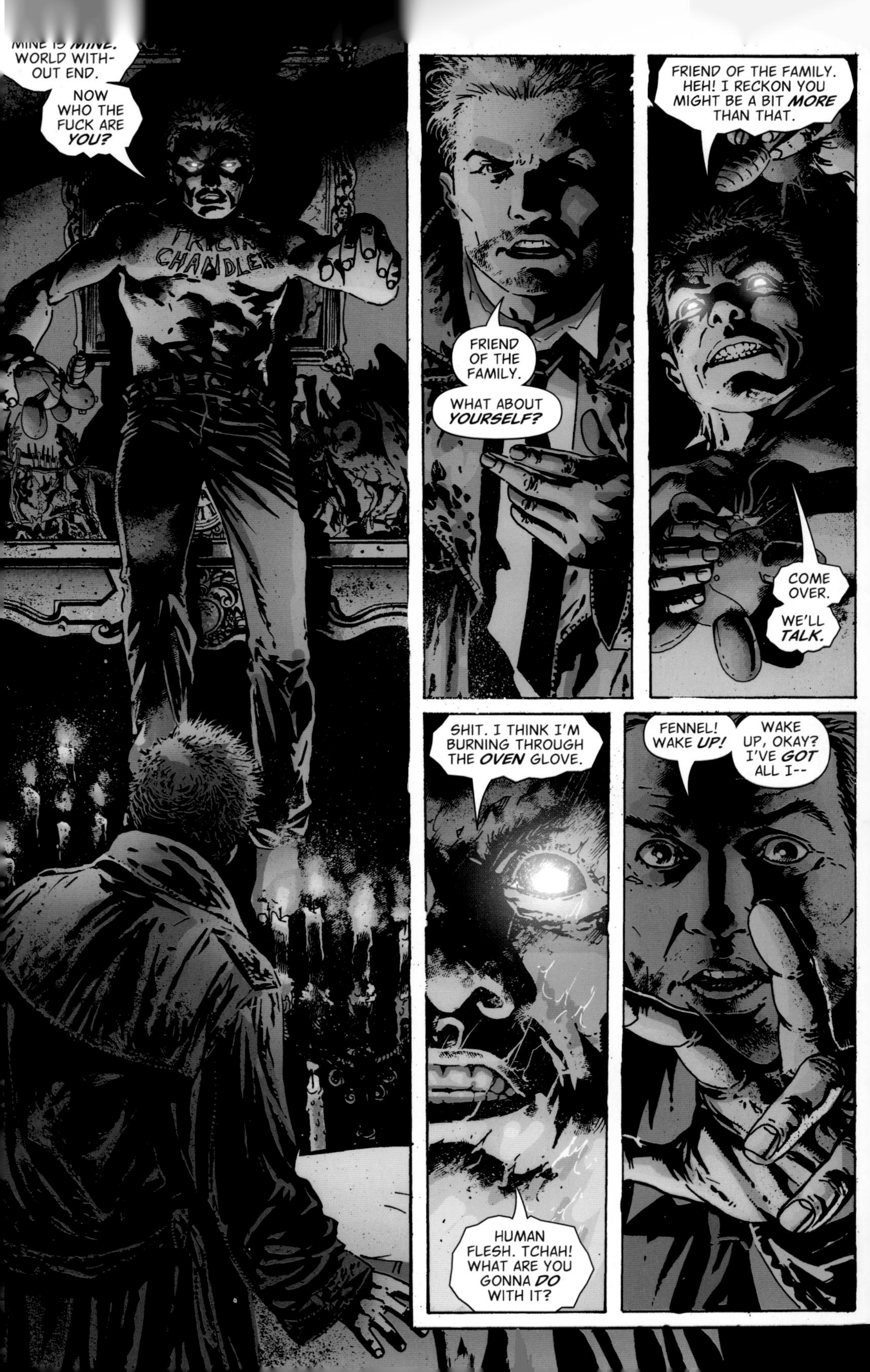

MINE IS MINE. WORLD WITHOUT END.
NOW WHO THE FUCK ARE YOU?
FRIEND OF THE FAMILY.
WHAT ABOUT YOURSELF?
FRIEND OF THE FAMILY. HEH! I RECKON YOU MIGHT BE A BIT MORE THAN THAT.
COME OVER.
WE'LL TALK.
SHIT. I THINK I'M BURNING THROUGH THE OVEN GLOVE.
HUMAN FLESH. TCHAH! WHAT ARE YOU GONNA DO WITH IT?
FENNEL! WAKE UP!
WAKE UP, OKAY? I'VE GOT ALL I--

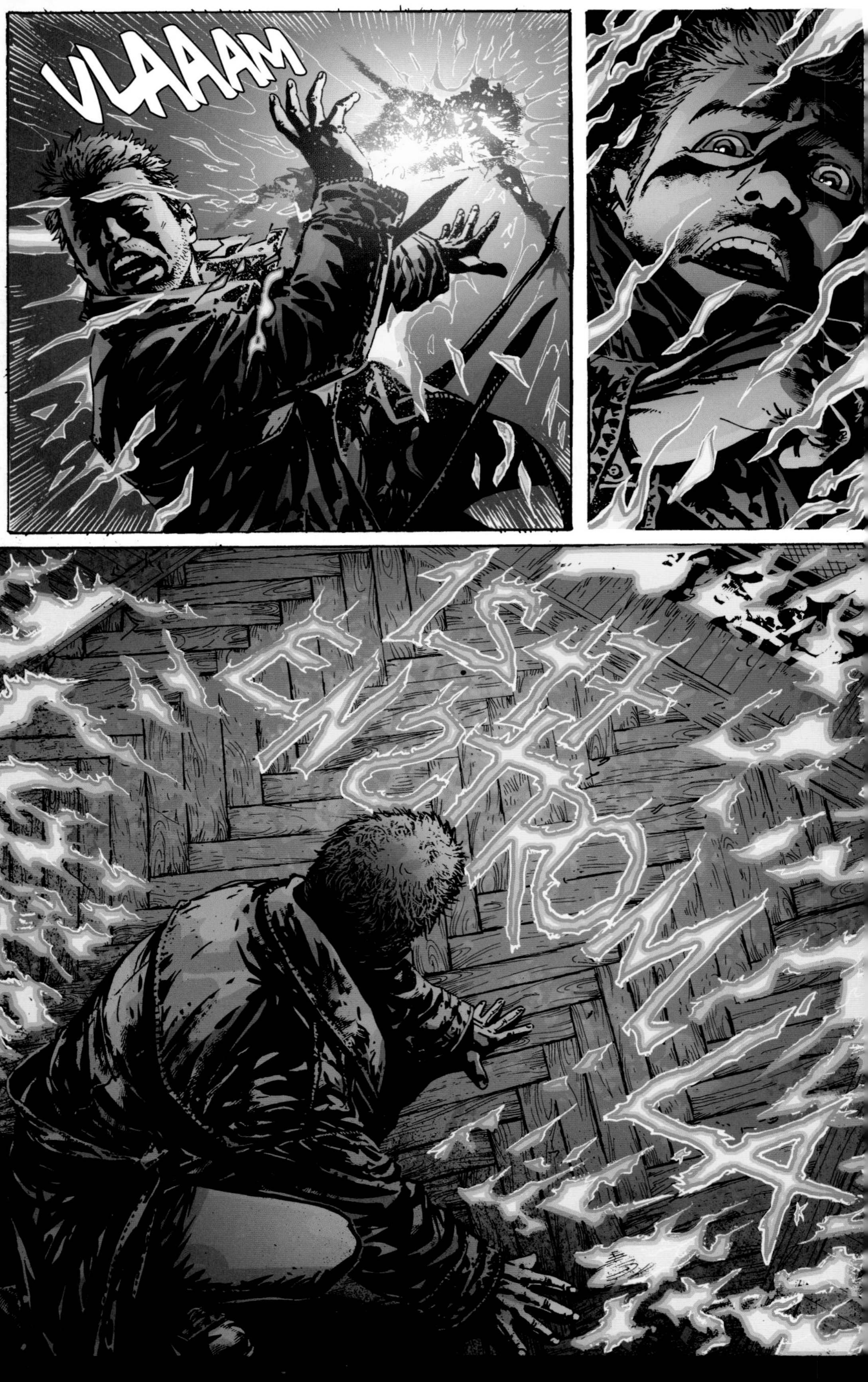
VLAAAM

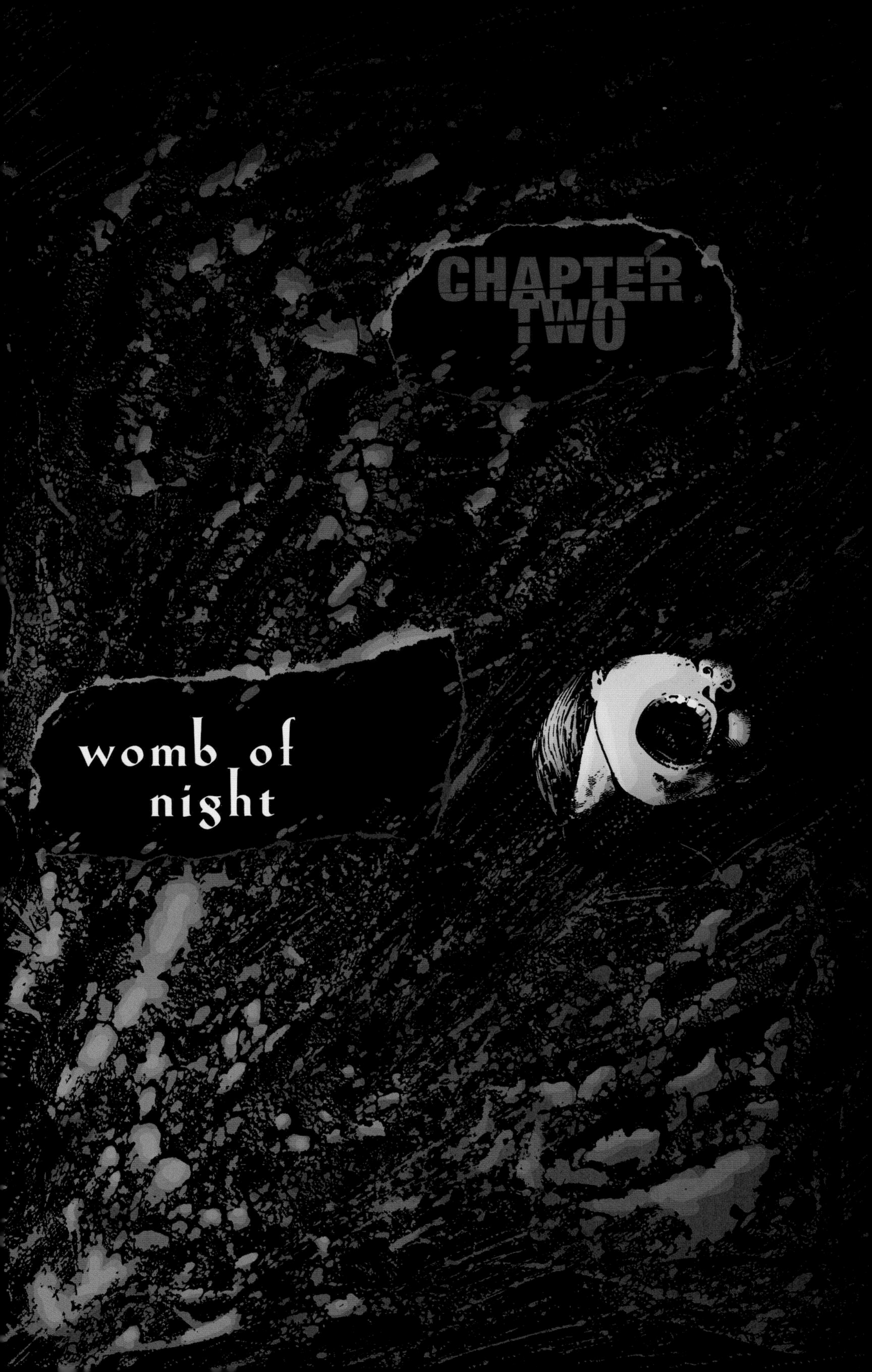
CHAPTER TWO
womb of night

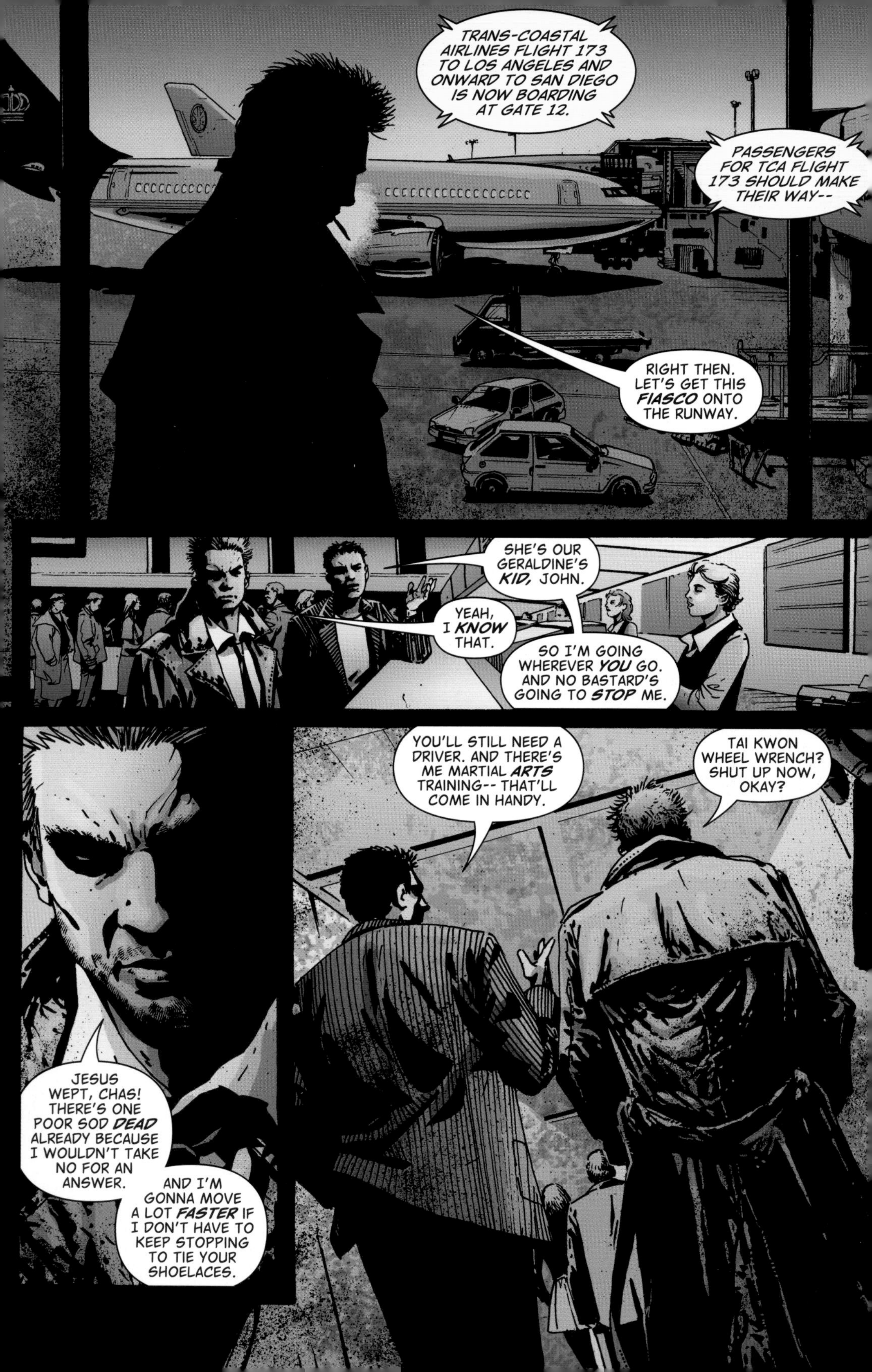
TRANS-COASTAL AIRLINES FLIGHT 173 TO LOS ANGELES AND ONWARD TO SAN DIEGO IS NOW BOARDING AT GATE 12.
PASSENGERS FOR TCA FLIGHT 173 SHOULD MAKE THEIR WAY--
RIGHT THEN. LET'S GET THIS FIASCO ONTO THE RUNWAY.
SHE'S OUR GERALDINE'S KID, JOHN.
YEAH, I KNOW THAT.
SO I'M GOING WHEREVER YOU GO. AND NO BASTARD'S GOING TO STOP ME.
JESUS WEPT, CHAS! THERE'S ONE POOR SOD DEAD ALREADY BECAUSE I WOULDN'T TAKE NO FOR AN ANSWER.
AND I'M GONNA MOVE A LOT FASTER IF I DON'T HAVE TO KEEP STOPPING TO TIE YOUR SHOELACES.
YOU'LL STILL NEED A DRIVER. AND THERE'S ME MARTIAL ARTS TRAINING-- THAT'LL COME IN HANDY.
TAI KWON WHEEL WRENCH? SHUT UP NOW, OKAY?

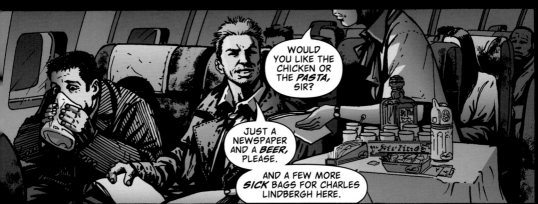

WOULD YOU LIKE THE CHICKEN OR THE *PASTA*, SIR?

JUST A NEWSPAPER AND A *BEER*, PLEASE.

AND A FEW MORE *SICK* BAGS FOR CHARLES LINDBERGH HERE.

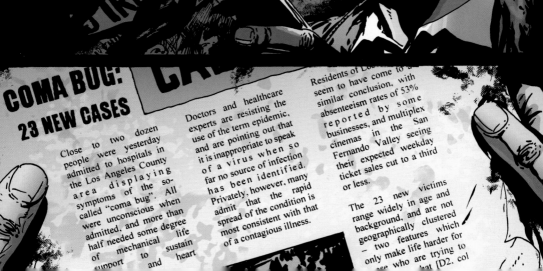

COMA BUG: 23 NEW CASES

Close to two dozen people were yesterday admitted to hospitals in the Los Angeles County area displaying symptoms of the so-called "coma bug". All were unconscious when admitted, and more than half needed some degree of mechanical life support to sustain heart

Doctors and healthcare experts are resisting the use of the term epidemic, and are pointing out that it is inappropriate to speak of a virus when so far no source of infection has been identified. Privately, however, many admit that the rapid spread of the condition is most consistent with that of a contagious illness.

Residents of Los seem to have come to a similar conclusion, with absenteeism rates of 53% reported by some businesses, and multiplex cinemas in the San Fernando Valley seeing their expected weekday ticket sales cut to a third or less.

The 23 new victims range widely in age and background, and are not geographically clustered — two features which only make life harder for those who are trying to [D2. col

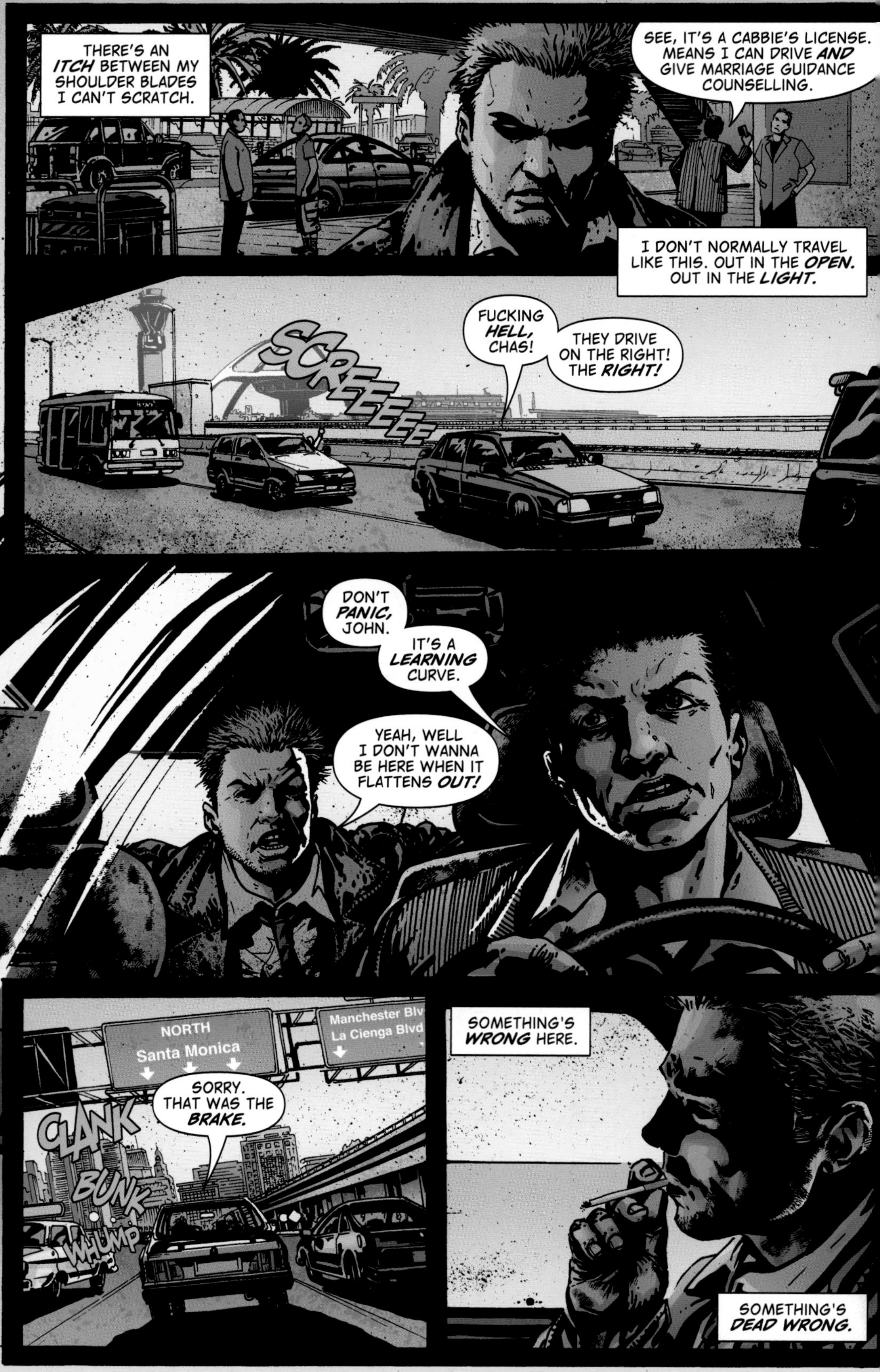
THERE'S AN ITCH BETWEEN MY SHOULDER BLADES I CAN'T SCRATCH.
SEE, IT'S A CABBIE'S LICENSE. MEANS I CAN DRIVE AND GIVE MARRIAGE GUIDANCE COUNSELLING.
I DON'T NORMALLY TRAVEL LIKE THIS. OUT IN THE OPEN. OUT IN THE LIGHT.
SCREEEEEE
FUCKING HELL, CHAS!
THEY DRIVE ON THE RIGHT! THE RIGHT!
DON'T PANIC, JOHN.
IT'S A LEARNING CURVE.
YEAH, WELL I DON'T WANNA BE HERE WHEN IT FLATTENS OUT!
NORTH
Santa Monica
Manchester Blvd
La Cienga Blvd
SORRY. THAT WAS THE BRAKE.
CLANK
BUNK
WHUMP
SOMETHING'S WRONG HERE.
SOMETHING'S DEAD WRONG.

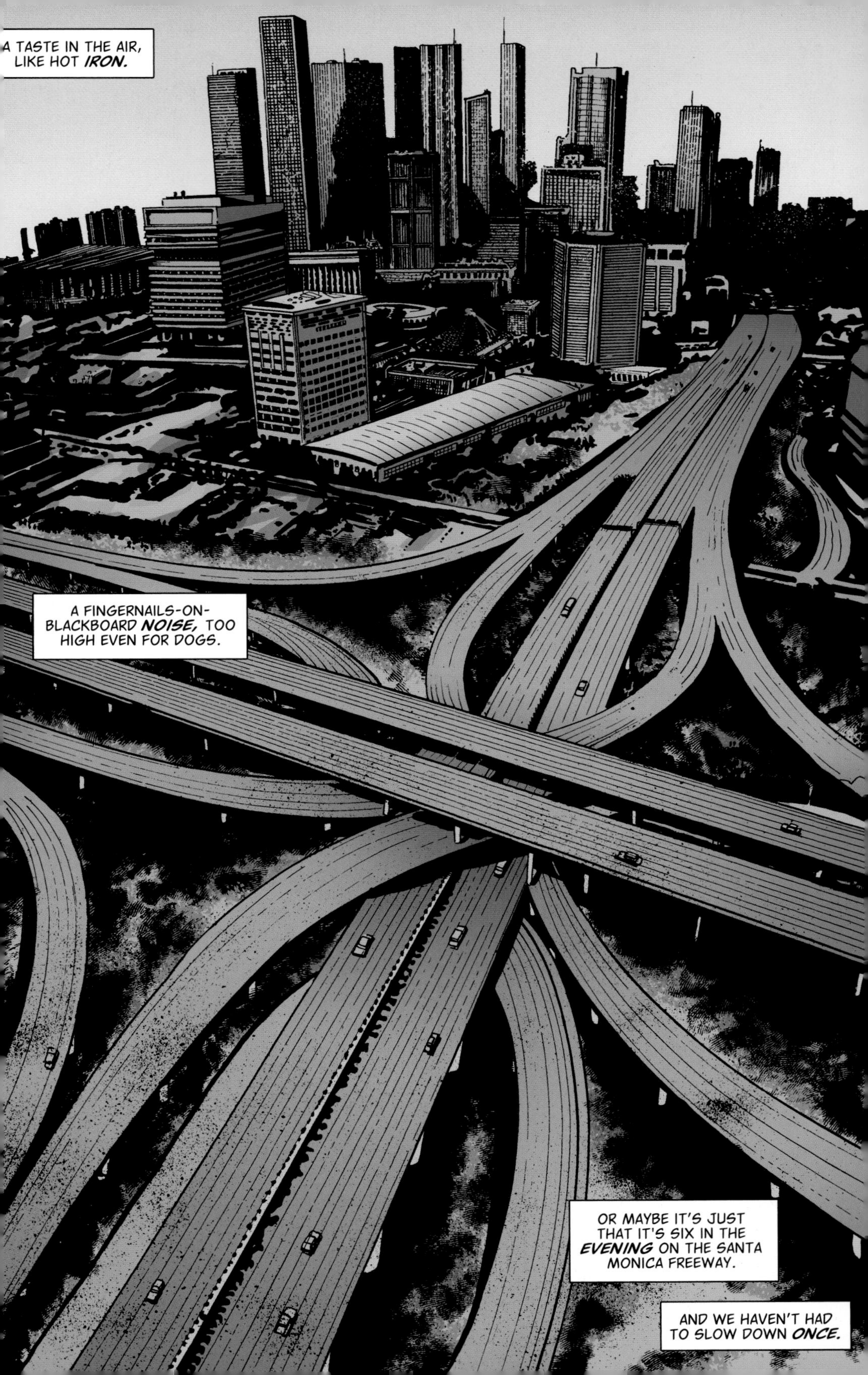
A TASTE IN THE AIR, LIKE HOT IRON.
A FINGERNAILS-ON-BLACKBOARD NOISE, TOO HIGH EVEN FOR DOGS.
OR MAYBE IT'S JUST THAT IT'S SIX IN THE EVENING ON THE SANTA MONICA FREEWAY.
AND WE HAVEN'T HAD TO SLOW DOWN ONCE.

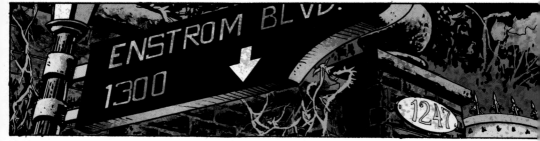

1247 ENSTROM. WE'RE HERE.

BLEEDIN' HELL, JOHN! ISN'T THIS WHERE *WOTSISNAME* USED TO LIVE?

NO. THAT WAS SOMEWHERE *ELSE*.

YES?

JOHN CONSTANTINE. AND THE LOVELY MRS. CONSTANTINE.

A MOMENT, PLEASE.

VMMMMMM

I SAW SOME OF THIS KIT ON *ANTIQUES ROADSHOW.*

IT DIDN'T GO DOWN TOO WELL.

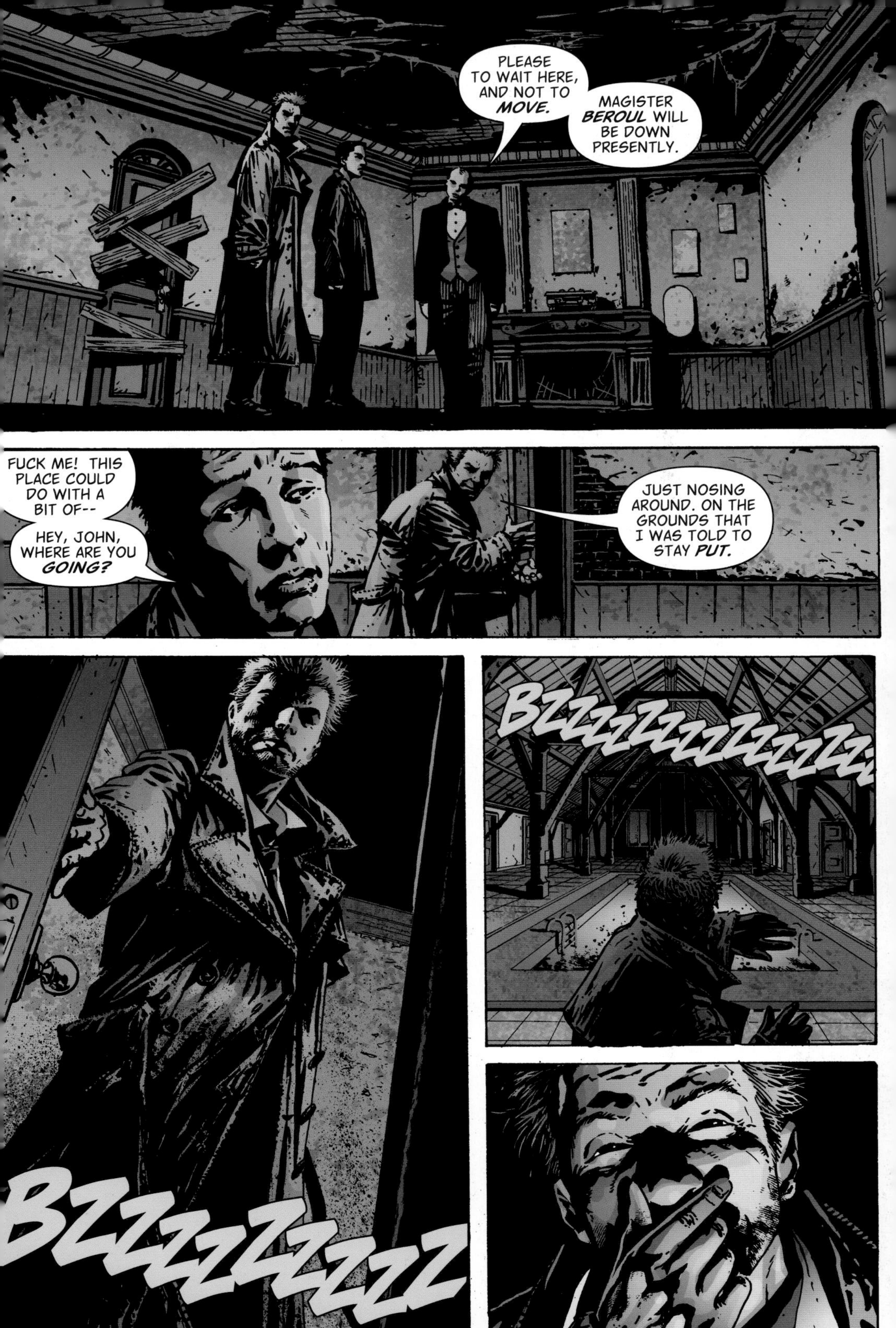

PLEASE TO WAIT HERE, AND NOT TO MOVE.
MAGISTER BEROUL WILL BE DOWN PRESENTLY.
FUCK ME! THIS PLACE COULD DO WITH A BIT OF--
HEY, JOHN, WHERE ARE YOU GOING?
JUST NOSING AROUND. ON THE GROUNDS THAT I WAS TOLD TO STAY PUT.
BZZZZZZZZZ
BZZZZZZZZZZZZZ

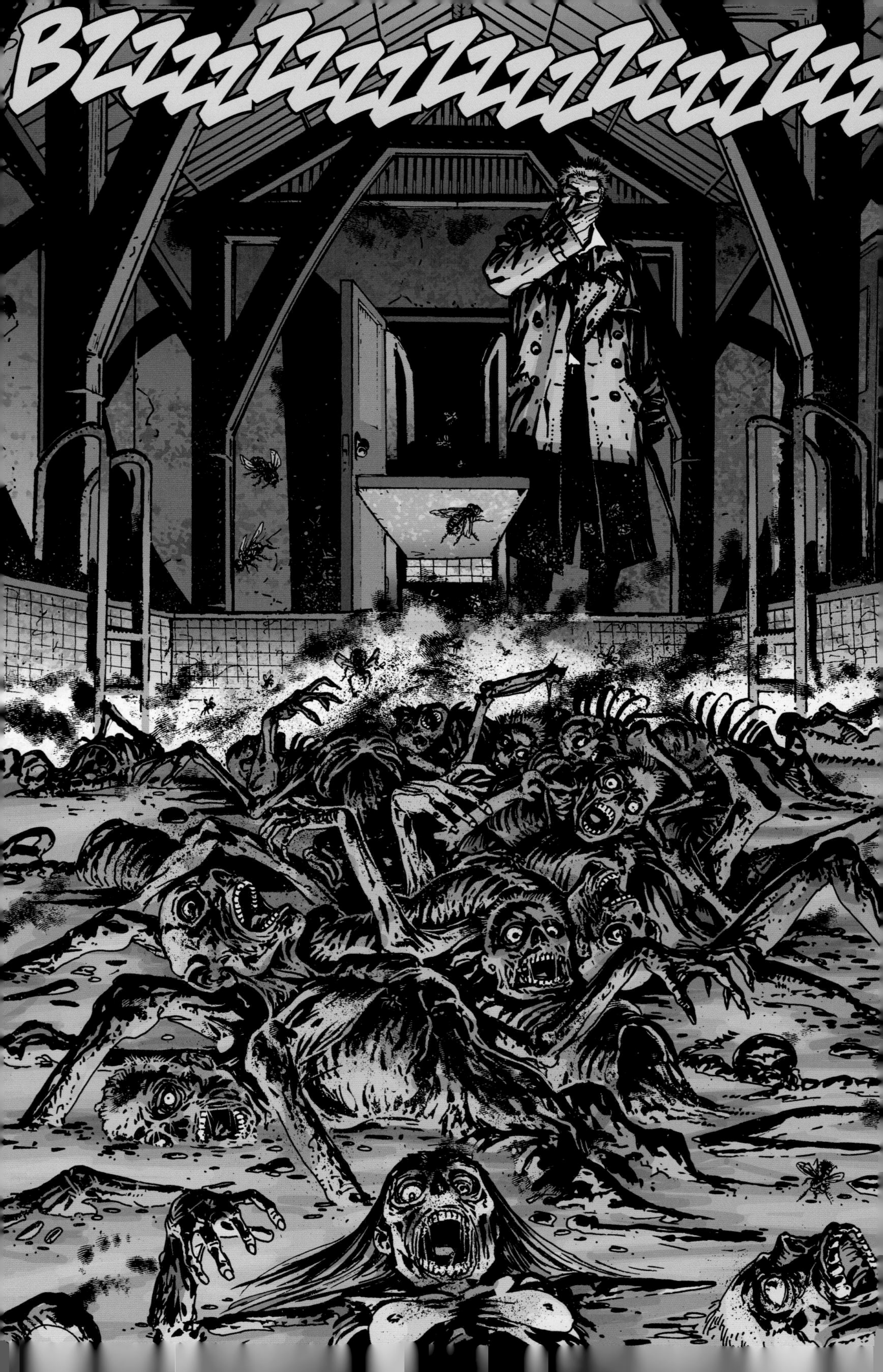
BZZzzZzzzzZzzzzZzzzzZzz

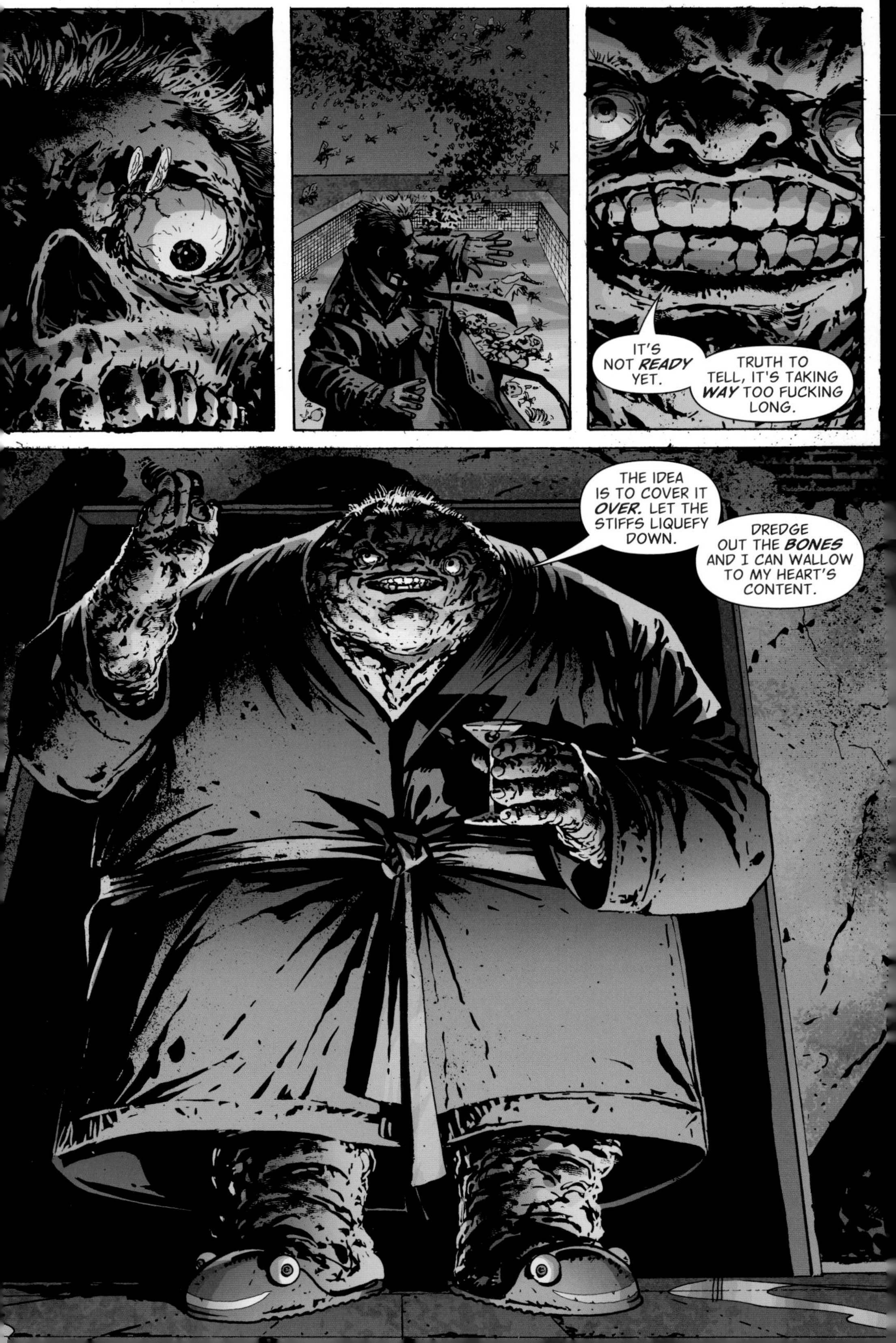
IT'S NOT READY YET.
TRUTH TO TELL, IT'S TAKING WAY TOO FUCKING LONG.
THE IDEA IS TO COVER IT OVER. LET THE STIFFS LIQUEFY DOWN.
DREDGE OUT THE BONES AND I CAN WALLOW TO MY HEART'S CONTENT.

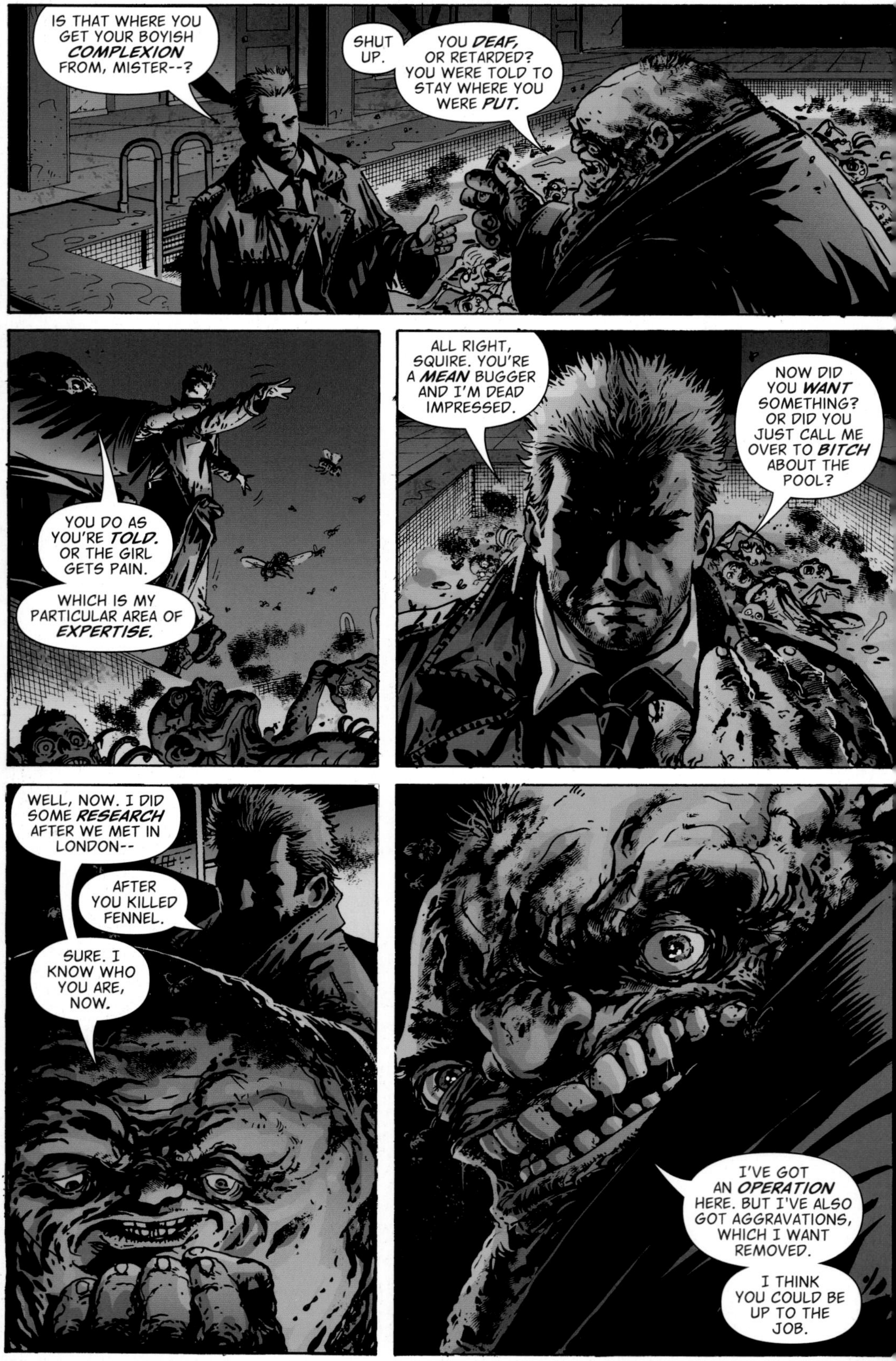
IS THAT WHERE YOU GET YOUR BOYISH COMPLEXION FROM, MISTER--?
SHUT UP.
YOU DEAF, OR RETARDED? YOU WERE TOLD TO STAY WHERE YOU WERE PUT.
YOU DO AS YOU'RE TOLD. OR THE GIRL GETS PAIN.
WHICH IS MY PARTICULAR AREA OF EXPERTISE.
ALL RIGHT, SQUIRE. YOU'RE A MEAN BUGGER AND I'M DEAD IMPRESSED.
NOW DID YOU WANT SOMETHING? OR DID YOU JUST CALL ME OVER TO BITCH ABOUT THE POOL?
WELL, NOW. I DID SOME RESEARCH AFTER WE MET IN LONDON--
AFTER YOU KILLED FENNEL.
SURE. I KNOW WHO YOU ARE, NOW.
I'VE GOT AN OPERATION HERE. BUT I'VE ALSO GOT AGGRAVATIONS, WHICH I WANT REMOVED.
I THINK YOU COULD BE UP TO THE JOB.

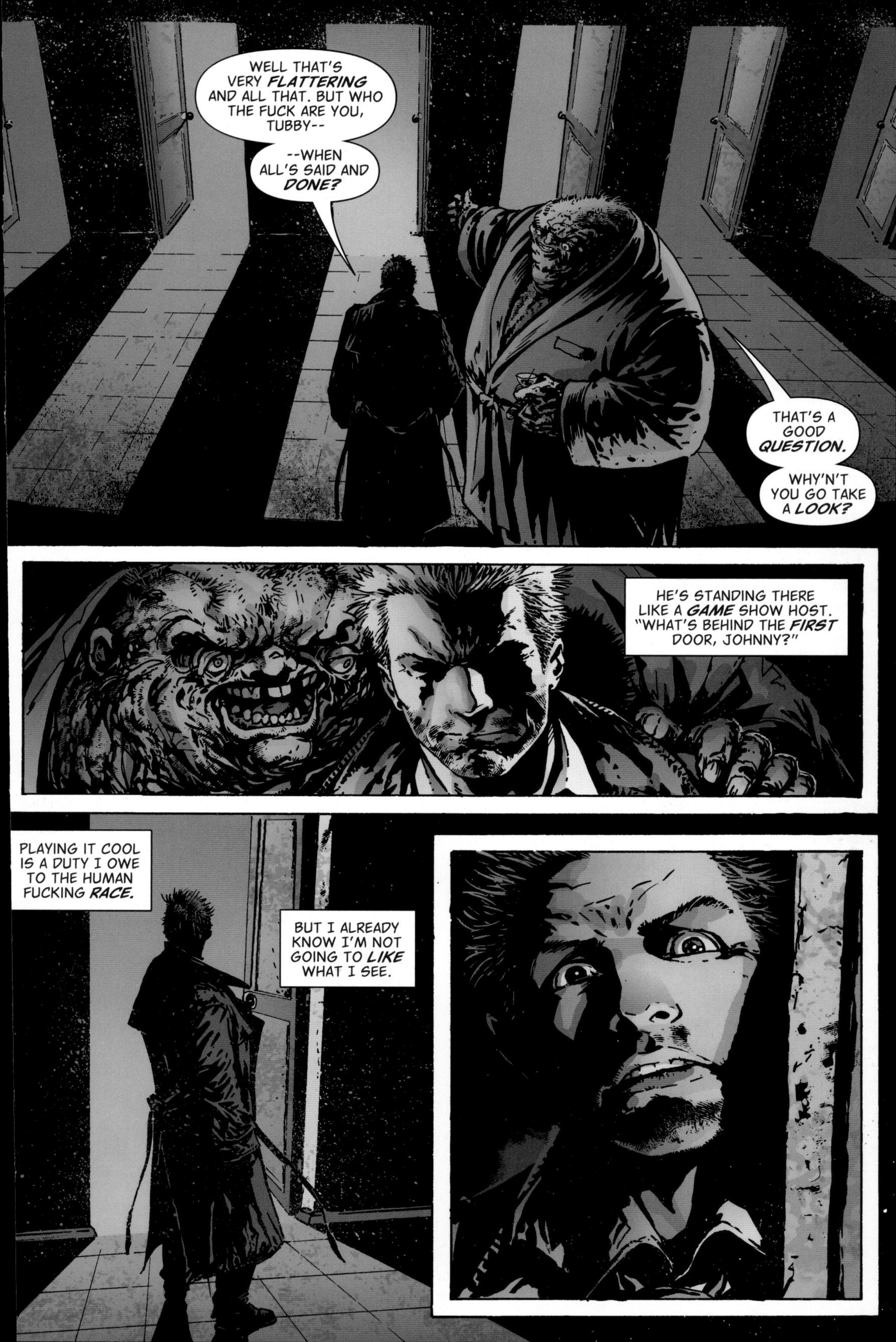
WELL THAT'S VERY FLATTERING AND ALL THAT. BUT WHO THE FUCK ARE YOU, TUBBY--
--WHEN ALL'S SAID AND DONE?
THAT'S A GOOD QUESTION.
WHY'N'T YOU GO TAKE A LOOK?
HE'S STANDING THERE LIKE A GAME SHOW HOST. "WHAT'S BEHIND THE FIRST DOOR, JOHNNY?"
PLAYING IT COOL IS A DUTY I OWE TO THE HUMAN FUCKING RACE.
BUT I ALREADY KNOW I'M NOT GOING TO LIKE WHAT I SEE.

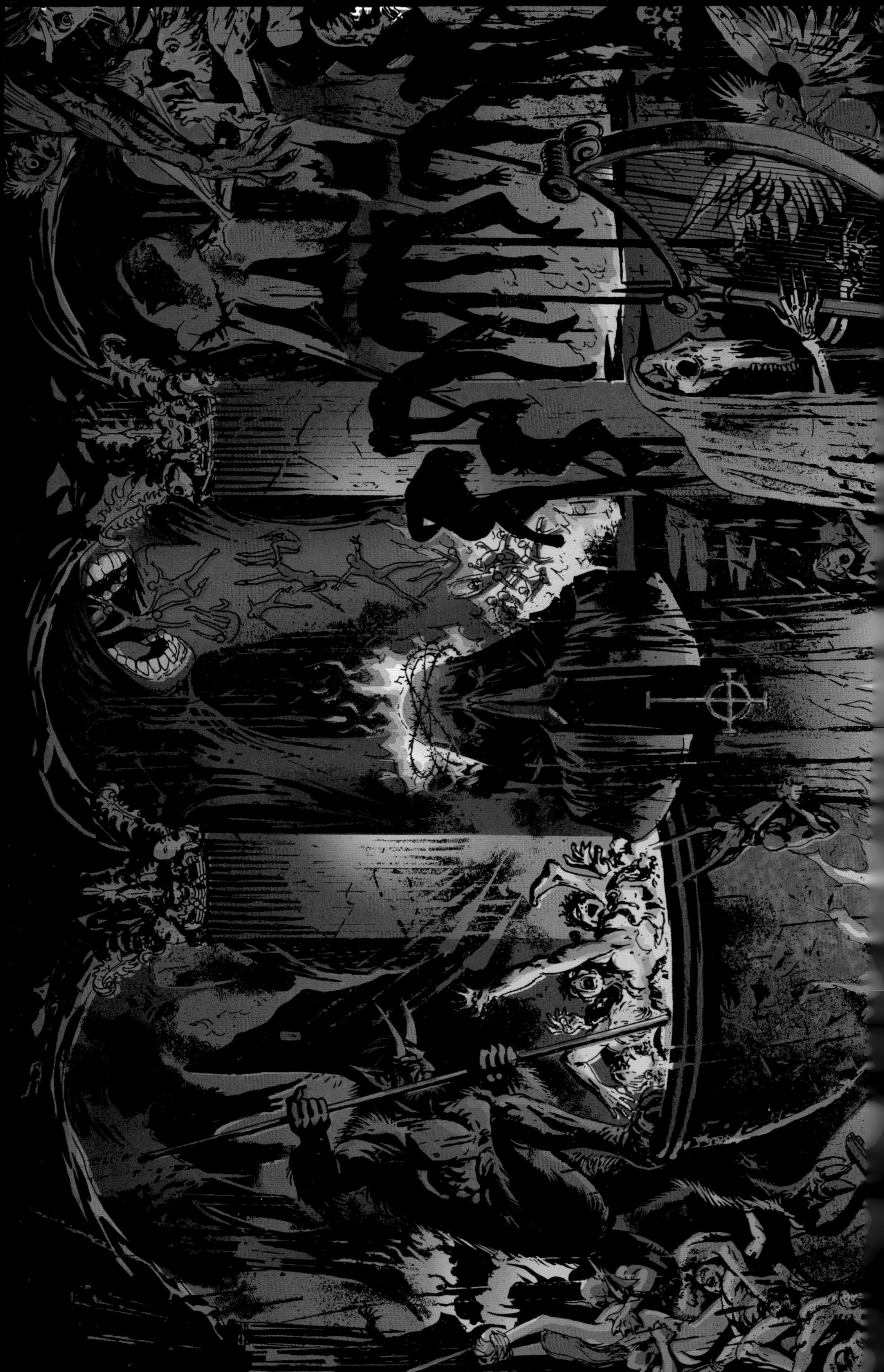

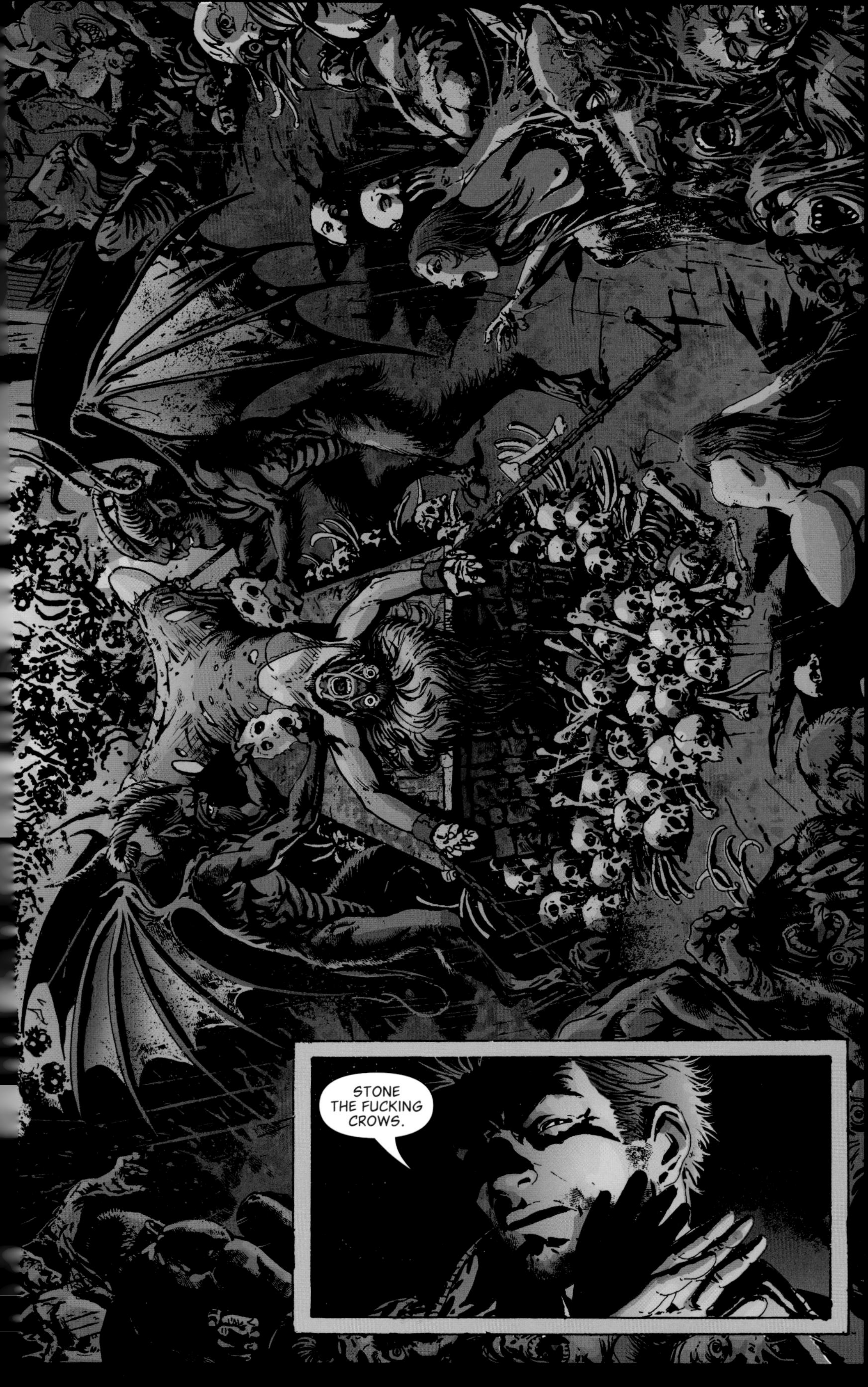
STONE THE FUCKING CROWS.

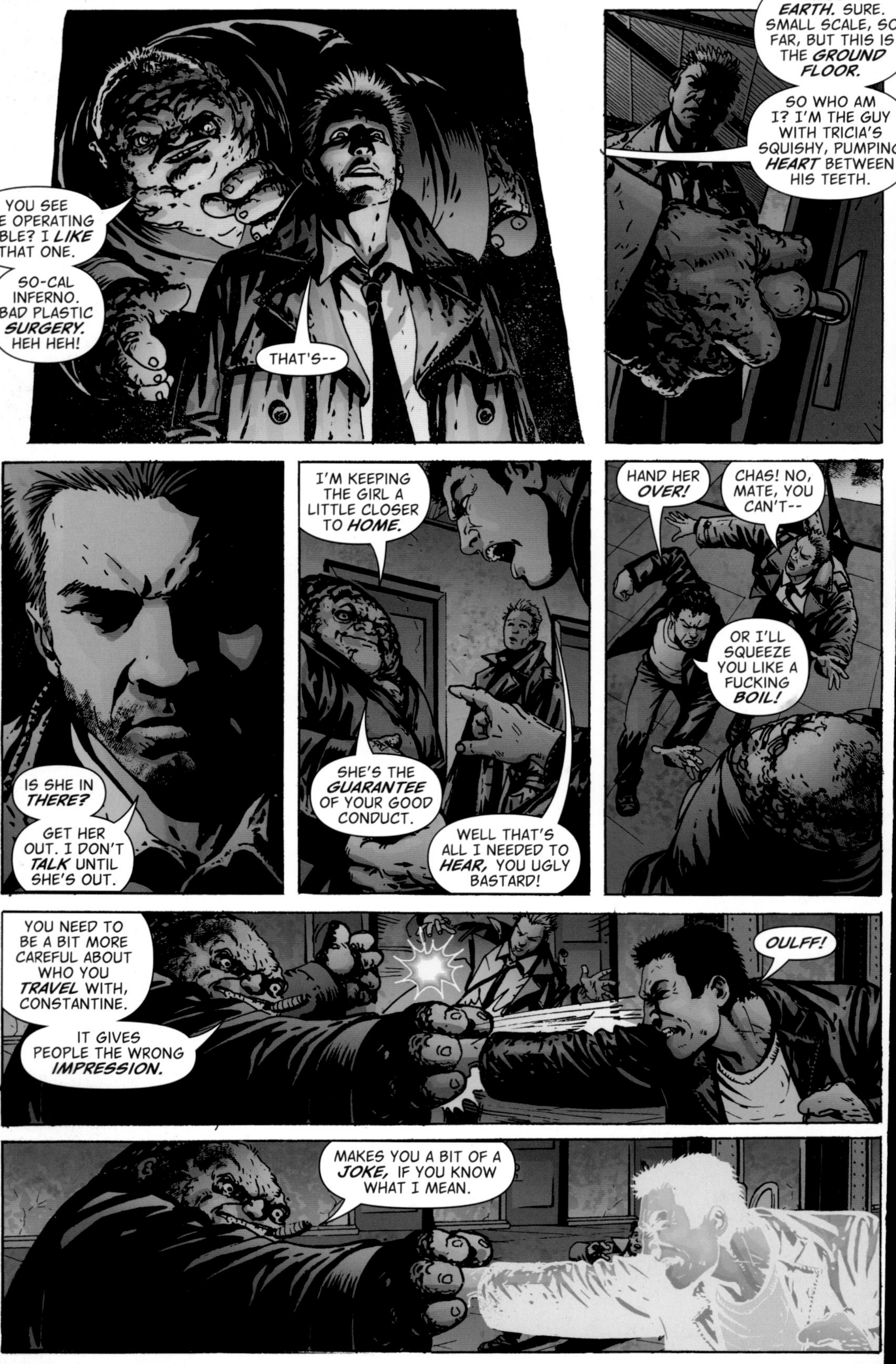
YOU SEE THE OPERATING TABLE? I LIKE THAT ONE.
SO-CAL INFERNO. BAD PLASTIC SURGERY. HEH HEH!
THAT'S--
--HELL ON EARTH. SURE. SMALL SCALE, SO FAR, BUT THIS IS THE GROUND FLOOR.
SO WHO AM I? I'M THE GUY WITH TRICIA'S SQUISHY, PUMPING HEART BETWEEN HIS TEETH.
IS SHE IN THERE?
GET HER OUT. I DON'T TALK UNTIL SHE'S OUT.
I'M KEEPING THE GIRL A LITTLE CLOSER TO HOME.
SHE'S THE GUARANTEE OF YOUR GOOD CONDUCT.
WELL THAT'S ALL I NEEDED TO HEAR, YOU UGLY BASTARD!
HAND HER OVER!
CHAS! NO, MATE, YOU CAN'T--
OR I'LL SQUEEZE YOU LIKE A FUCKING BOIL!
YOU NEED TO BE A BIT MORE CAREFUL ABOUT WHO YOU TRAVEL WITH, CONSTANTINE.
IT GIVES PEOPLE THE WRONG IMPRESSION.
OULFF!
MAKES YOU A BIT OF A JOKE, IF YOU KNOW WHAT I MEAN.

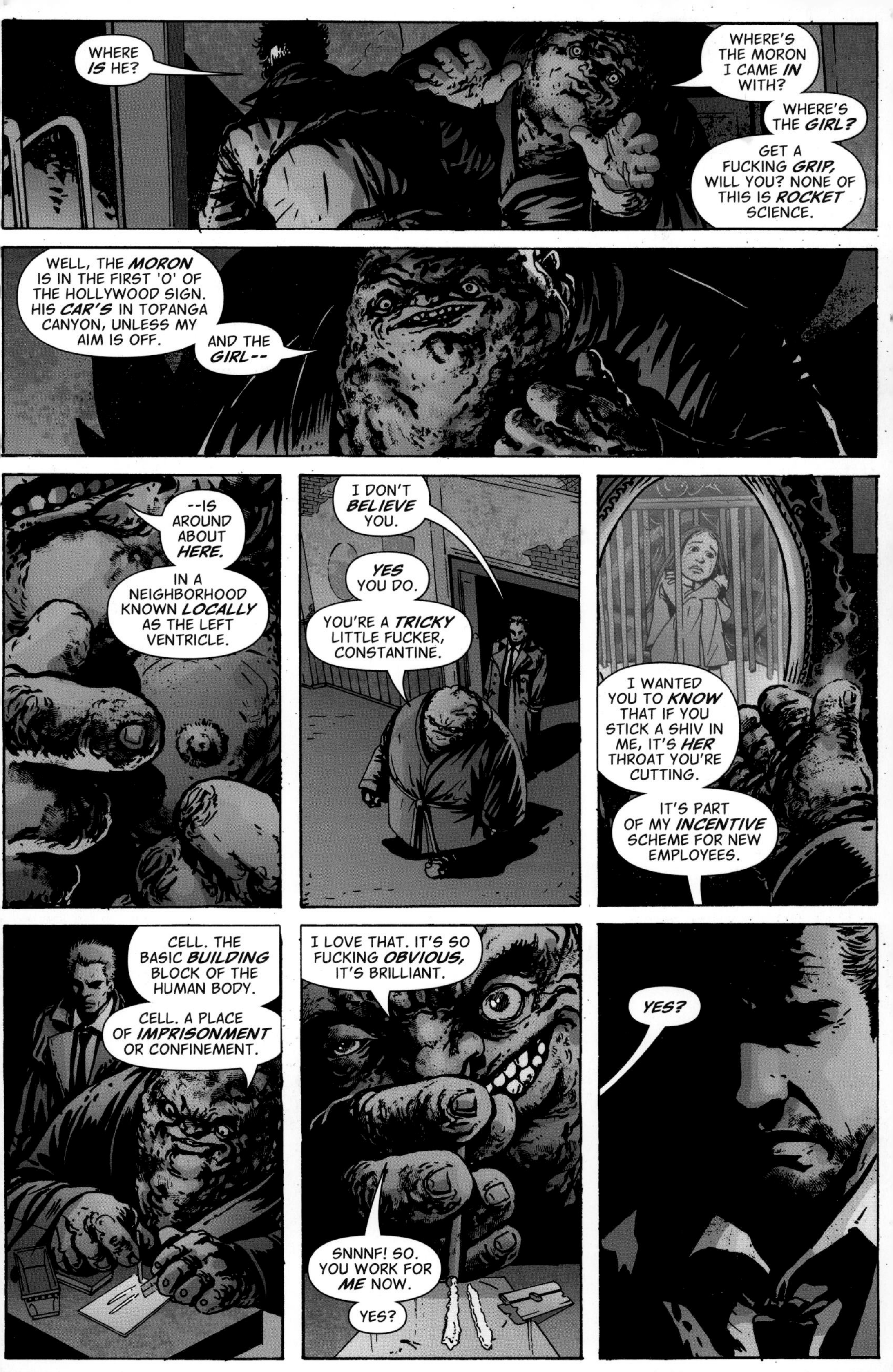
WHERE IS HE?
WHERE'S THE MORON I CAME IN WITH?
WHERE'S THE GIRL?
GET A FUCKING GRIP, WILL YOU? NONE OF THIS IS ROCKET SCIENCE.
WELL, THE MORON IS IN THE FIRST 'O' OF THE HOLLYWOOD SIGN. HIS CAR'S IN TOPANGA CANYON, UNLESS MY AIM IS OFF.
AND THE GIRL--
--IS AROUND ABOUT HERE.
IN A NEIGHBORHOOD KNOWN LOCALLY AS THE LEFT VENTRICLE.
I DON'T BELIEVE YOU.
YES YOU DO.
YOU'RE A TRICKY LITTLE FUCKER, CONSTANTINE.
I WANTED YOU TO KNOW THAT IF YOU STICK A SHIV IN ME, IT'S HER THROAT YOU'RE CUTTING.
IT'S PART OF MY INCENTIVE SCHEME FOR NEW EMPLOYEES.
CELL. THE BASIC BUILDING BLOCK OF THE HUMAN BODY.
CELL. A PLACE OF IMPRISONMENT OR CONFINEMENT.
I LOVE THAT. IT'S SO FUCKING OBVIOUS, IT'S BRILLIANT.
SNNNF! SO. YOU WORK FOR ME NOW.
YES?
YES?

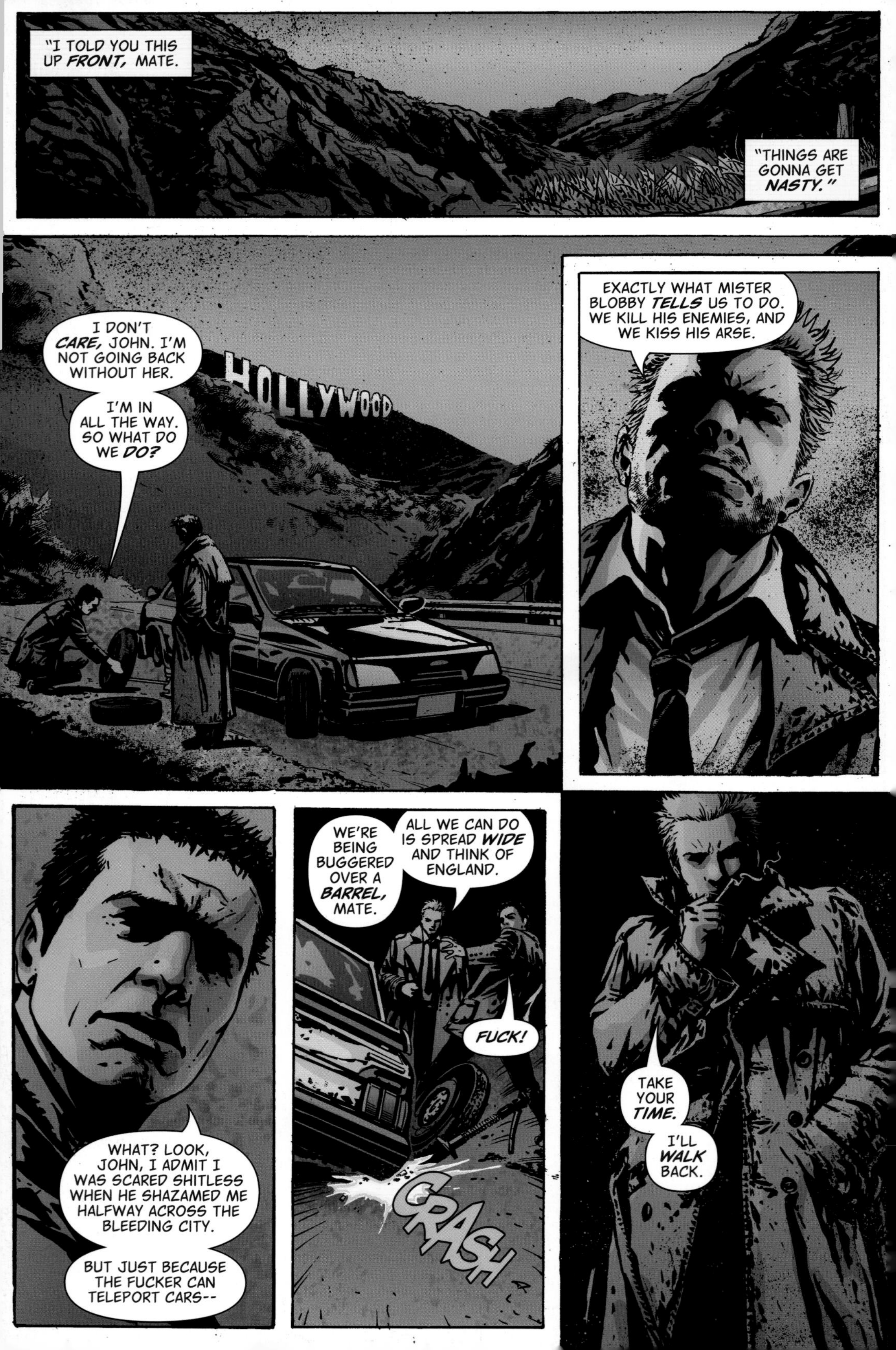
"I TOLD YOU THIS UP FRONT, MATE.
"THINGS ARE GONNA GET NASTY."
HOLLYWOOD
I DON'T CARE, JOHN. I'M NOT GOING BACK WITHOUT HER.
I'M IN ALL THE WAY. SO WHAT DO WE DO?
EXACTLY WHAT MISTER BLOBBY TELLS US TO DO. WE KILL HIS ENEMIES, AND WE KISS HIS ARSE.
WHAT? LOOK, JOHN, I ADMIT I WAS SCARED SHITLESS WHEN HE SHAZAMED ME HALFWAY ACROSS THE BLEEDING CITY.
BUT JUST BECAUSE THE FUCKER CAN TELEPORT CARS--
WE'RE BEING BUGGERED OVER A BARREL, MATE.
ALL WE CAN DO IS SPREAD WIDE AND THINK OF ENGLAND.
FUCK!
CRASH
TAKE YOUR TIME.
I'LL WALK BACK.

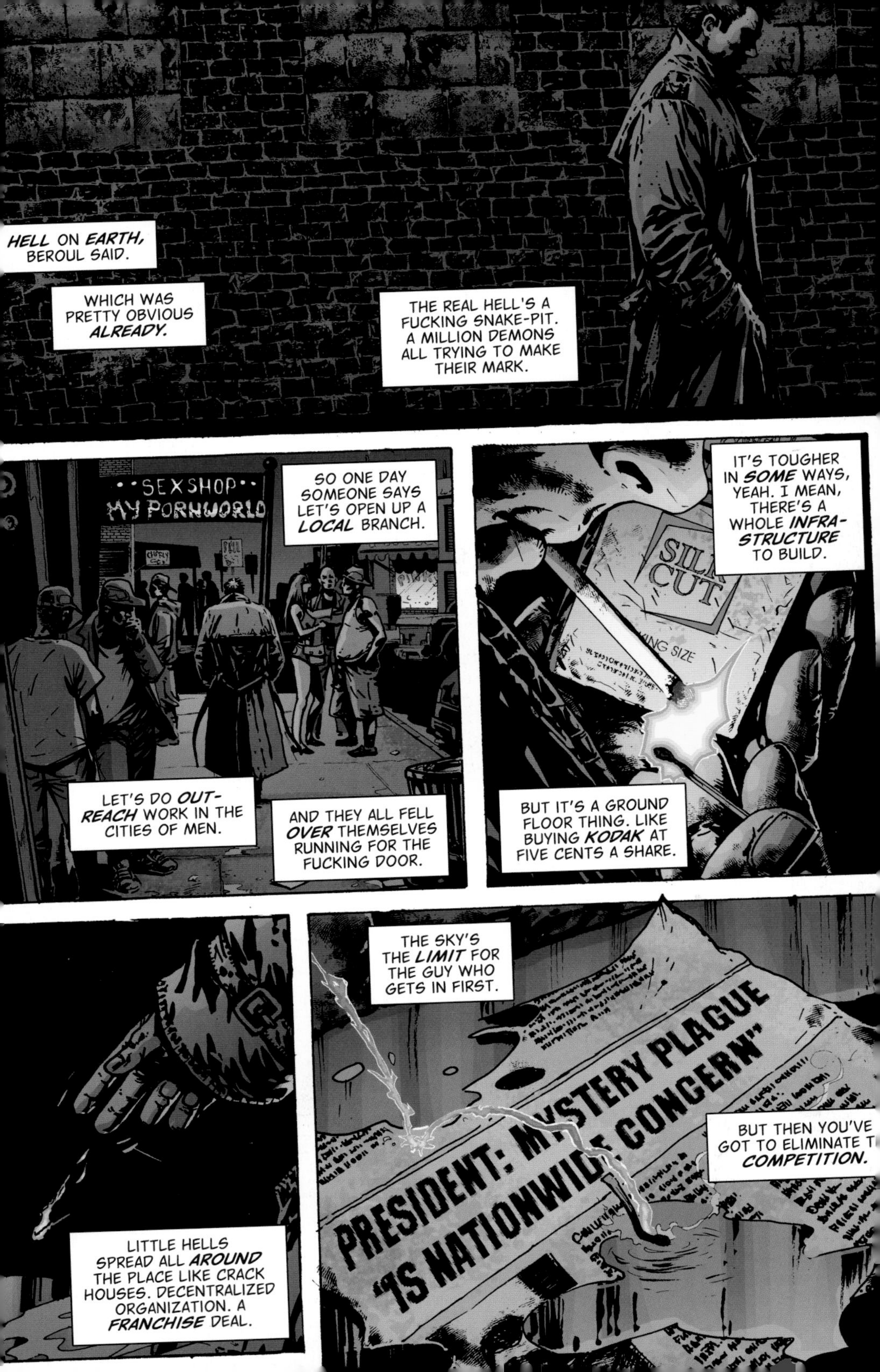
HELL ON EARTH, BEROUL SAID.
WHICH WAS PRETTY OBVIOUS ALREADY.
THE REAL HELL'S A FUCKING SNAKE-PIT. A MILLION DEMONS ALL TRYING TO MAKE THEIR MARK.
• • SEXSHOP • •
MY PORNWORLD
SO ONE DAY SOMEONE SAYS LET'S OPEN UP A LOCAL BRANCH.
LET'S DO OUT-REACH WORK IN THE CITIES OF MEN.
AND THEY ALL FELL OVER THEMSELVES RUNNING FOR THE FUCKING DOOR.
IT'S TOUGHER IN SOME WAYS, YEAH. I MEAN, THERE'S A WHOLE INFRA-STRUCTURE TO BUILD.
CUT
BUT IT'S A GROUND FLOOR THING. LIKE BUYING KODAK AT FIVE CENTS A SHARE.
LITTLE HELLS SPREAD ALL AROUND THE PLACE LIKE CRACK HOUSES. DECENTRALIZED ORGANIZATION. A FRANCHISE DEAL.
THE SKY'S THE LIMIT FOR THE GUY WHO GETS IN FIRST.
PRESIDENT: MYSTERY PLAGUE
"IS NATIONWIDE CONCERN"
BUT THEN YOU'VE GOT TO ELIMINATE T
COMPETITION.

CHAPTER THREE

blood of sacrifice

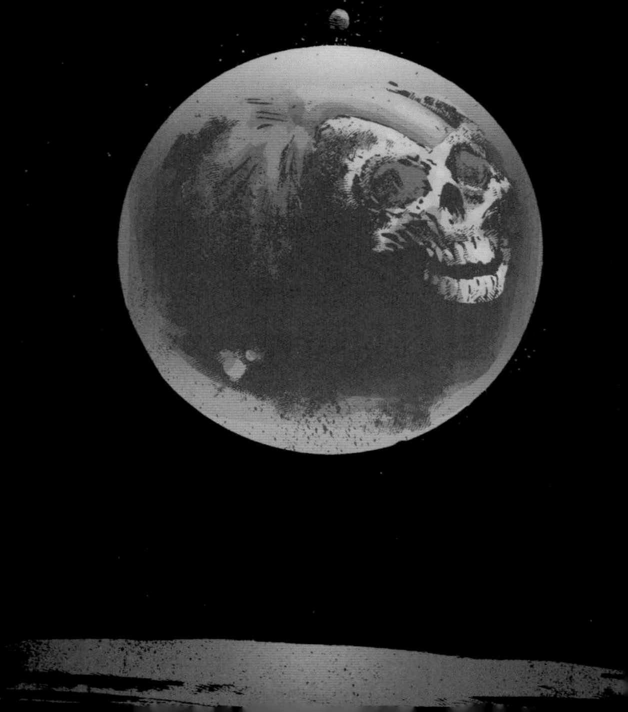

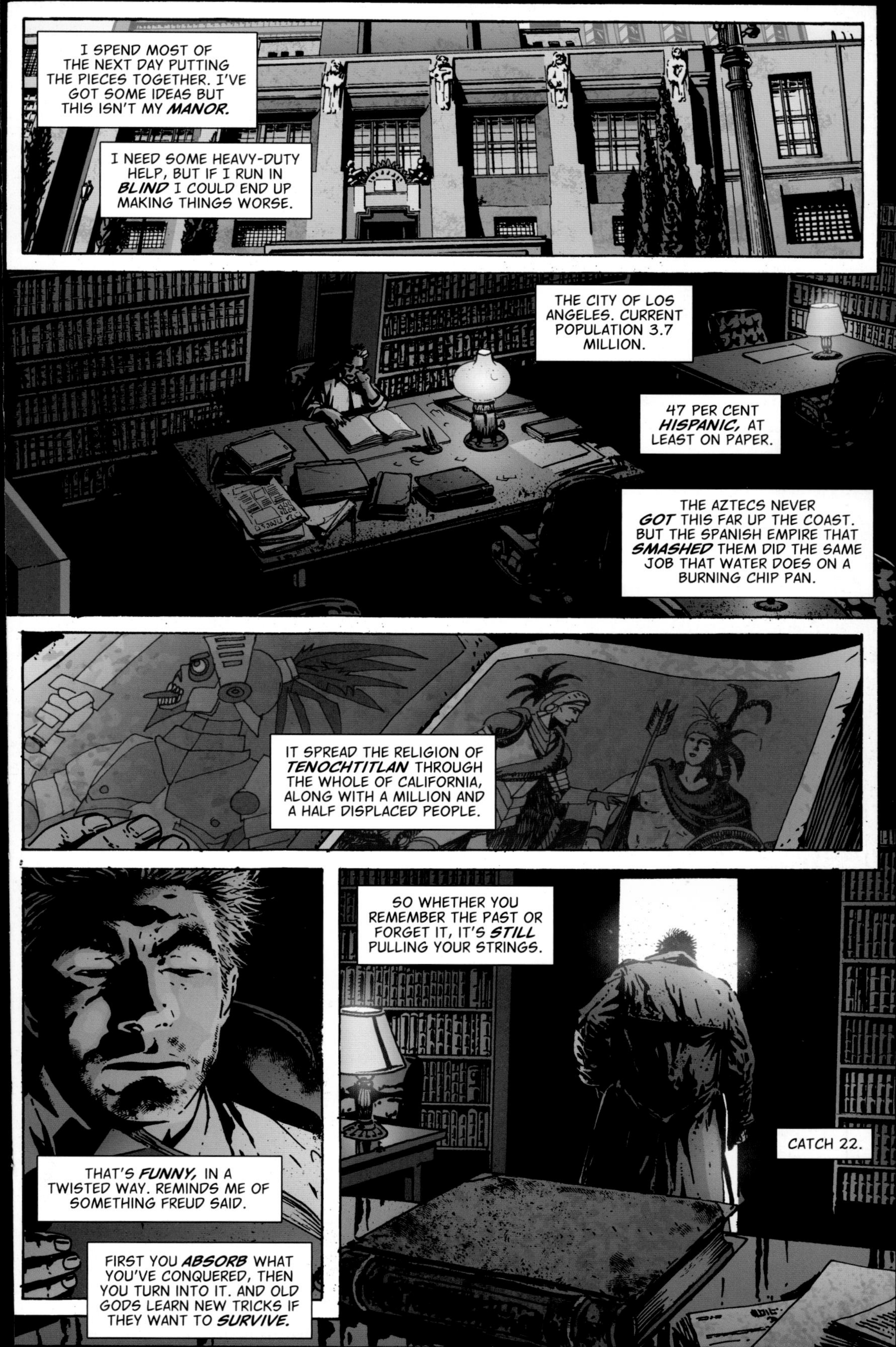
I SPEND MOST OF THE NEXT DAY PUTTING THE PIECES TOGETHER. I'VE GOT SOME IDEAS BUT THIS ISN'T MY MANOR.
I NEED SOME HEAVY-DUTY HELP, BUT IF I RUN IN BLIND I COULD END UP MAKING THINGS WORSE.
THE CITY OF LOS ANGELES. CURRENT POPULATION 3.7 MILLION.
47 PER CENT HISPANIC, AT LEAST ON PAPER.
THE AZTECS NEVER GOT THIS FAR UP THE COAST. BUT THE SPANISH EMPIRE THAT SMASHED THEM DID THE SAME JOB THAT WATER DOES ON A BURNING CHIP PAN.
IT SPREAD THE RELIGION OF TENOCHTITLAN THROUGH THE WHOLE OF CALIFORNIA, ALONG WITH A MILLION AND A HALF DISPLACED PEOPLE.
THAT'S FUNNY, IN A TWISTED WAY. REMINDS ME OF SOMETHING FREUD SAID.
FIRST YOU ABSORB WHAT YOU'VE CONQUERED, THEN YOU TURN INTO IT. AND OLD GODS LEARN NEW TRICKS IF THEY WANT TO SURVIVE.
SO WHETHER YOU REMEMBER THE PAST OR FORGET IT, IT'S STILL PULLING YOUR STRINGS.
CATCH 22.

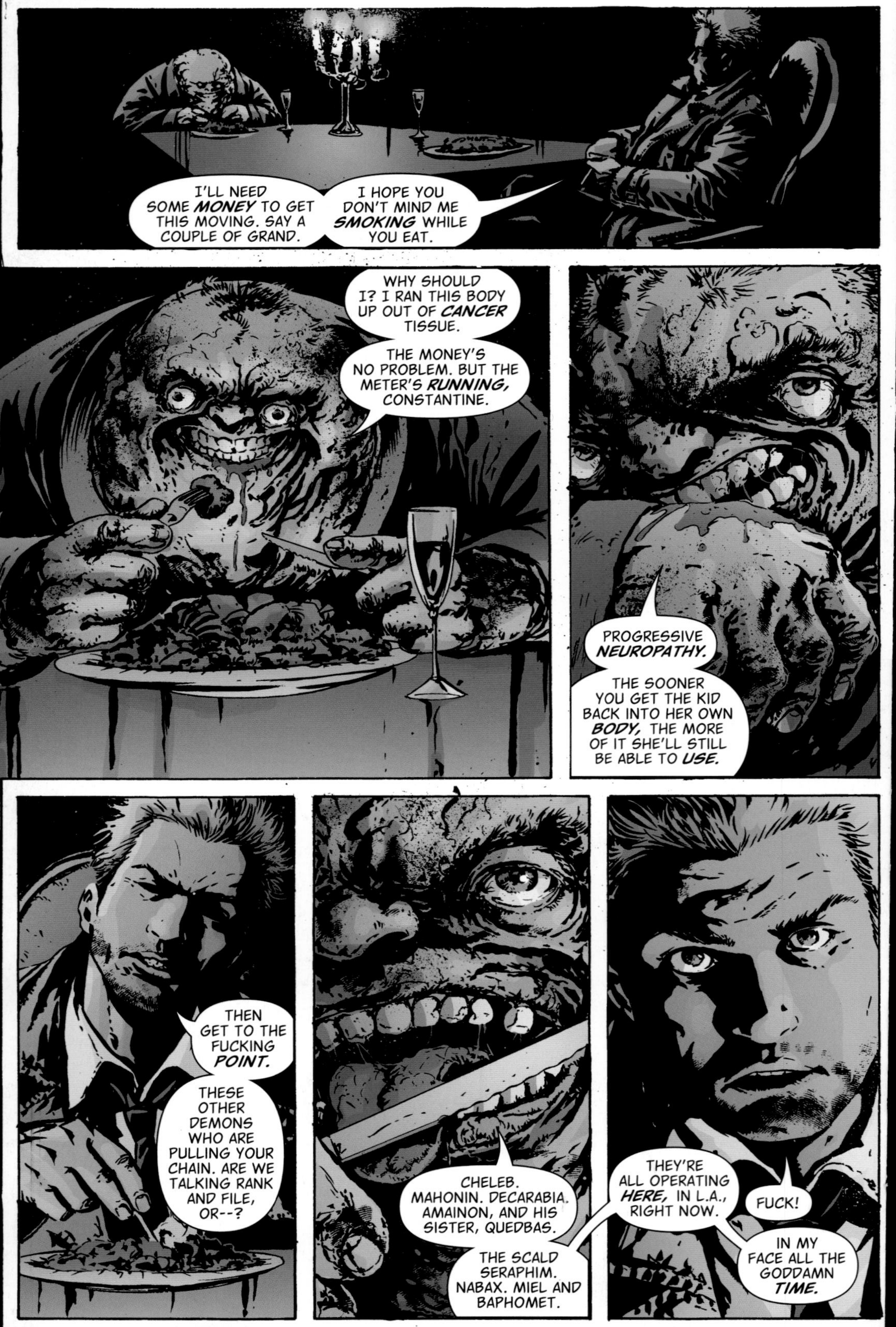
I'LL NEED SOME *MONEY* TO GET THIS MOVING. SAY A COUPLE OF GRAND.
I HOPE YOU DON'T MIND ME *SMOKING* WHILE YOU EAT.
WHY SHOULD I? I RAN THIS BODY UP OUT OF *CANCER* TISSUE.
THE MONEY'S NO PROBLEM. BUT THE METER'S *RUNNING,* CONSTANTINE.
PROGRESSIVE *NEUROPATHY.*
THE SOONER YOU GET THE KID BACK INTO HER OWN *BODY,* THE MORE OF IT SHE'LL STILL BE ABLE TO *USE.*
THEN GET TO THE FUCKING *POINT.*
THESE OTHER DEMONS WHO ARE PULLING YOUR CHAIN. ARE WE TALKING RANK AND FILE, OR--?
CHELEB. MAHONIN. DECARABIA. AMAINON, AND HIS SISTER, QUEDBAS.
THE SCALD SERAPHIM. NABAX. MIEL AND BAPHOMET.
THEY'RE ALL OPERATING *HERE,* IN L.A., RIGHT NOW.
FUCK!
IN MY FACE ALL THE GODDAMN *TIME.*

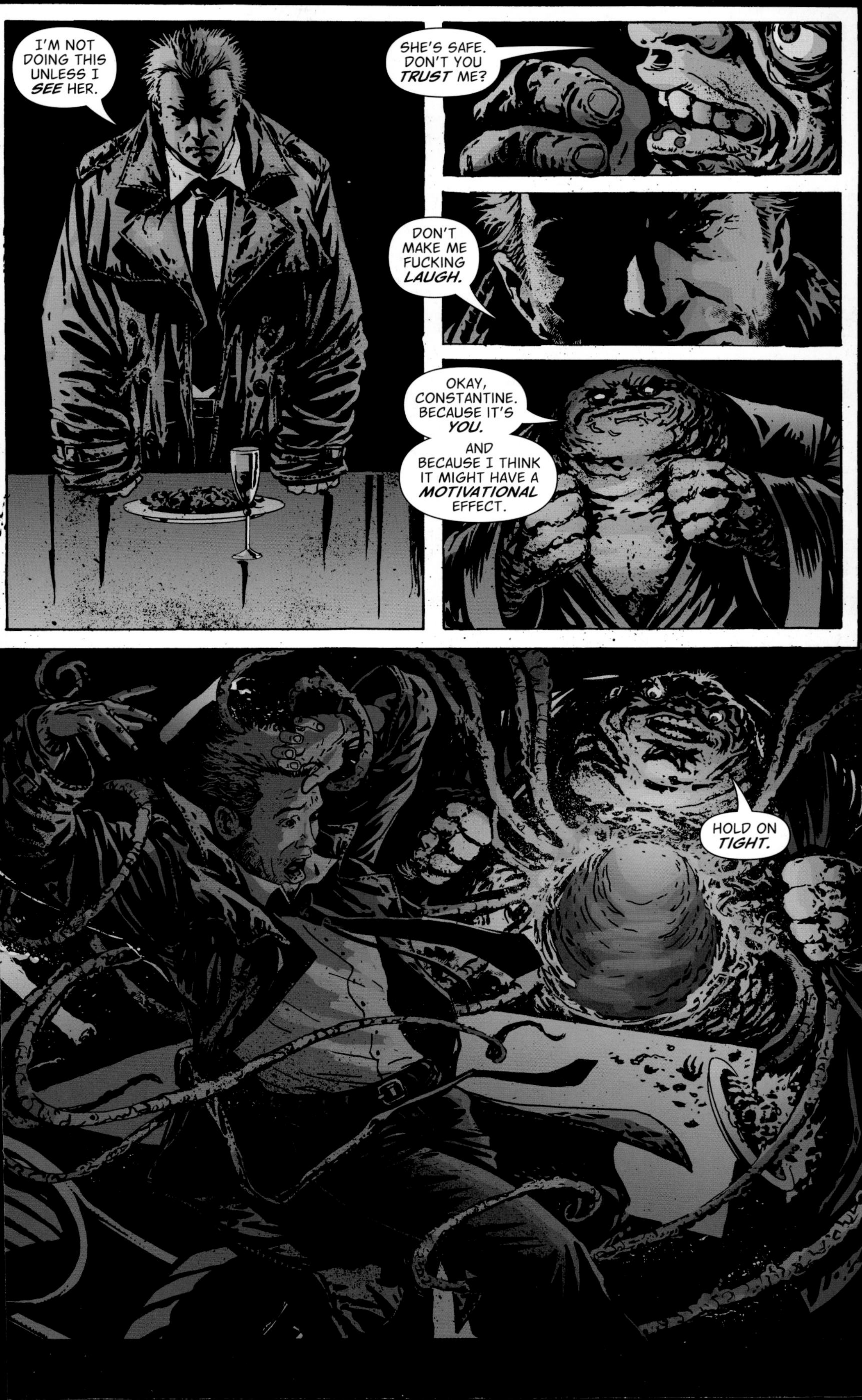
I'M NOT DOING THIS UNLESS I *SEE* HER.
SHE'S SAFE. DON'T YOU *TRUST* ME?
DON'T MAKE ME FUCKING *LAUGH.*
OKAY, CONSTANTINE. BECAUSE IT'S *YOU.*
AND BECAUSE I THINK IT MIGHT HAVE A *MOTIVATIONAL* EFFECT.
HOLD ON *TIGHT.*

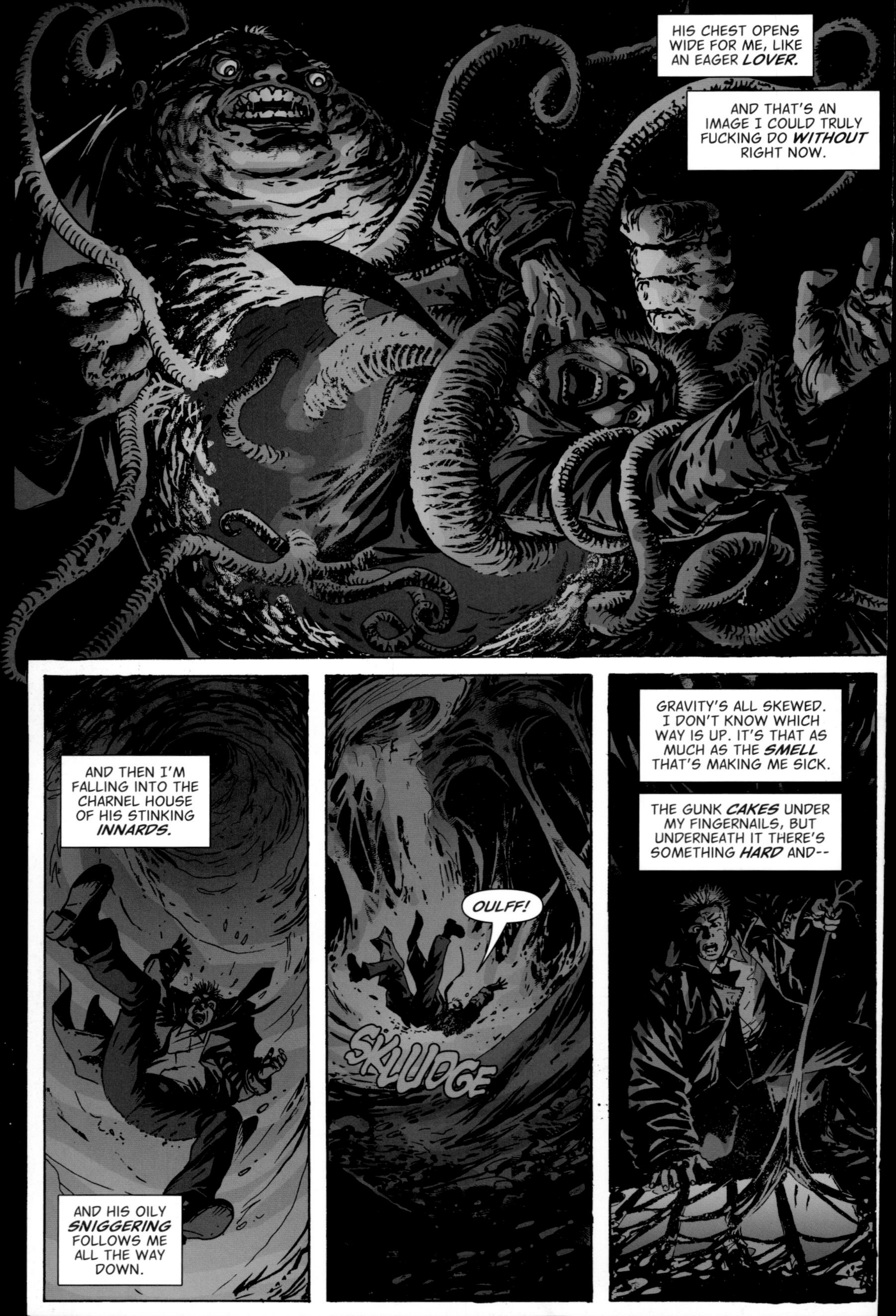
HIS CHEST OPENS WIDE FOR ME, LIKE AN EAGER LOVER.
AND THAT'S AN IMAGE I COULD TRULY FUCKING DO WITHOUT RIGHT NOW.
AND THEN I'M FALLING INTO THE CHARNEL HOUSE OF HIS STINKING INNARDS.
AND HIS OILY SNIGGERING FOLLOWS ME ALL THE WAY DOWN.
OULFF!
SKLUDGE
GRAVITY'S ALL SKEWED. I DON'T KNOW WHICH WAY IS UP. IT'S THAT AS MUCH AS THE SMELL THAT'S MAKING ME SICK.
THE GUNK CAKES UNDER MY FINGERNAILS, BUT UNDERNEATH IT THERE'S SOMETHING HARD AND--

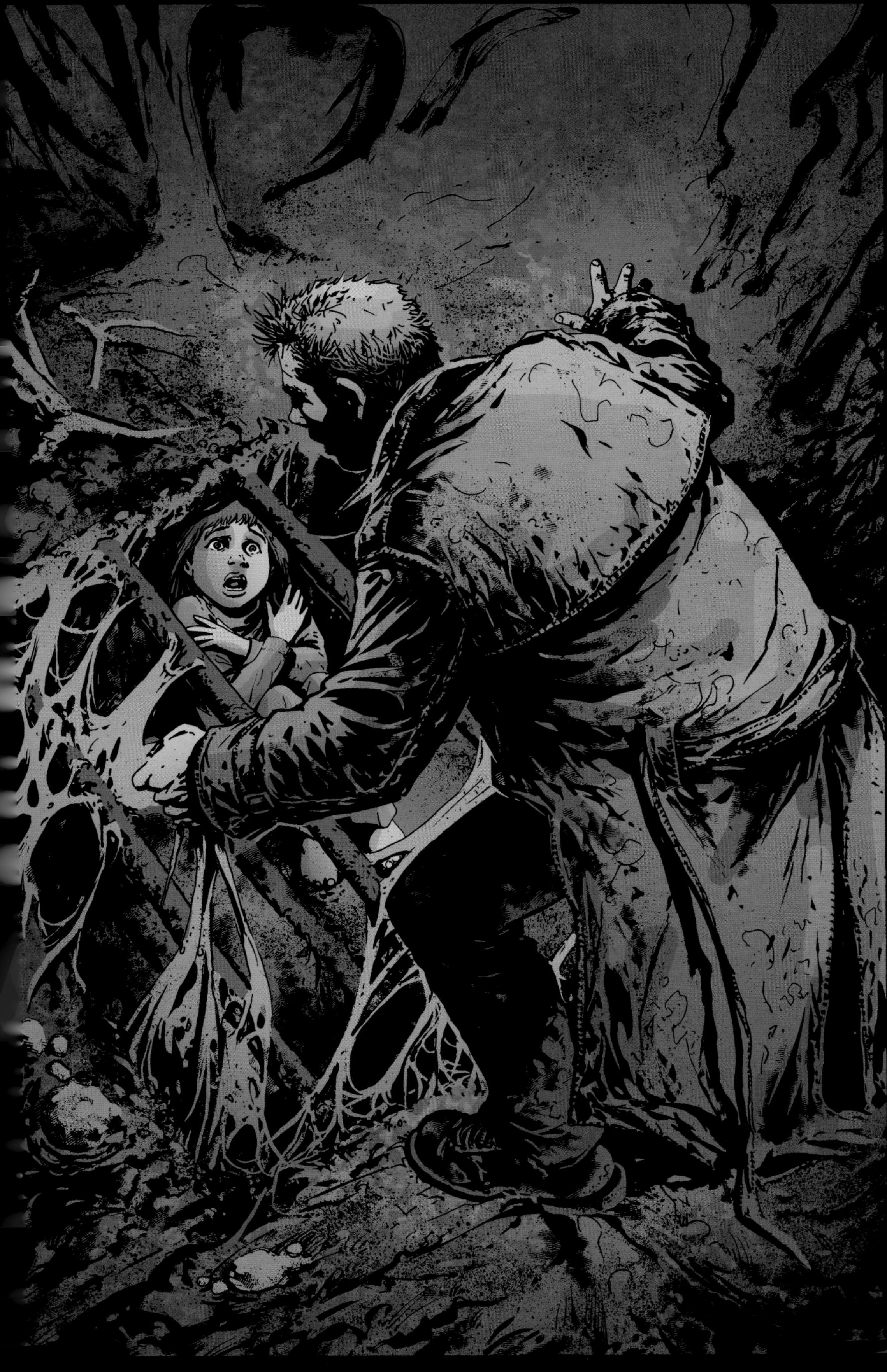

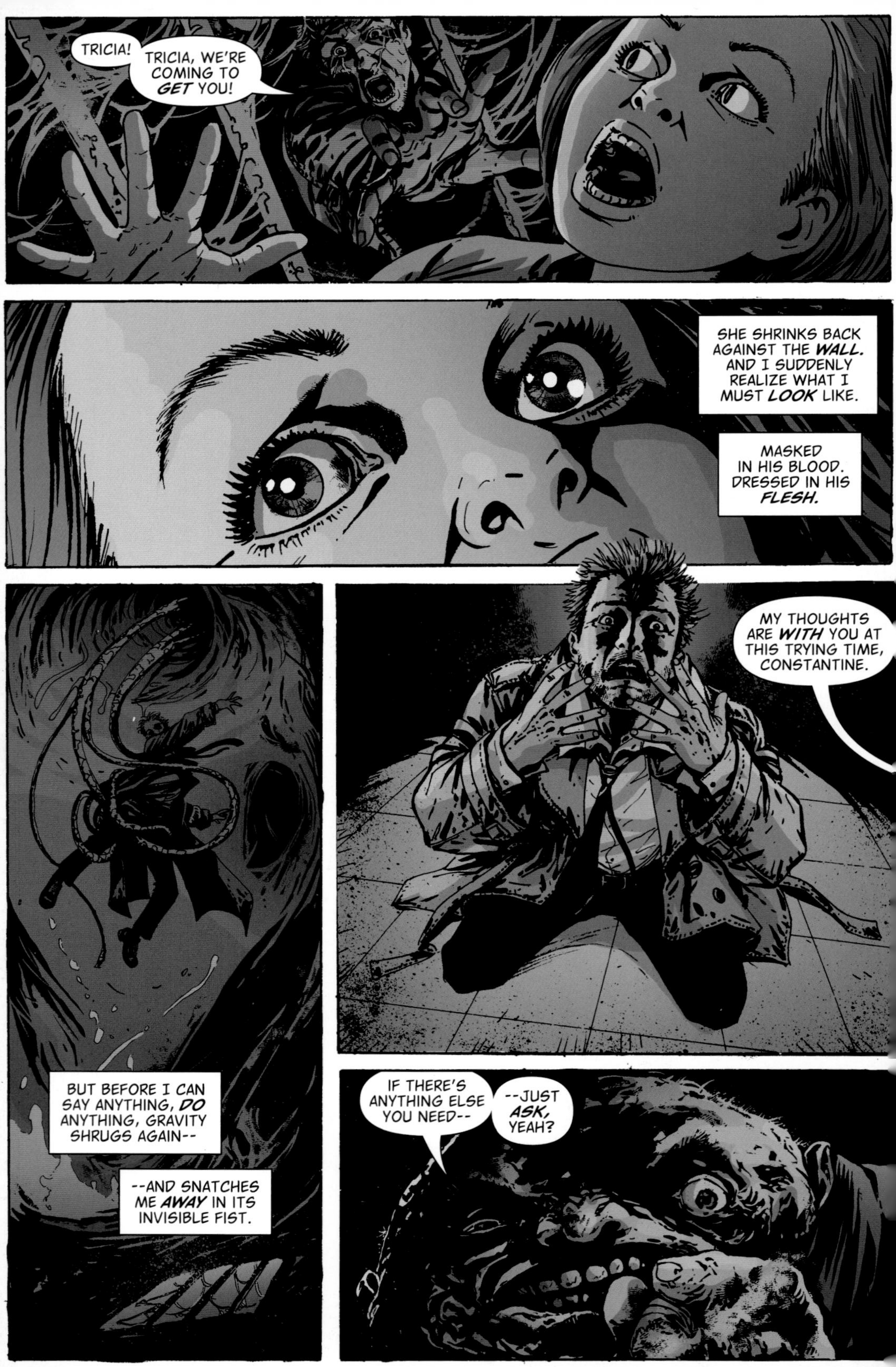
TRICIA!
TRICIA, WE'RE COMING TO *GET* YOU!
SHE SHRINKS BACK AGAINST THE *WALL.* AND I SUDDENLY REALIZE WHAT I MUST *LOOK* LIKE.
MASKED IN HIS BLOOD. DRESSED IN HIS *FLESH.*
BUT BEFORE I CAN SAY ANYTHING, *DO* ANYTHING, GRAVITY SHRUGS AGAIN--
--AND SNATCHES ME *AWAY* IN ITS INVISIBLE FIST.
MY THOUGHTS ARE *WITH* YOU AT THIS TRYING TIME, CONSTANTINE.
IF THERE'S ANYTHING ELSE YOU NEED--
--JUST *ASK,* YEAH?

THOUGHT I'D FEEL BETTER OUT ON THE *STREETS.*

BUT THEY'RE NOT *MY* STREETS. THEY DON'T *OPEN* THE SAME WAY.

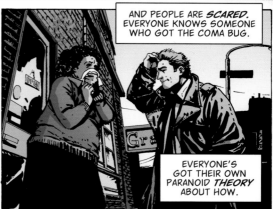

AND PEOPLE ARE *SCARED.* EVERYONE KNOWS SOMEONE WHO GOT THE COMA BUG.

EVERYONE'S GOT THEIR OWN PARANOID *THEORY* ABOUT HOW.

BUT THERE *IS* A TRAIL. AND I FOLLOW IT. OUT OF THE VALLEY, THROUGH EAST L.A. TO MONTEREY PARK.

A LOT OF THE TIME I'M GLAD OF THE DAYLIGHT. AND THAT'S A *NOVELTY* FOR ME.

THE CITY *BREATHES* GASOLINE AND CHURCH INCENSE.

SOBS AND KEENS TO ITSELF IN *SIRENS.*

AND IT LOOKS OVER MY *SHOULDER* AS I WALK.

I FUCKING *HATE* THAT.

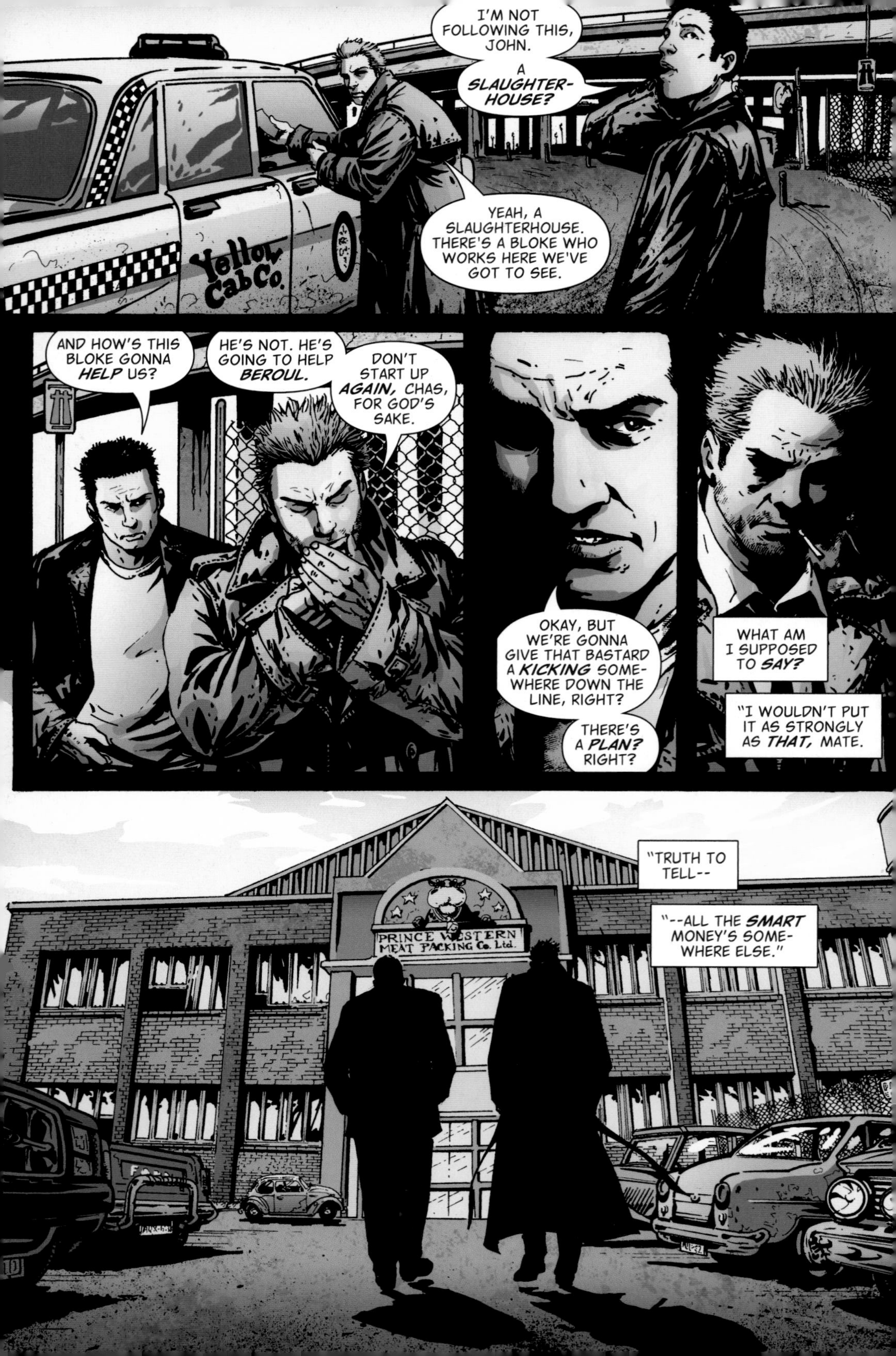

I'M NOT FOLLOWING THIS, JOHN.
A SLAUGHTER-HOUSE?
YEAH, A SLAUGHTERHOUSE. THERE'S A BLOKE WHO WORKS HERE WE'VE GOT TO SEE.
Yellow Cab Co.
AND HOW'S THIS BLOKE GONNA HELP US?
HE'S NOT. HE'S GOING TO HELP BEROUL.
DON'T START UP AGAIN, CHAS, FOR GOD'S SAKE.
OKAY, BUT WE'RE GONNA GIVE THAT BASTARD A KICKING SOME-WHERE DOWN THE LINE, RIGHT?
THERE'S A PLAN? RIGHT?
WHAT AM I SUPPOSED TO SAY?
"I WOULDN'T PUT IT AS STRONGLY AS THAT, MATE.
"TRUTH TO TELL--
"--ALL THE SMART MONEY'S SOME-WHERE ELSE."
PRINCE WESTERN MEAT PACKING Co. Ltd.

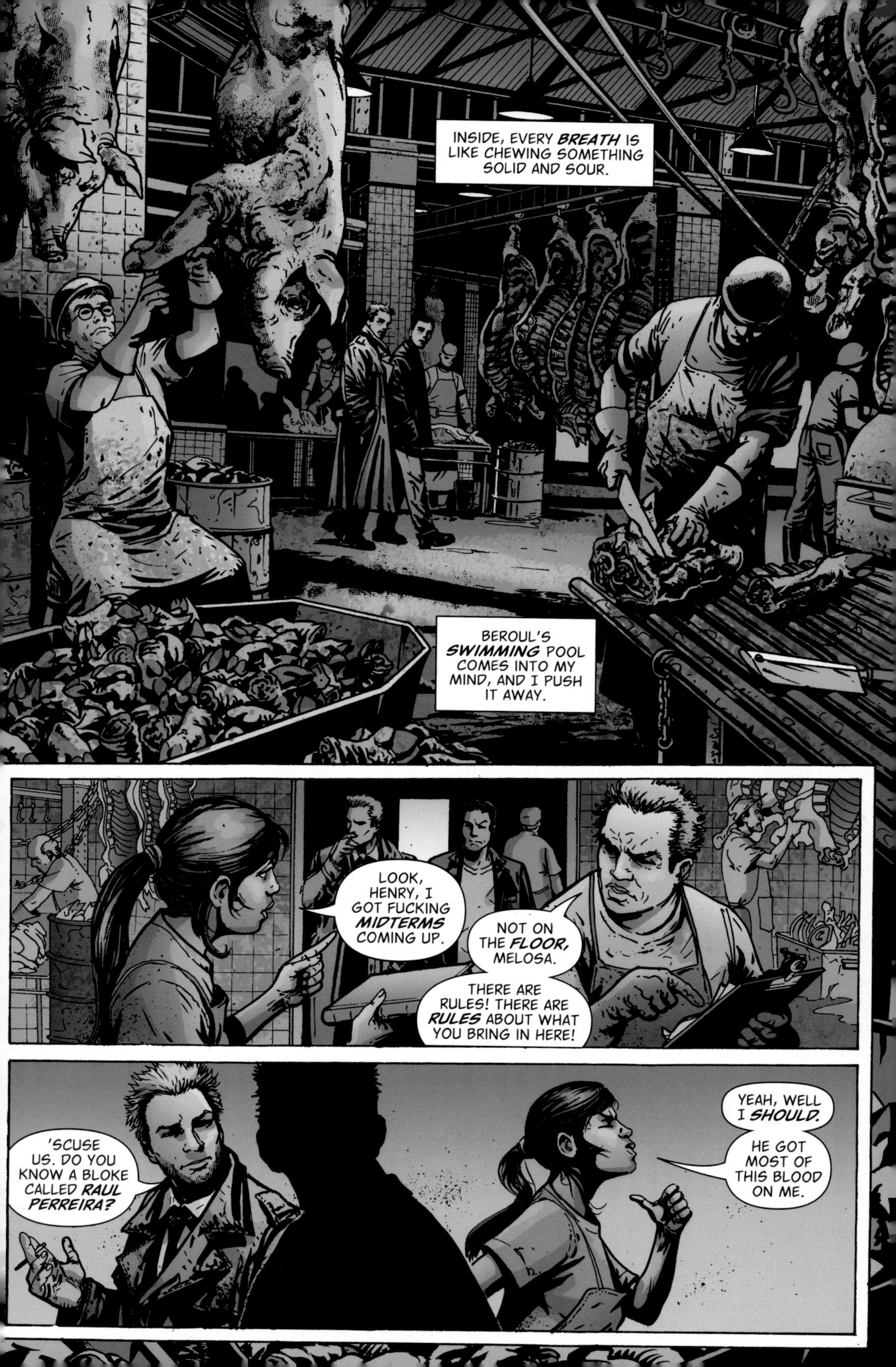
INSIDE, EVERY BREATH IS LIKE CHEWING SOMETHING SOLID AND SOUR.
BEROUL'S SWIMMING POOL COMES INTO MY MIND, AND I PUSH IT AWAY.
LOOK, HENRY, I GOT FUCKING MIDTERMS COMING UP.
NOT ON THE FLOOR, MELOSA.
THERE ARE RULES! THERE ARE RULES ABOUT WHAT YOU BRING IN HERE!
'SCUSE US. DO YOU KNOW A BLOKE CALLED RAUL PERREIRA?
YEAH, WELL I SHOULD.
HE GOT MOST OF THIS BLOOD ON ME.

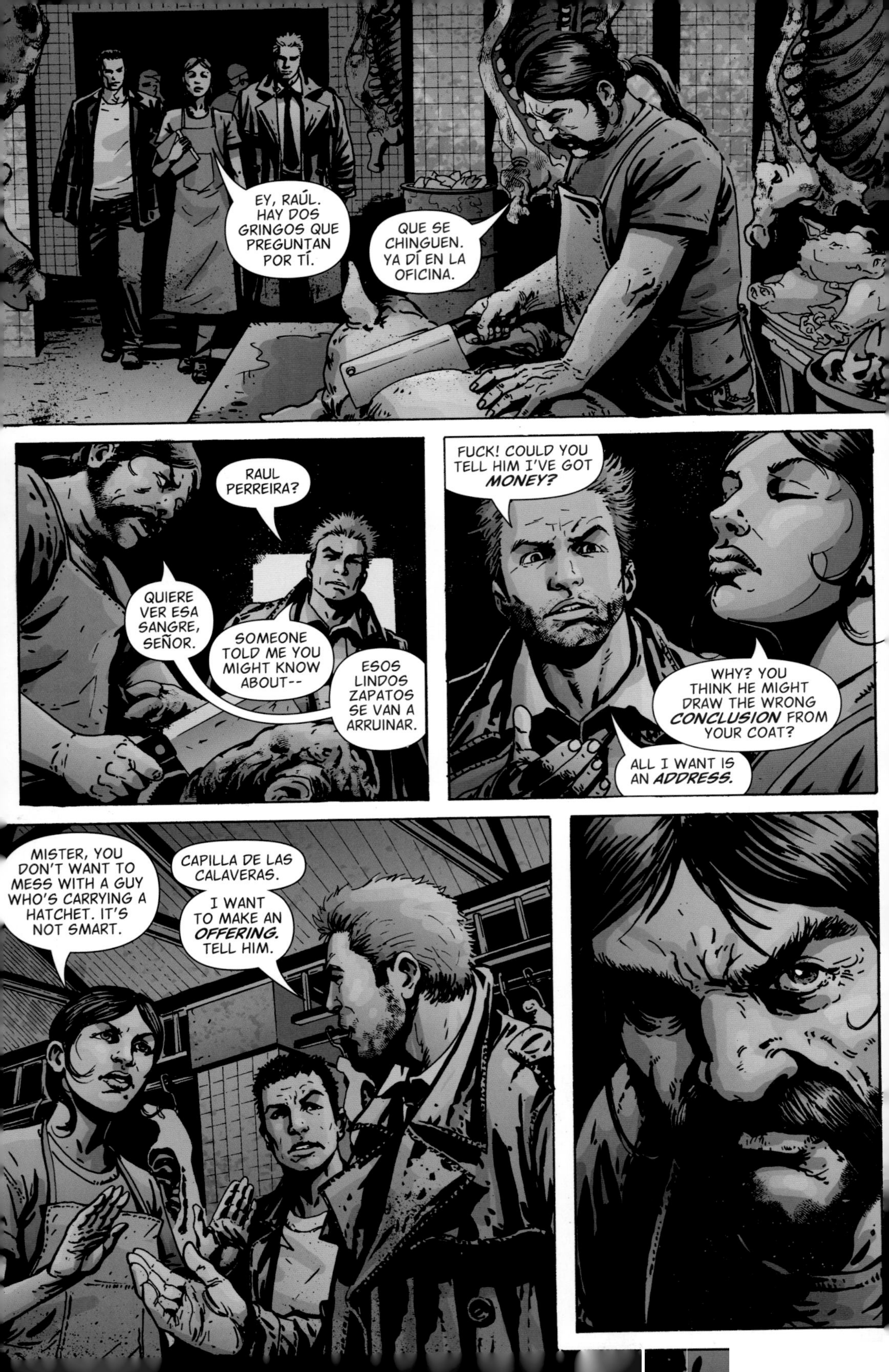
EY, RAÚL. HAY DOS GRINGOS QUE PREGUNTAN POR TÍ.
QUE SE CHINGUEN. YA DÍ EN LA OFICINA.
RAUL PERREIRA?
QUIERE VER ESA SANGRE, SEÑOR.
SOMEONE TOLD ME YOU MIGHT KNOW ABOUT--
ESOS LINDOS ZAPATOS SE VAN A ARRUINAR.
FUCK! COULD YOU TELL HIM I'VE GOT MONEY?
WHY? YOU THINK HE MIGHT DRAW THE WRONG CONCLUSION FROM YOUR COAT?
ALL I WANT IS AN ADDRESS.
MISTER, YOU DON'T WANT TO MESS WITH A GUY WHO'S CARRYING A HATCHET. IT'S NOT SMART.
CAPILLA DE LAS CALAVERAS.
I WANT TO MAKE AN OFFERING. TELL HIM.

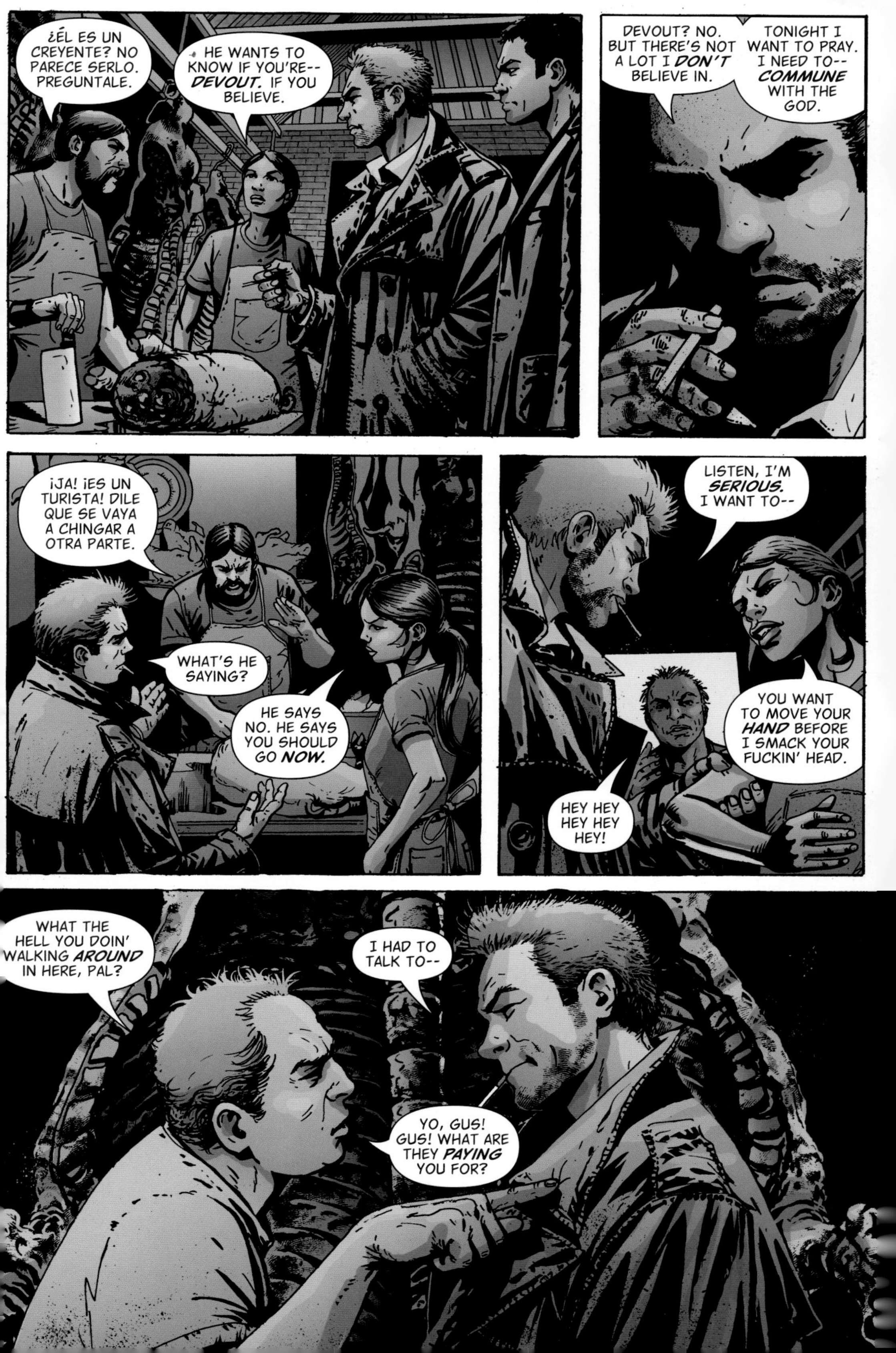

¿ÉL ES UN CREYENTE? NO PARECE SERLO. PREGUNTALE.
HE WANTS TO KNOW IF YOU'RE-- DEVOUT. IF YOU BELIEVE.
DEVOUT? NO. BUT THERE'S NOT A LOT I DON'T BELIEVE IN.
TONIGHT I WANT TO PRAY. I NEED TO-- COMMUNE WITH THE GOD.
¡JA! ¡ES UN TURISTA! DILE QUE SE VAYA A CHINGAR A OTRA PARTE.
WHAT'S HE SAYING?
HE SAYS NO. HE SAYS YOU SHOULD GO NOW.
LISTEN, I'M SERIOUS. I WANT TO--
YOU WANT TO MOVE YOUR HAND BEFORE I SMACK YOUR FUCKIN' HEAD.
HEY HEY HEY HEY HEY!
WHAT THE HELL YOU DOIN' WALKING AROUND IN HERE, PAL?
I HAD TO TALK TO--
YO, GUS! GUS! WHAT ARE THEY PAYING YOU FOR?

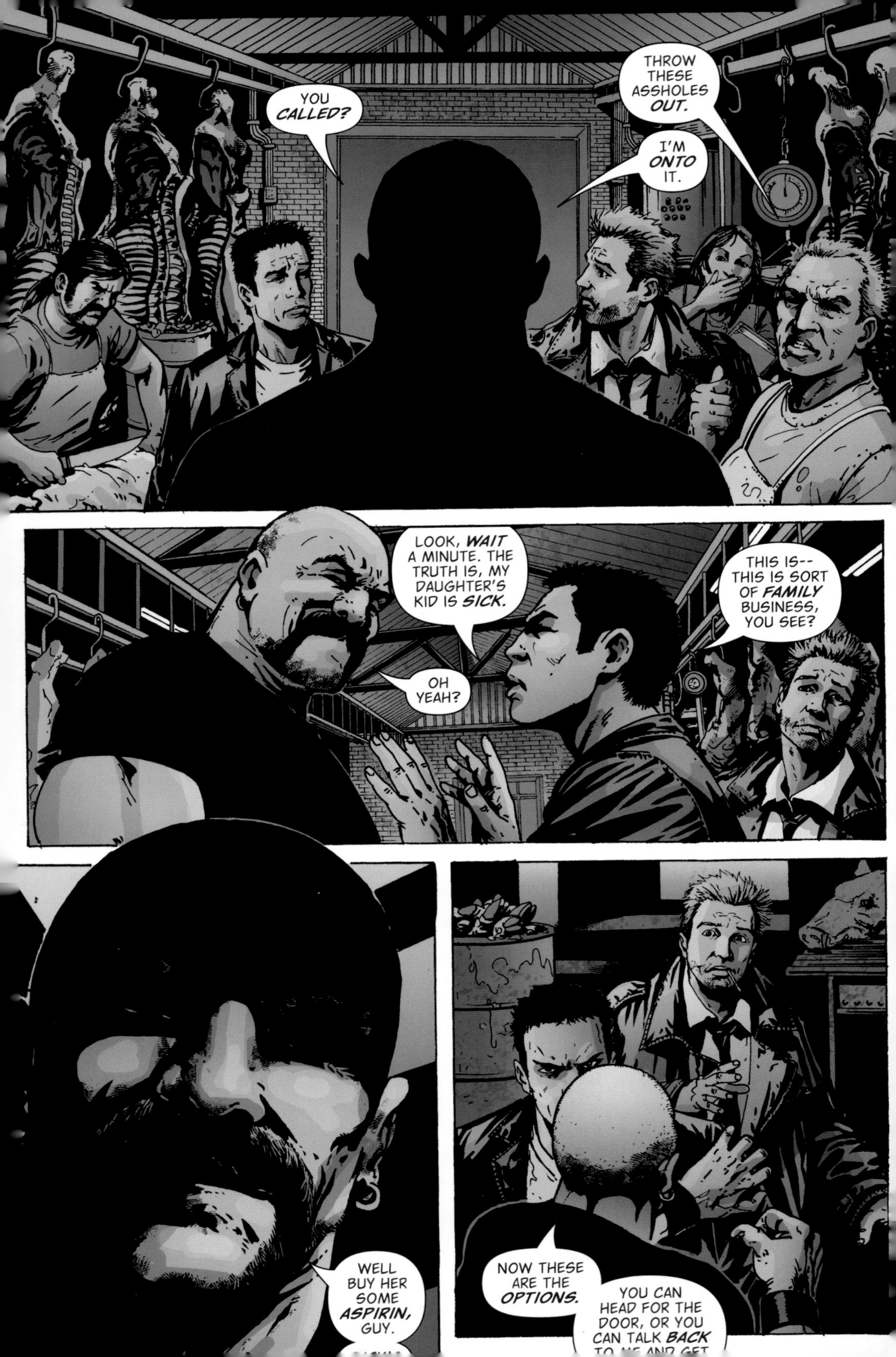
YOU CALLED?
THROW THESE ASSHOLES OUT.
I'M ONTO IT.
LOOK, WAIT A MINUTE. THE TRUTH IS, MY DAUGHTER'S KID IS SICK.
OH YEAH?
THIS IS-- THIS IS SORT OF FAMILY BUSINESS, YOU SEE?
WELL BUY HER SOME ASPIRIN, GUY.
NOW THESE ARE THE OPTIONS.
YOU CAN HEAD FOR THE DOOR, OR YOU CAN TALK BACK

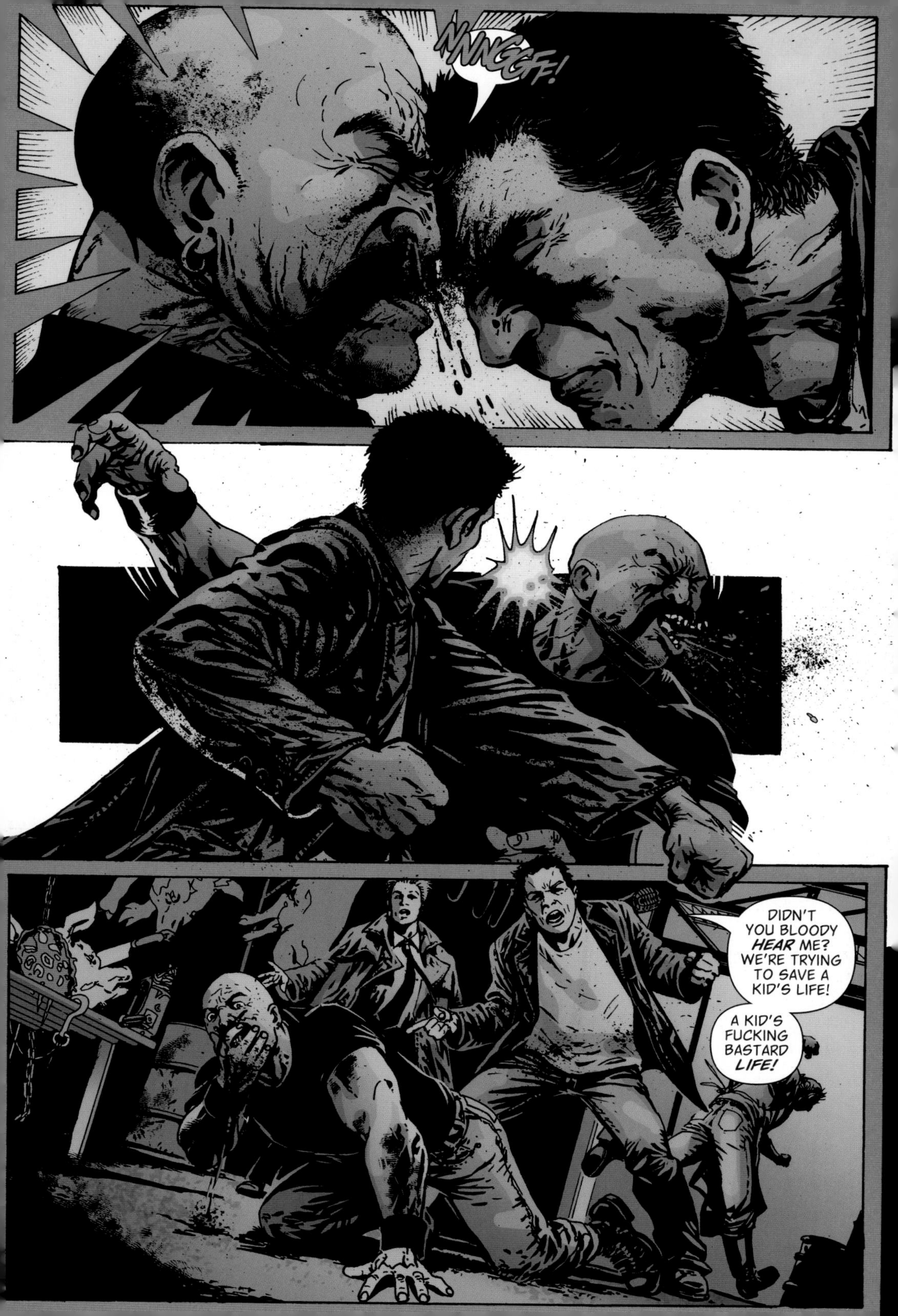
NNNGGFF!
DIDN'T YOU BLOODY HEAR ME? WE'RE TRYING TO SAVE A KID'S LIFE!
A KID'S FUCKING BASTARD LIFE!

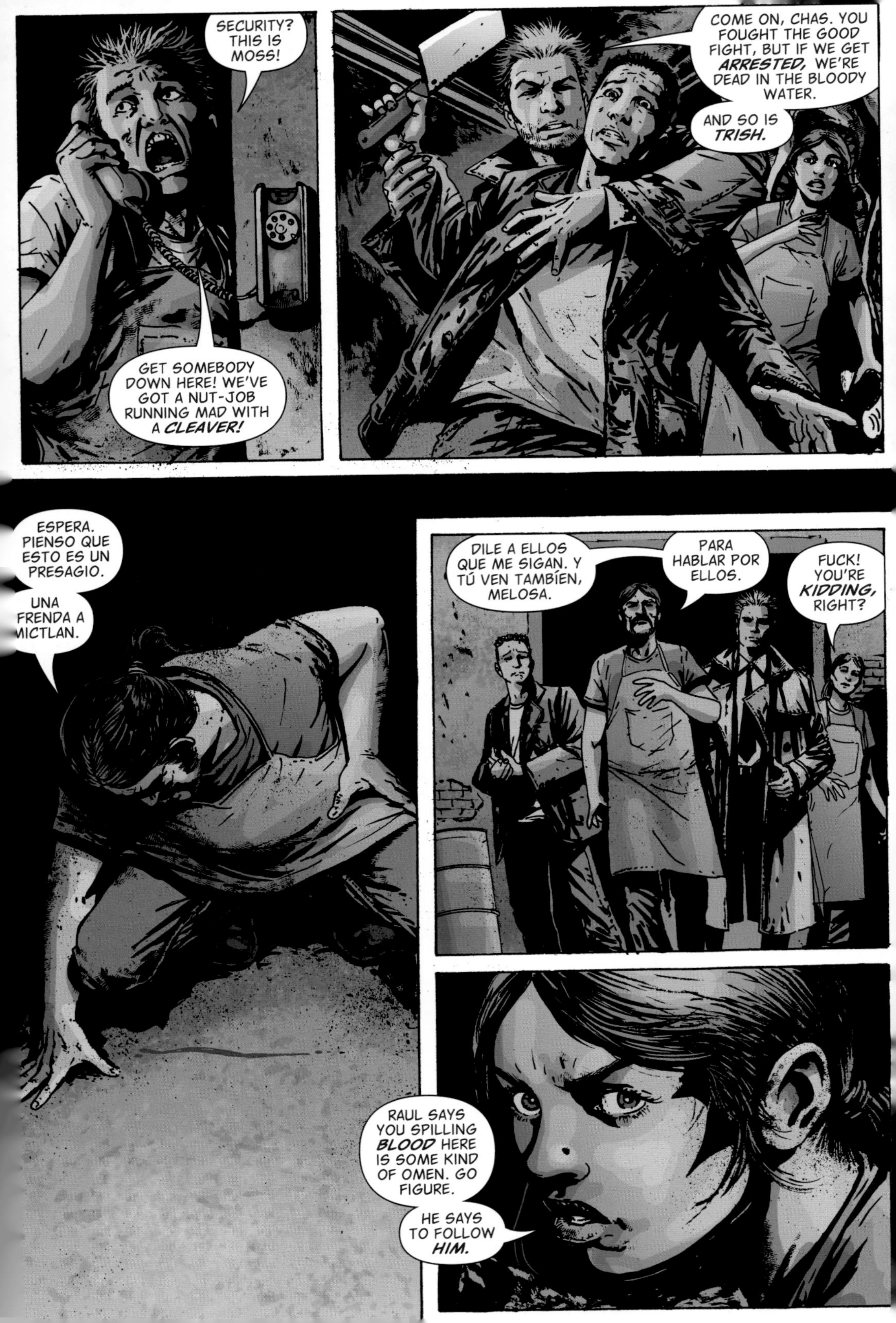
SECURITY? THIS IS MOSS!
GET SOMEBODY DOWN HERE! WE'VE GOT A NUT-JOB RUNNING MAD WITH A *CLEAVER!*
COME ON, CHAS. YOU FOUGHT THE GOOD FIGHT, BUT IF WE GET *ARRESTED,* WE'RE DEAD IN THE BLOODY WATER.
AND SO IS *TRISH.*
ESPERA. PIENSO QUE ESTO ES UN PRESAGIO.
UNA FRENDA A MICTLAN.
DILE A ELLOS QUE ME SIGAN. Y TÚ VEN TAMBÍEN, MELOSA.
PARA HABLAR POR ELLOS.
FUCK! YOU'RE *KIDDING,* RIGHT?
RAUL SAYS YOU SPILLING *BLOOD* HERE IS SOME KIND OF OMEN. GO FIGURE.
HE SAYS TO FOLLOW *HIM.*

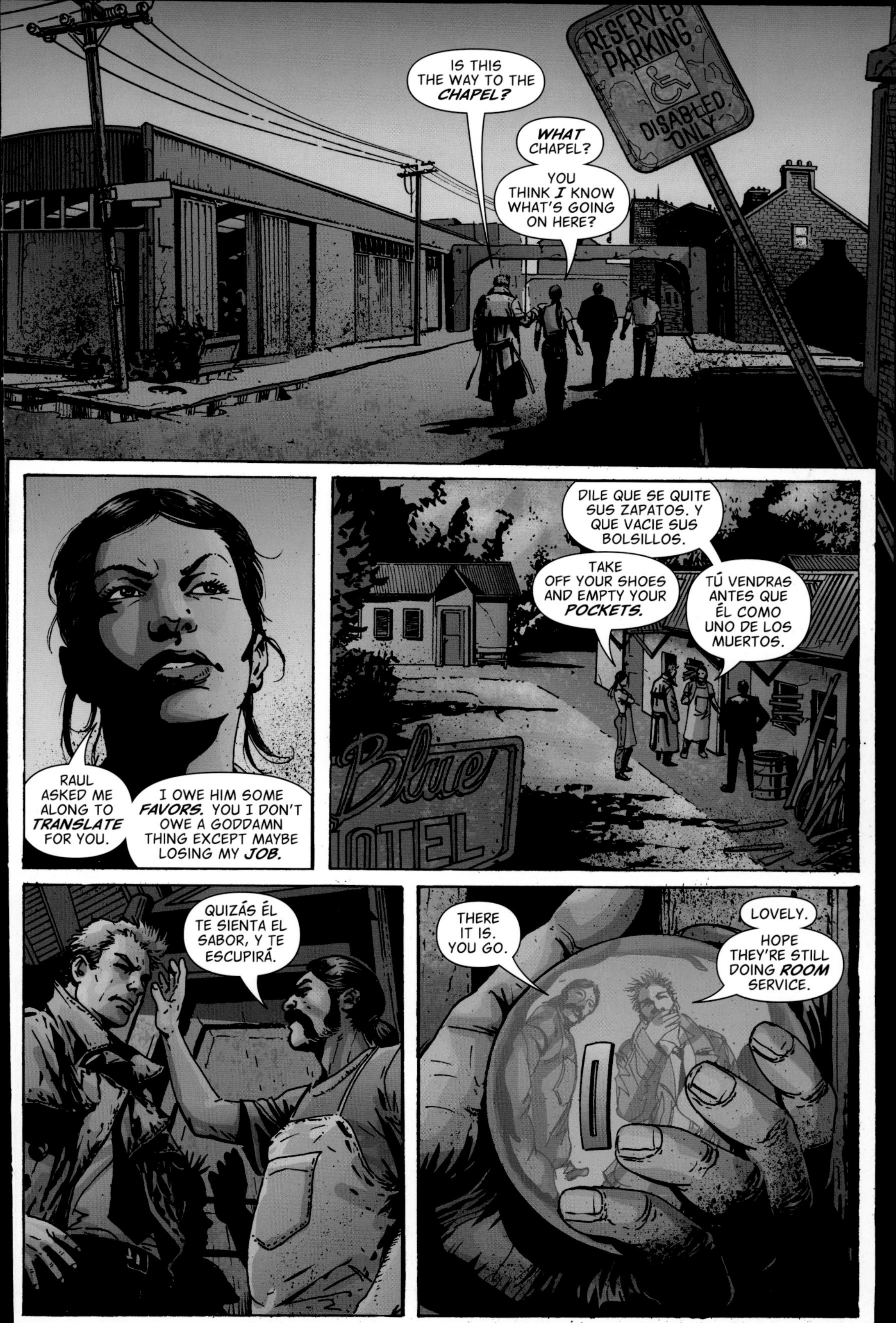

RESERVED PARKING
DISABLED ONLY
IS THIS THE WAY TO THE CHAPEL?
WHAT CHAPEL?
YOU THINK I KNOW WHAT'S GOING ON HERE?
RAUL ASKED ME ALONG TO TRANSLATE FOR YOU.
I OWE HIM SOME FAVORS. YOU I DON'T OWE A GODDAMN THING EXCEPT MAYBE LOSING MY JOB.
DILE QUE SE QUITE SUS ZAPATOS. Y QUE VACIE SUS BOLSILLOS.
TAKE OFF YOUR SHOES AND EMPTY YOUR POCKETS.
TÚ VENDRAS ANTES QUE ÉL COMO UNO DE LOS MUERTOS.
Blue
OTEL
QUIZÁS ÉL TE SIENTA EL SABOR, Y TE ESCUPIRÁ.
THERE IT IS. YOU GO.
LOVELY.
HOPE THEY'RE STILL DOING ROOM SERVICE.

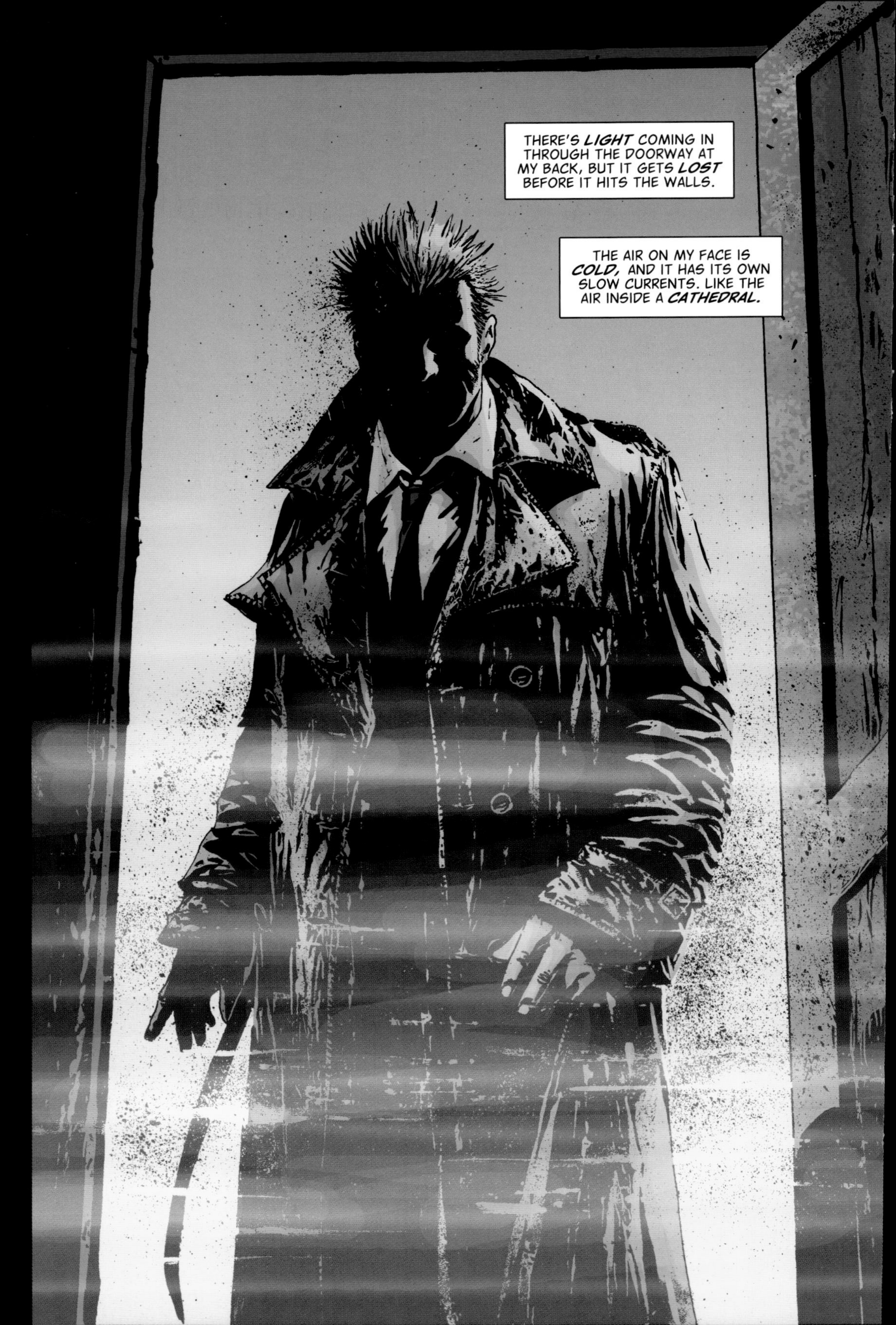
THERE'S *LIGHT* COMING IN THROUGH THE DOORWAY AT MY BACK, BUT IT GETS *LOST* BEFORE IT HITS THE WALLS.
THE AIR ON MY FACE IS *COLD,* AND IT HAS ITS OWN SLOW CURRENTS. LIKE THE AIR INSIDE A *CATHEDRAL.*

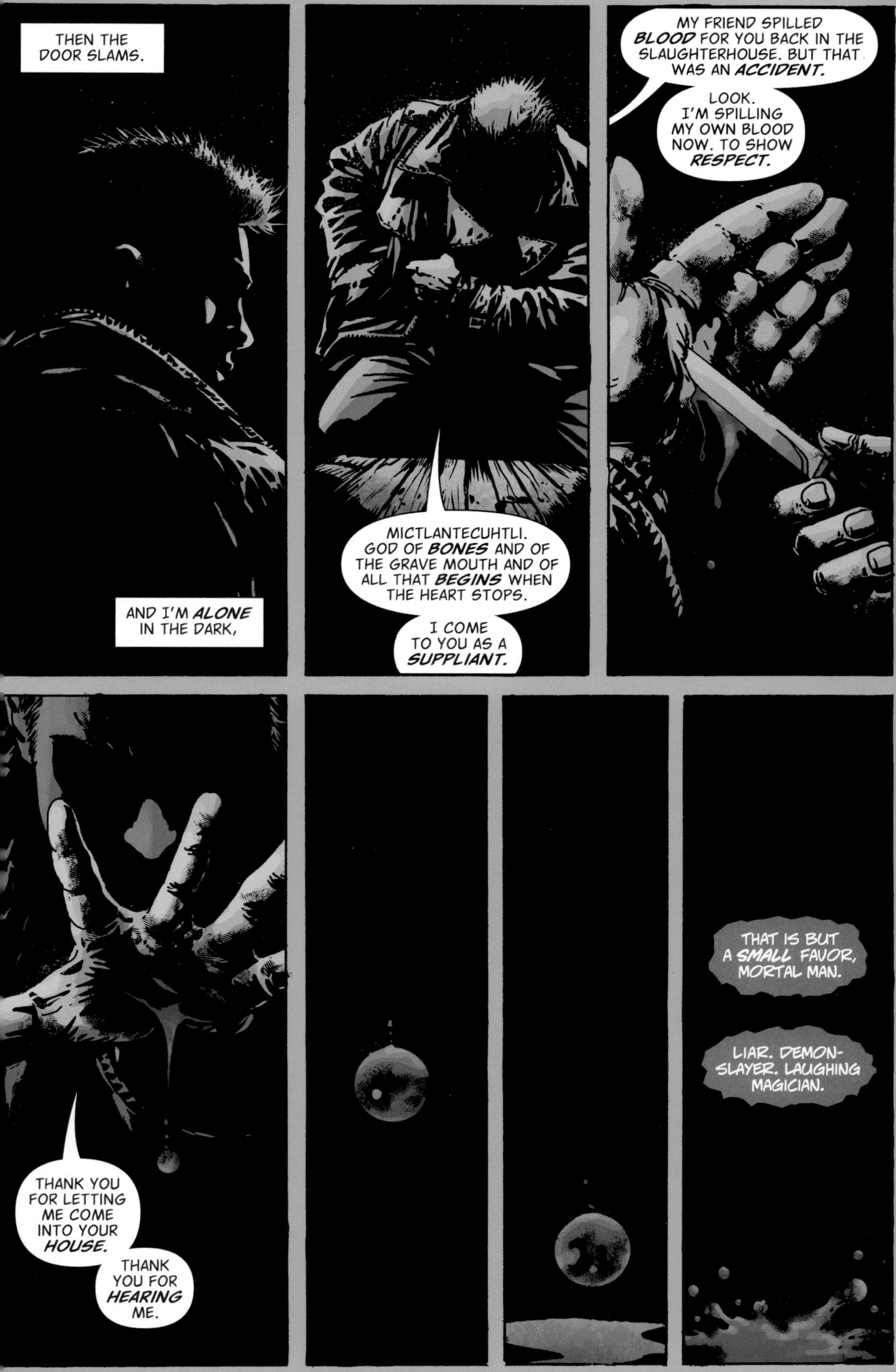
THEN THE DOOR SLAMS.
AND I'M ALONE IN THE DARK,
MICTLANTECUHTLI. GOD OF BONES AND OF THE GRAVE MOUTH AND OF ALL THAT BEGINS WHEN THE HEART STOPS.
I COME TO YOU AS A SUPPLIANT.
MY FRIEND SPILLED BLOOD FOR YOU BACK IN THE SLAUGHTERHOUSE. BUT THAT WAS AN ACCIDENT.
LOOK. I'M SPILLING MY OWN BLOOD NOW. TO SHOW RESPECT.
THANK YOU FOR LETTING ME COME INTO YOUR HOUSE.
THANK YOU FOR HEARING ME.
THAT IS BUT A SMALL FAVOR, MORTAL MAN.
LIAR. DEMON-SLAYER. LAUGHING MAGICIAN.

WITH NO BREATH OR HEARTBEAT DINNING IN MY EARS--

--WITH THE NOISY TIDES OF BLOOD ALL DRIED, ALL STILLED--

I HEAR EVERYTHING.

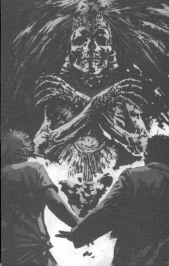

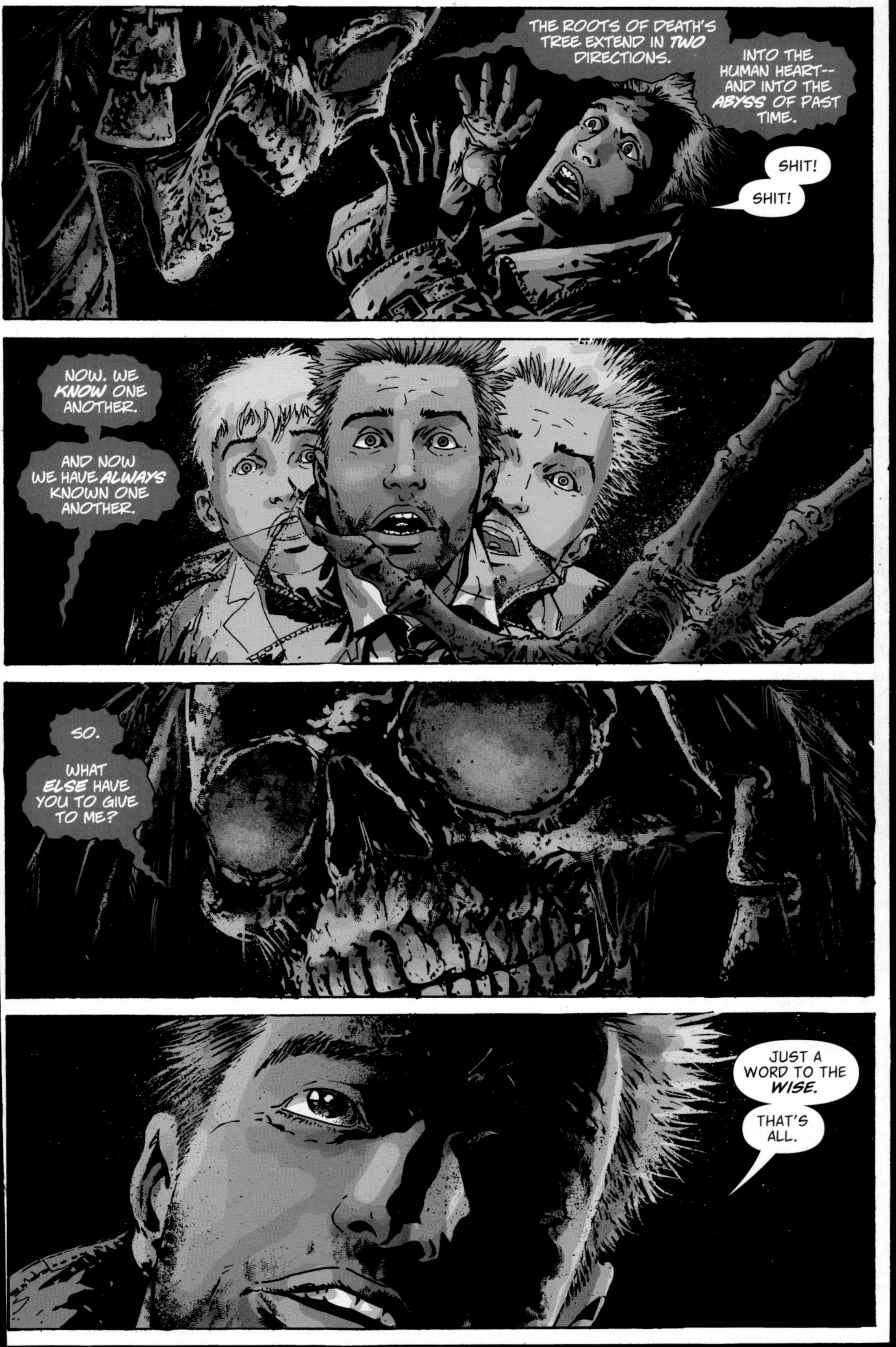
THE ROOTS OF DEATH'S TREE EXTEND IN TWO DIRECTIONS.
INTO THE HUMAN HEART-- AND INTO THE ABYSS OF PAST TIME.
SHIT!
SHIT!
NOW. WE KNOW ONE ANOTHER.
AND NOW WE HAVE ALWAYS KNOWN ONE ANOTHER.
SO.
WHAT ELSE HAVE YOU TO GIVE TO ME?
JUST A WORD TO THE WISE.
THAT'S ALL.

YOU WANNA **SMOKE?**

... THANKS.

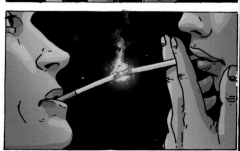

SO HEY. YOU HIS **BODYGUARD,** OR WHAT?

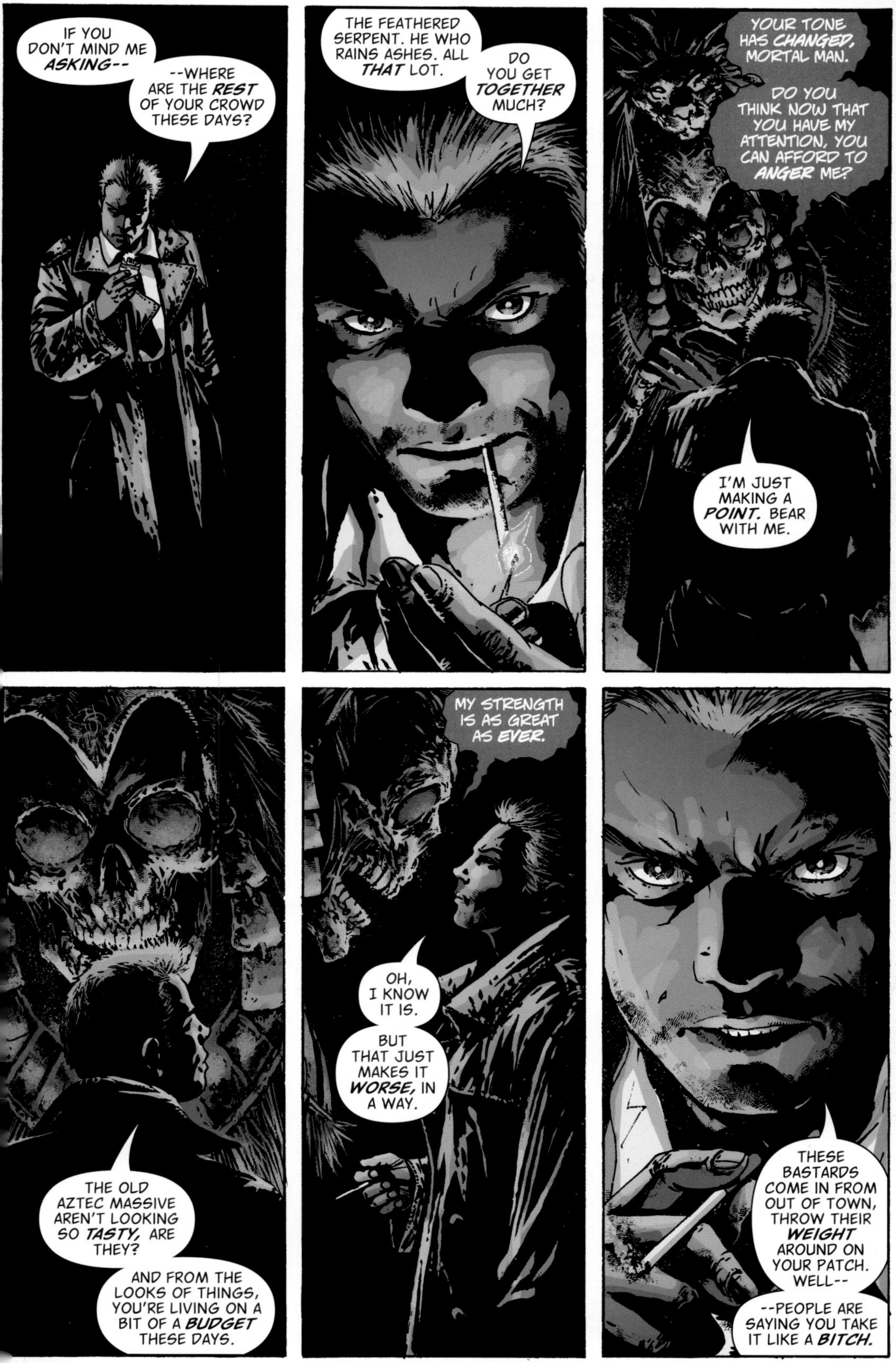
IF YOU DON'T MIND ME ASKING--
--WHERE ARE THE REST OF YOUR CROWD THESE DAYS?
THE FEATHERED SERPENT. HE WHO RAINS ASHES. ALL THAT LOT.
DO YOU GET TOGETHER MUCH?
YOUR TONE HAS CHANGED, MORTAL MAN.
DO YOU THINK NOW THAT YOU HAVE MY ATTENTION, YOU CAN AFFORD TO ANGER ME?
I'M JUST MAKING A POINT. BEAR WITH ME.
THE OLD AZTEC MASSIVE AREN'T LOOKING SO TASTY, ARE THEY?
AND FROM THE LOOKS OF THINGS, YOU'RE LIVING ON A BIT OF A BUDGET THESE DAYS.
MY STRENGTH IS AS GREAT AS EVER.
OH, I KNOW IT IS.
BUT THAT JUST MAKES IT WORSE, IN A WAY.
THESE BASTARDS COME IN FROM OUT OF TOWN, THROW THEIR WEIGHT AROUND ON YOUR PATCH. WELL--
--PEOPLE ARE SAYING YOU TAKE IT LIKE A BITCH.

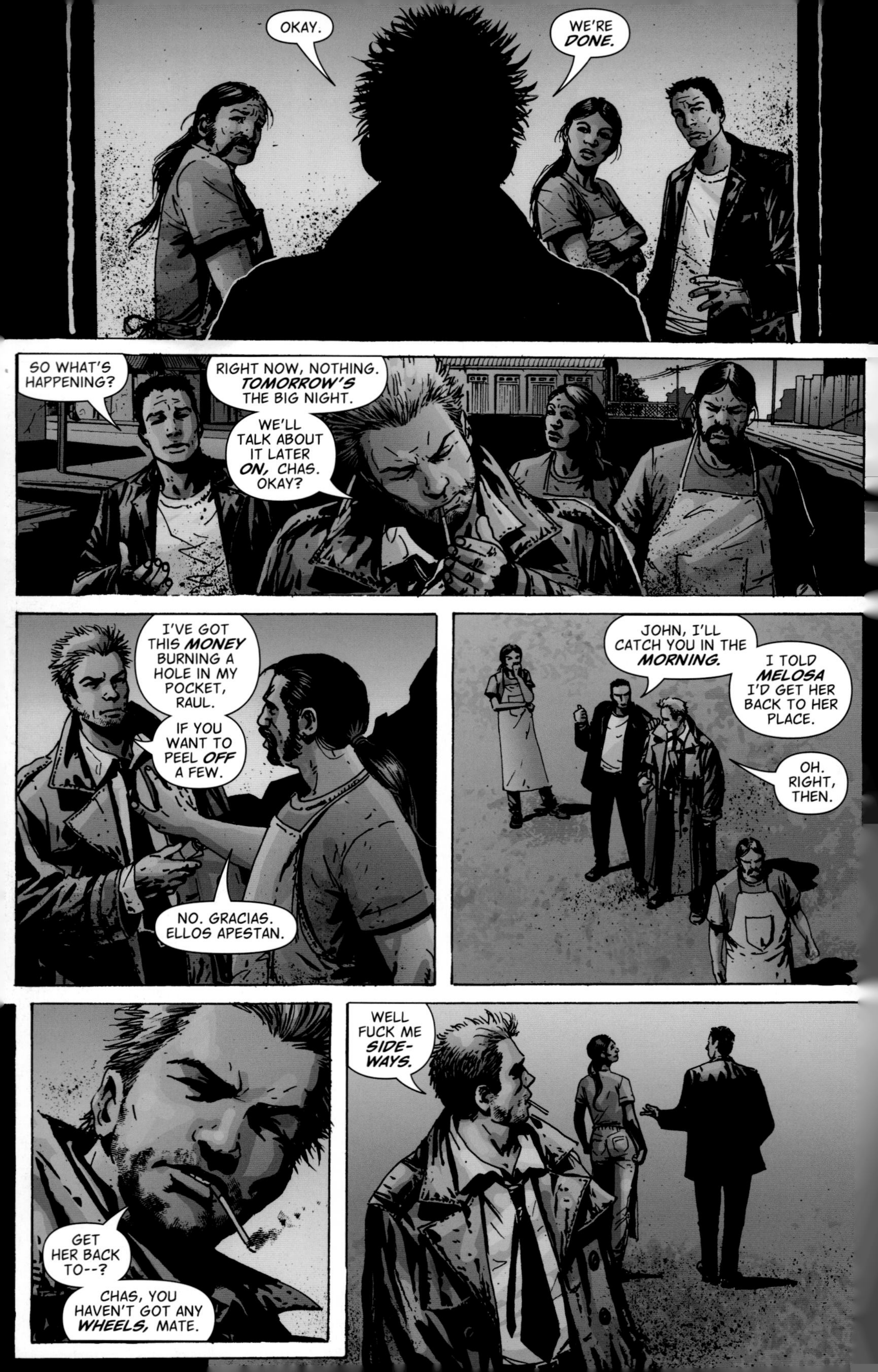
OKAY.
WE'RE *DONE.*
SO WHAT'S HAPPENING?
RIGHT NOW, NOTHING. ***TOMORROW'S*** THE BIG NIGHT.
WE'LL TALK ABOUT IT LATER ***ON,*** CHAS. OKAY?
I'VE GOT THIS ***MONEY*** BURNING A HOLE IN MY POCKET, RAUL.
IF YOU WANT TO PEEL ***OFF*** A FEW.
NO. GRACIAS. ELLOS APESTAN.
JOHN, I'LL CATCH YOU IN THE ***MORNING.***
I TOLD ***MELOSA*** I'D GET HER BACK TO HER PLACE.
OH. RIGHT, THEN.
GET HER BACK TO--?
CHAS, YOU HAVEN'T GOT ANY ***WHEELS,*** MATE.
WELL FUCK ME ***SIDE-WAYS.***

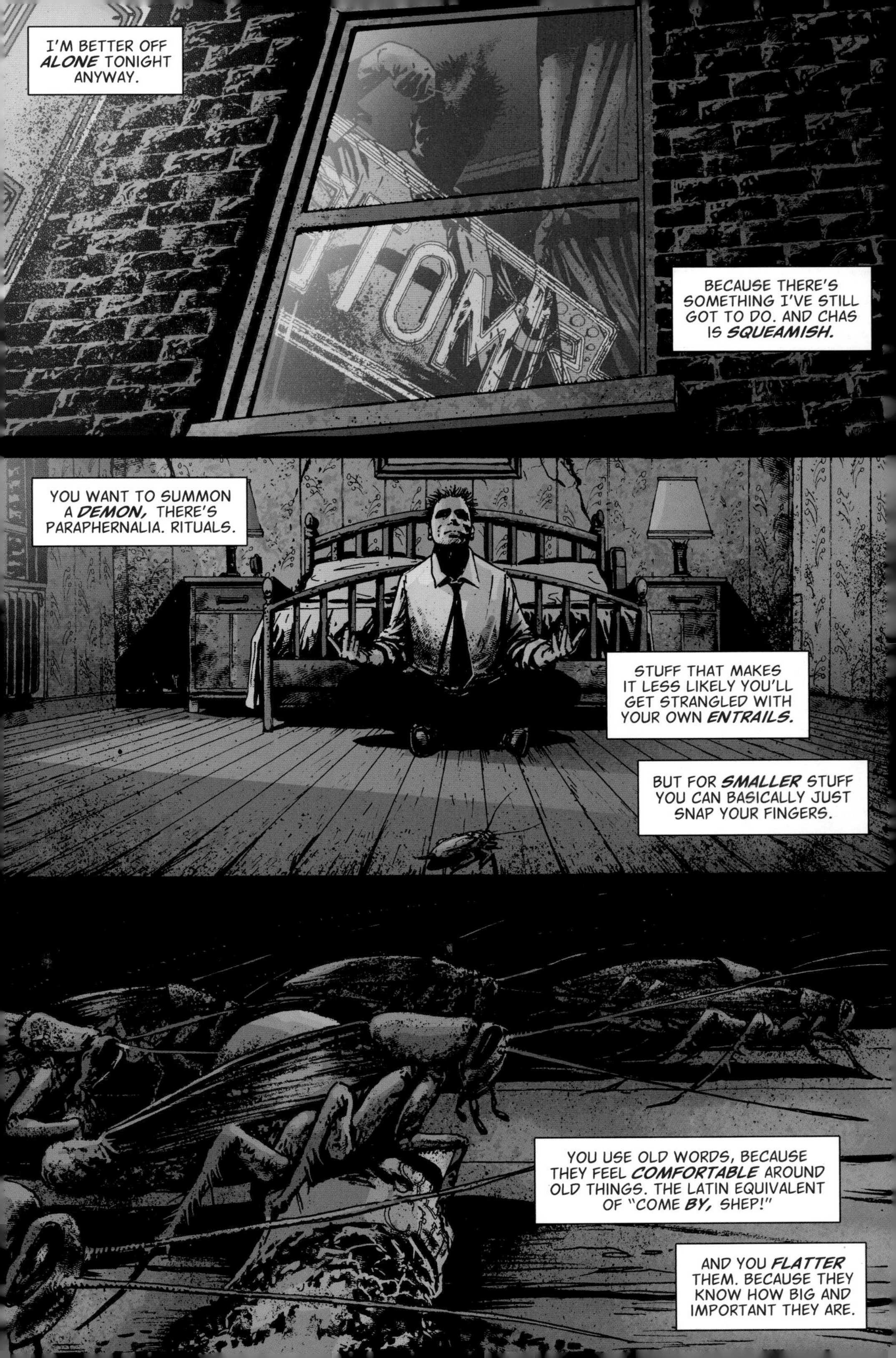
I'M BETTER OFF ALONE TONIGHT ANYWAY.
BECAUSE THERE'S SOMETHING I'VE STILL GOT TO DO. AND CHAS IS SQUEAMISH.
YOU WANT TO SUMMON A DEMON, THERE'S PARAPHERNALIA. RITUALS.
STUFF THAT MAKES IT LESS LIKELY YOU'LL GET STRANGLED WITH YOUR OWN ENTRAILS.
BUT FOR SMALLER STUFF YOU CAN BASICALLY JUST SNAP YOUR FINGERS.
YOU USE OLD WORDS, BECAUSE THEY FEEL COMFORTABLE AROUND OLD THINGS. THE LATIN EQUIVALENT OF "COME BY, SHEP!"
AND YOU FLATTER THEM. BECAUSE THEY KNOW HOW BIG AND IMPORTANT THEY ARE.

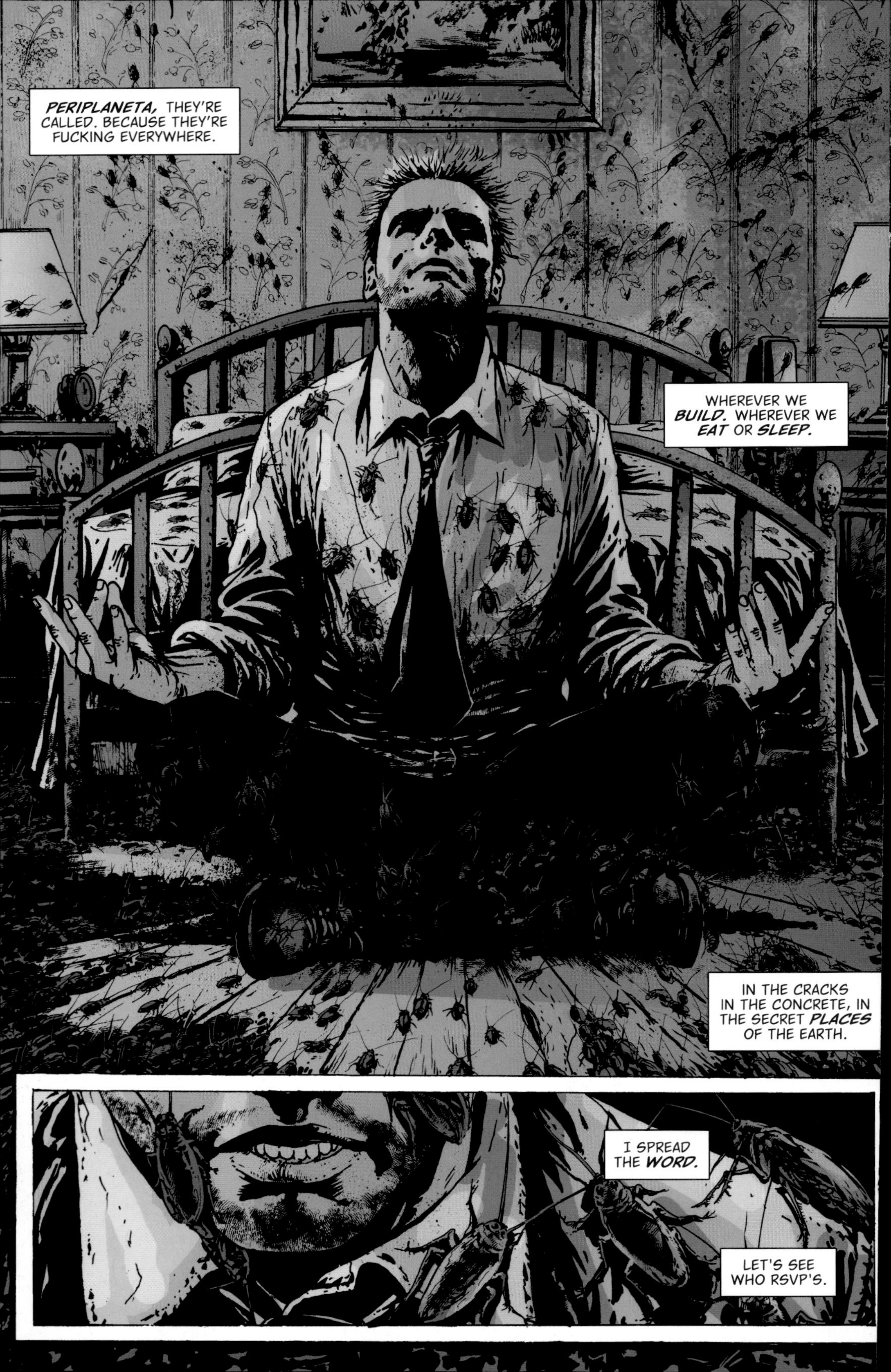
PERIPLANETA, THEY'RE CALLED. BECAUSE THEY'RE FUCKING EVERYWHERE.
WHEREVER WE BUILD. WHEREVER WE EAT OR SLEEP.
IN THE CRACKS IN THE CONCRETE, IN THE SECRET PLACES OF THE EARTH.
I SPREAD THE WORD.
LET'S SEE WHO RSVP'S.

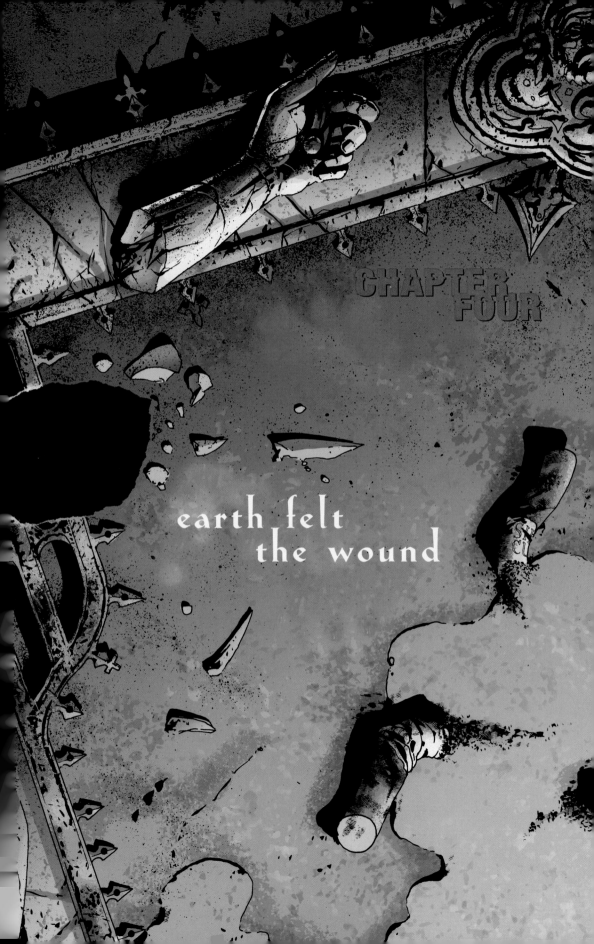

CHAPTER
FOUR

earth felt
the wound

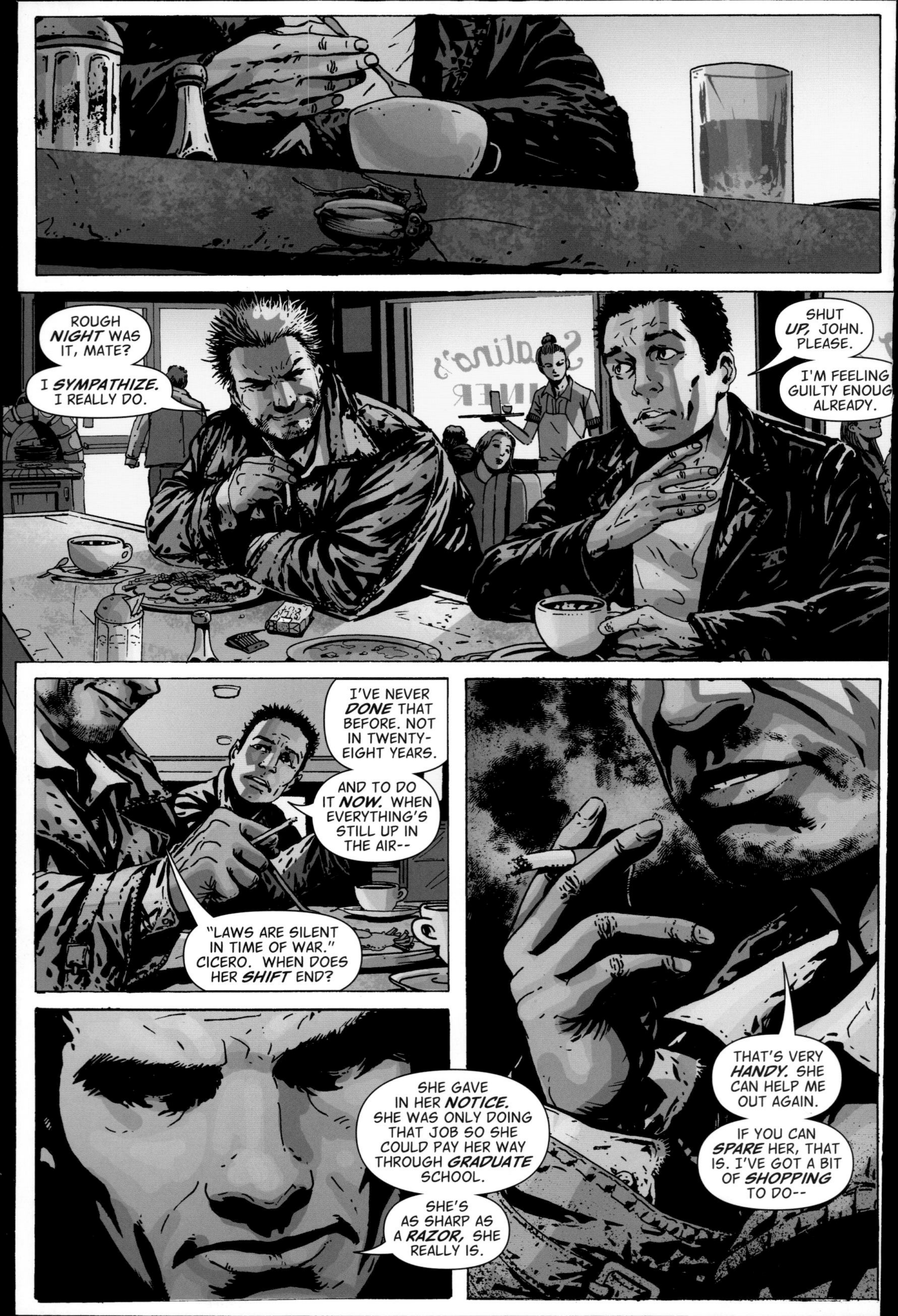

ROUGH NIGHT WAS IT, MATE?
I SYMPATHIZE. I REALLY DO.
SHUT UP, JOHN. PLEASE.
I'M FEELING GUILTY ENOUG ALREADY.
I'VE NEVER DONE THAT BEFORE. NOT IN TWENTY-EIGHT YEARS.
AND TO DO IT NOW. WHEN EVERYTHING'S STILL UP IN THE AIR--
"LAWS ARE SILENT IN TIME OF WAR." CICERO. WHEN DOES HER SHIFT END?
SHE GAVE IN HER NOTICE. SHE WAS ONLY DOING THAT JOB SO SHE COULD PAY HER WAY THROUGH GRADUATE SCHOOL.
SHE'S AS SHARP AS A RAZOR, SHE REALLY IS.
THAT'S VERY HANDY. SHE CAN HELP ME OUT AGAIN.
IF YOU CAN SPARE HER, THAT IS. I'VE GOT A BIT OF SHOPPING TO DO--

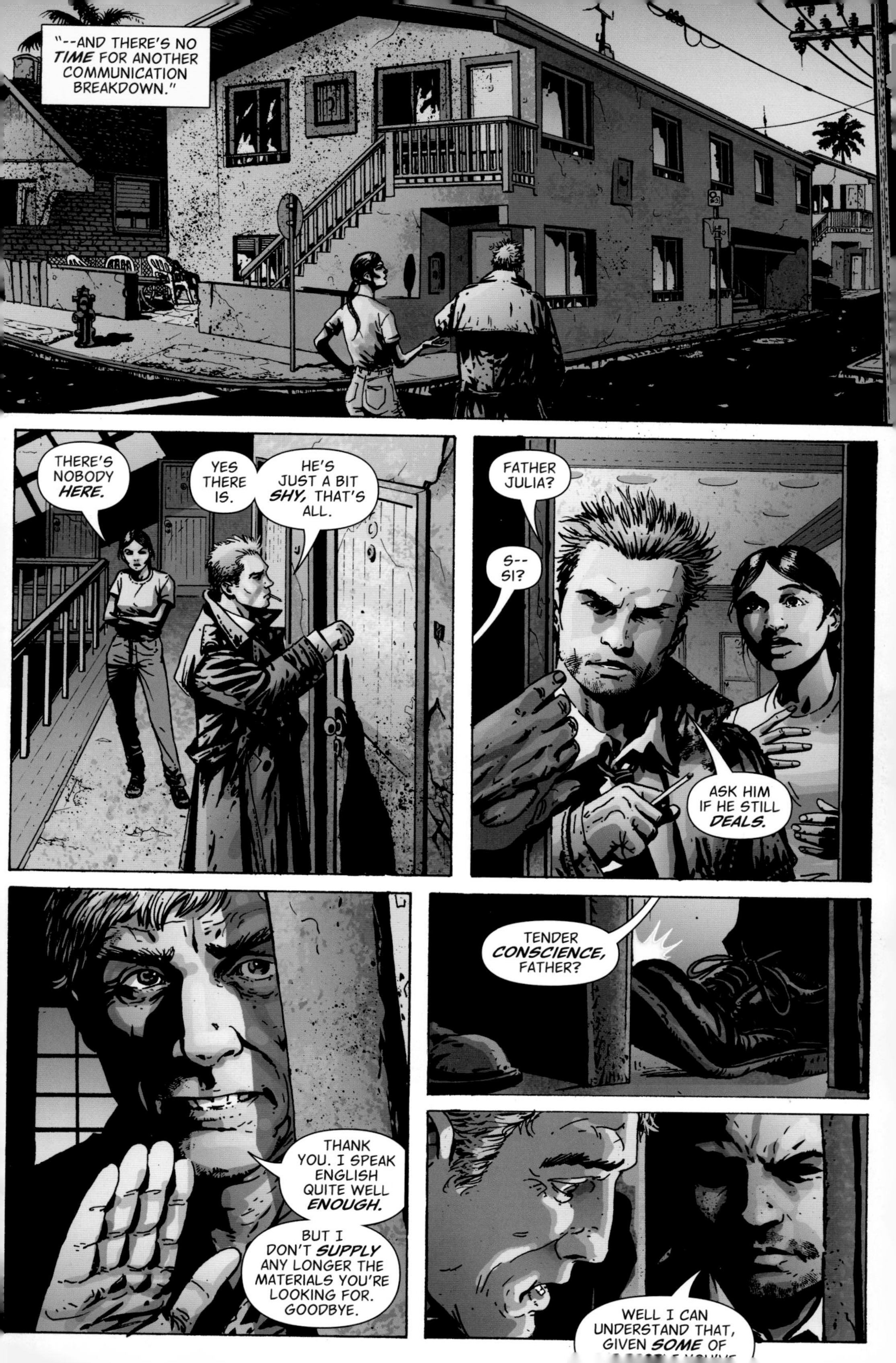
"--AND THERE'S NO *TIME* FOR ANOTHER COMMUNICATION BREAKDOWN."
THERE'S NOBODY *HERE.*
YES THERE IS.
HE'S JUST A BIT *SHY,* THAT'S ALL.
FATHER JULIA?
S-- SI?
ASK HIM IF HE STILL *DEALS.*
THANK YOU. I SPEAK ENGLISH QUITE WELL *ENOUGH.*
BUT I DON'T *SUPPLY* ANY LONGER THE MATERIALS YOU'RE LOOKING FOR. GOODBYE.
TENDER *CONSCIENCE,* FATHER?
WELL I CAN UNDERSTAND THAT, GIVEN *SOME* OF

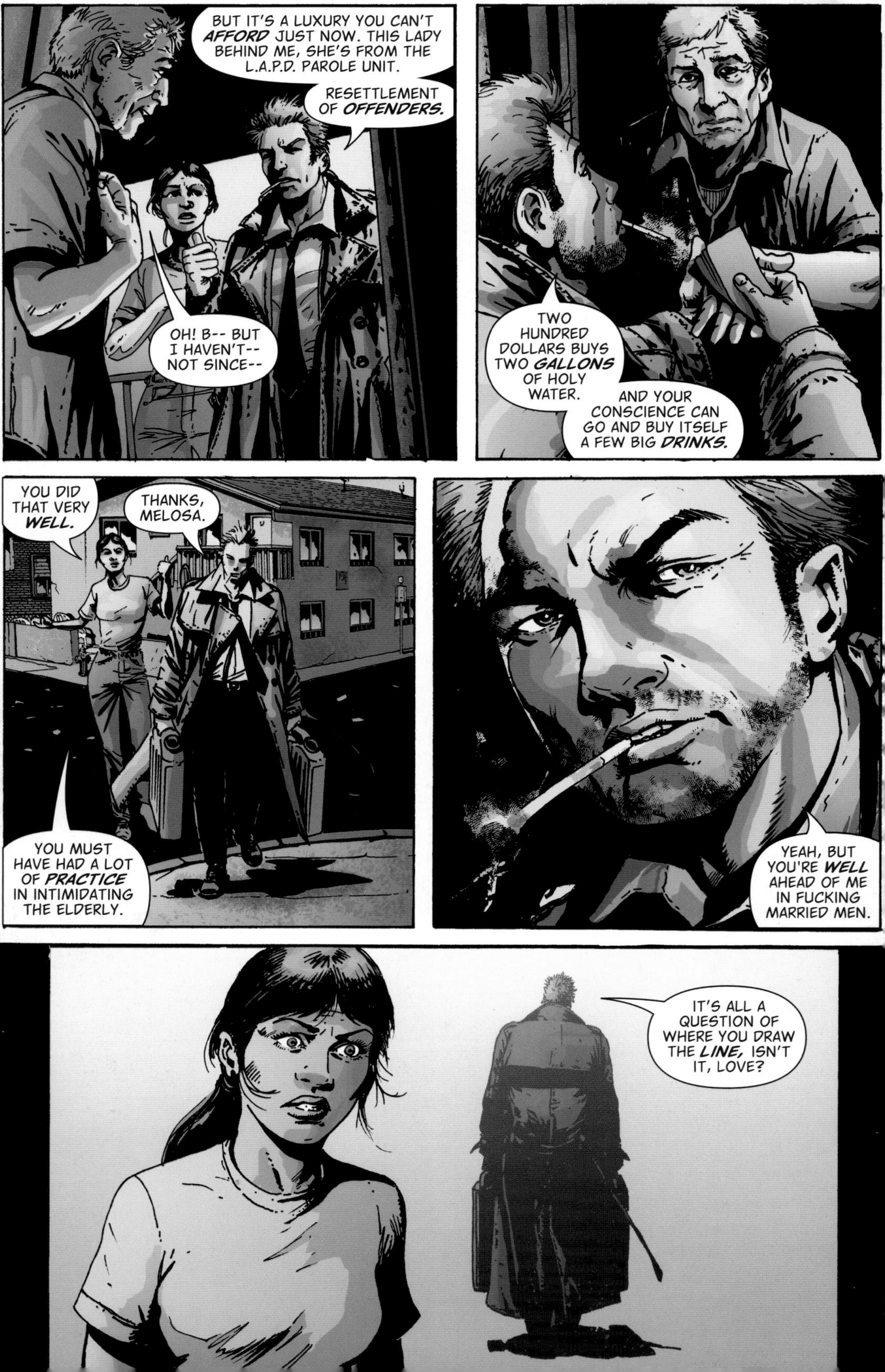
BUT IT'S A LUXURY YOU CAN'T *AFFORD* JUST NOW. THIS LADY BEHIND ME, SHE'S FROM THE L.A.P.D. PAROLE UNIT.
RESETTLEMENT OF *OFFENDERS.*
OH! B-- BUT I HAVEN'T-- NOT SINCE--
TWO HUNDRED DOLLARS BUYS TWO *GALLONS* OF HOLY WATER.
AND YOUR CONSCIENCE CAN GO AND BUY ITSELF A FEW BIG *DRINKS.*
YOU DID THAT VERY *WELL.*
THANKS, MELOSA.
YOU MUST HAVE HAD A LOT OF *PRACTICE* IN INTIMIDATING THE ELDERLY.
YEAH, BUT YOU'RE *WELL* AHEAD OF ME IN FUCKING MARRIED MEN.
IT'S ALL A QUESTION OF WHERE YOU DRAW THE *LINE,* ISN'T IT, LOVE?

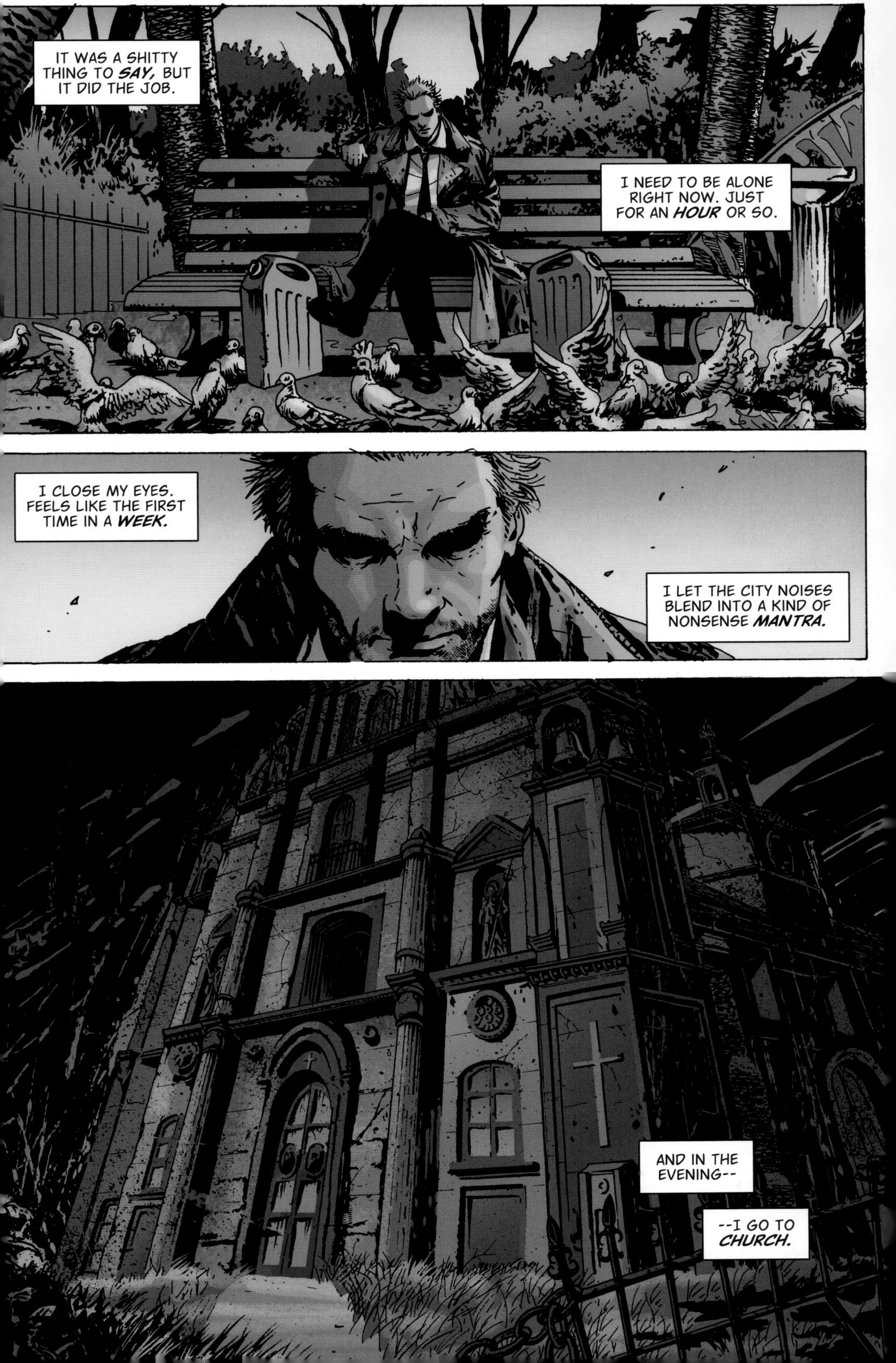
IT WAS A SHITTY THING TO *SAY,* BUT IT DID THE JOB.
I NEED TO BE ALONE RIGHT NOW. JUST FOR AN *HOUR* OR SO.
I CLOSE MY EYES. FEELS LIKE THE FIRST TIME IN A *WEEK.*
I LET THE CITY NOISES BLEND INTO A KIND OF NONSENSE *MANTRA.*
AND IN THE EVENING--
--I GO TO *CHURCH.*

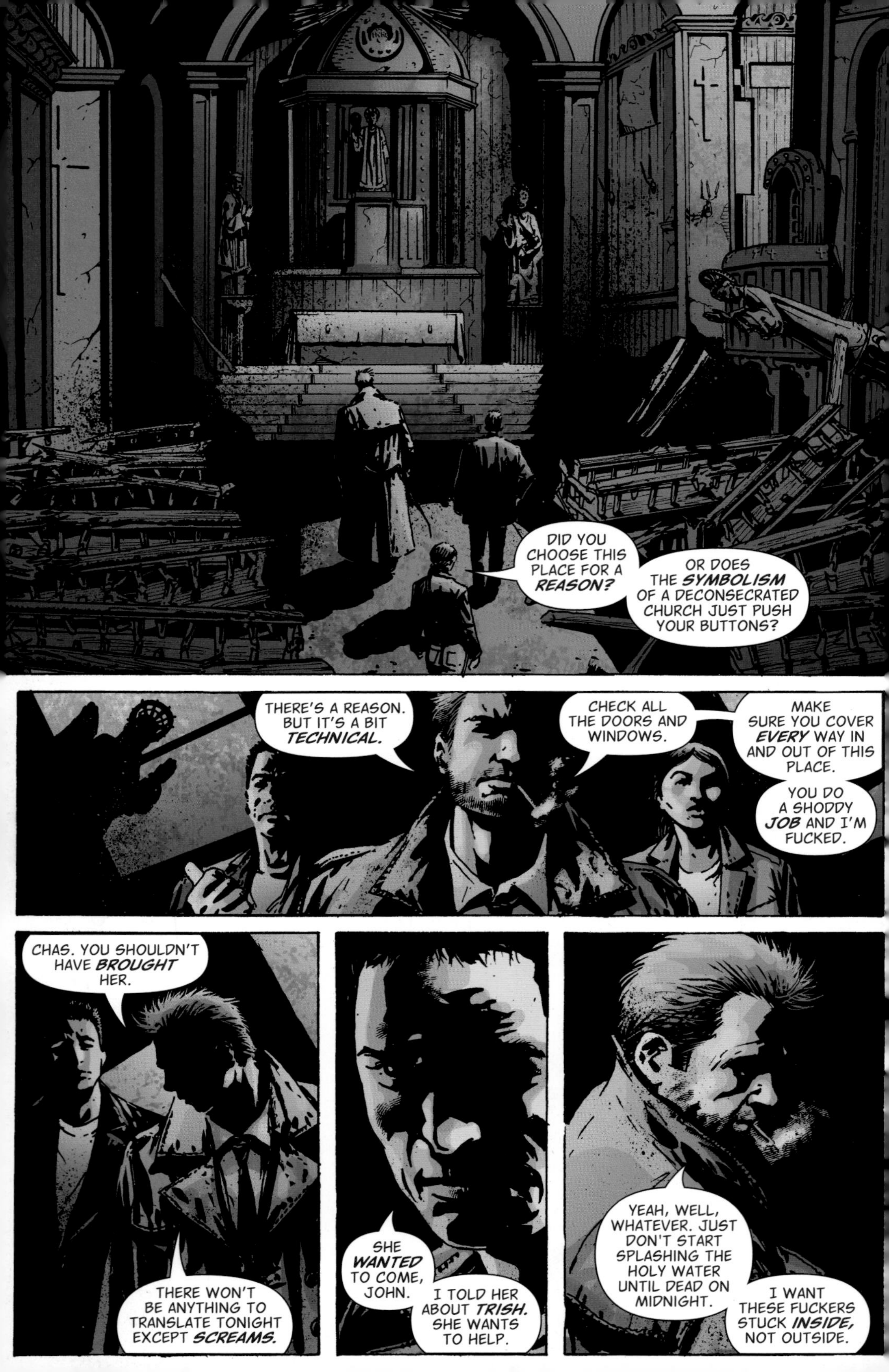
DID YOU CHOOSE THIS PLACE FOR A REASON?
OR DOES THE SYMBOLISM OF A DECONSECRATED CHURCH JUST PUSH YOUR BUTTONS?
THERE'S A REASON. BUT IT'S A BIT TECHNICAL.
CHECK ALL THE DOORS AND WINDOWS.
MAKE SURE YOU COVER EVERY WAY IN AND OUT OF THIS PLACE.
YOU DO A SHODDY JOB AND I'M FUCKED.
CHAS. YOU SHOULDN'T HAVE BROUGHT HER.
THERE WON'T BE ANYTHING TO TRANSLATE TONIGHT EXCEPT SCREAMS.
SHE WANTED TO COME, JOHN.
I TOLD HER ABOUT TRISH. SHE WANTS TO HELP.
YEAH, WELL, WHATEVER. JUST DON'T START SPLASHING THE HOLY WATER UNTIL DEAD ON MIDNIGHT.
I WANT THESE FUCKERS STUCK INSIDE, NOT OUTSIDE.

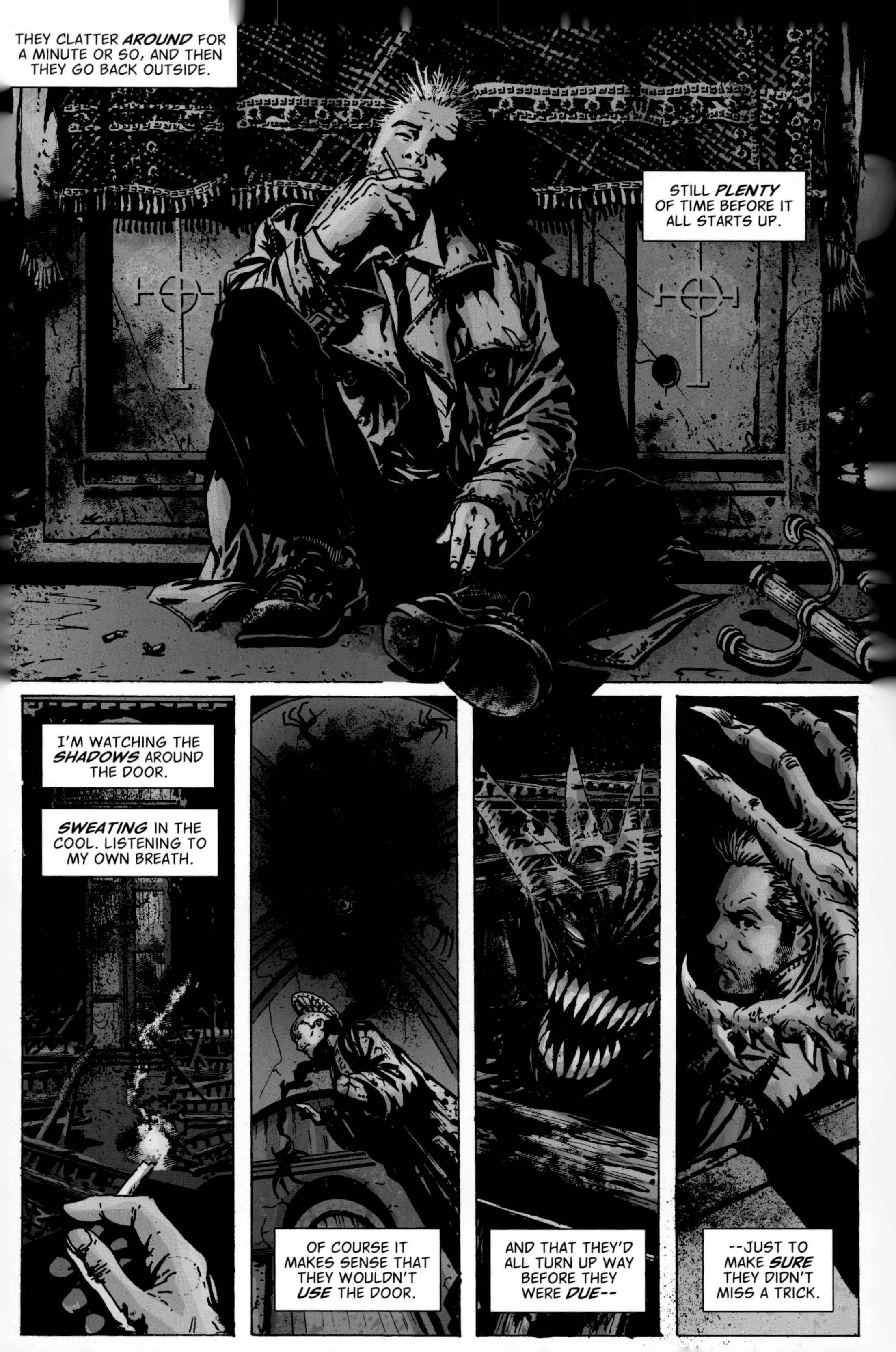
THEY CLATTER AROUND FOR A MINUTE OR SO, AND THEN THEY GO BACK OUTSIDE.
STILL PLENTY OF TIME BEFORE IT ALL STARTS UP.
I'M WATCHING THE SHADOWS AROUND THE DOOR.
SWEATING IN THE COOL. LISTENING TO MY OWN BREATH.
OF COURSE IT MAKES SENSE THAT THEY WOULDN'T USE THE DOOR.
AND THAT THEY'D ALL TURN UP WAY BEFORE THEY WERE DUE--
--JUST TO MAKE SURE THEY DIDN'T MISS A TRICK.

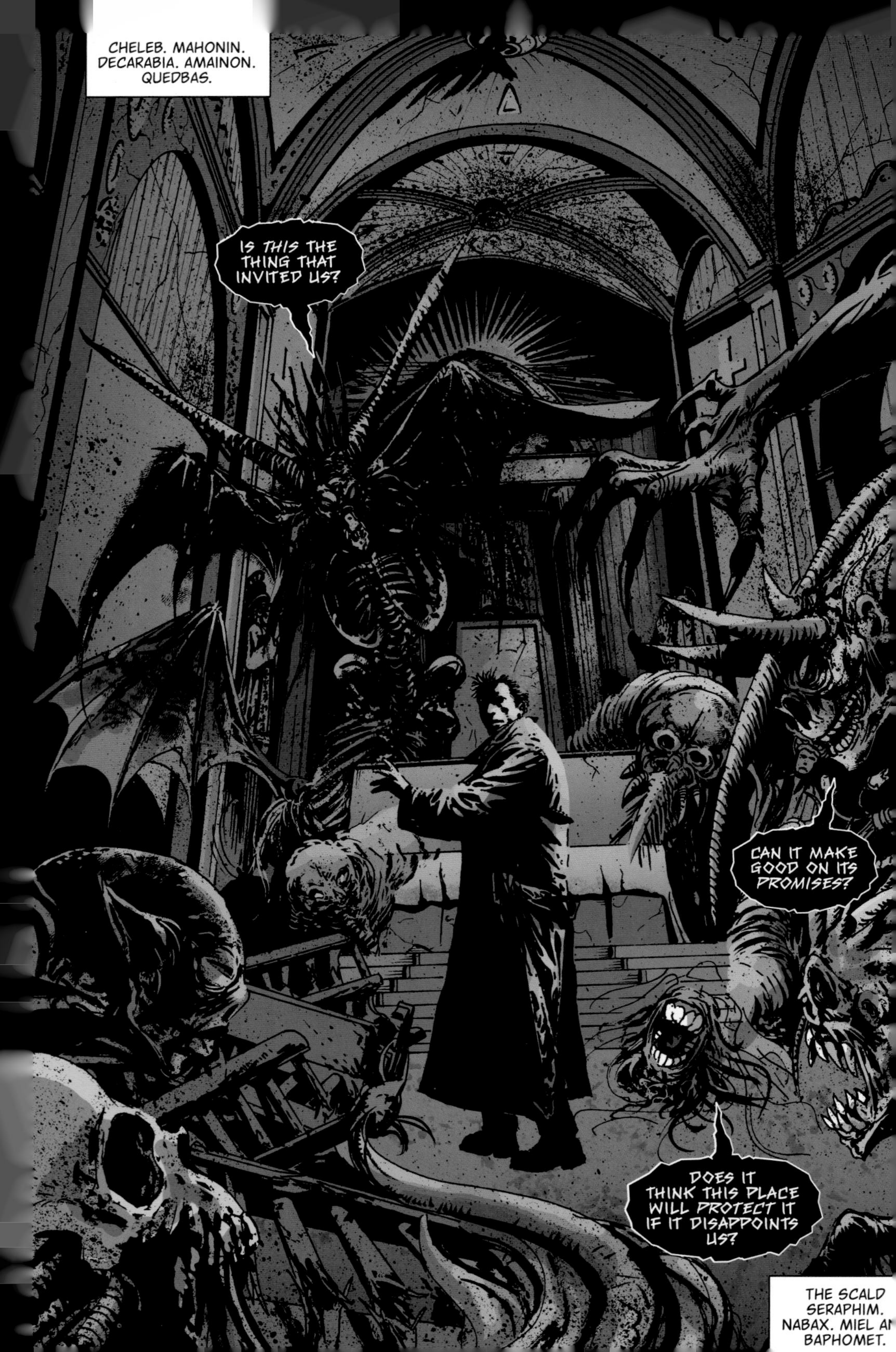
CHELEB. MAHONIN. DECARABIA. AMAINON. QUEDBAS.
IS THIS THE THING THAT INVITED US?
CAN IT MAKE GOOD ON ITS PROMISES?
DOES IT THINK THIS PLACE WILL PROTECT IT IF IT DISAPPOINTS US?
THE SCALD SERAPHIM. NABAX. MIEL A
BAPHOMET.

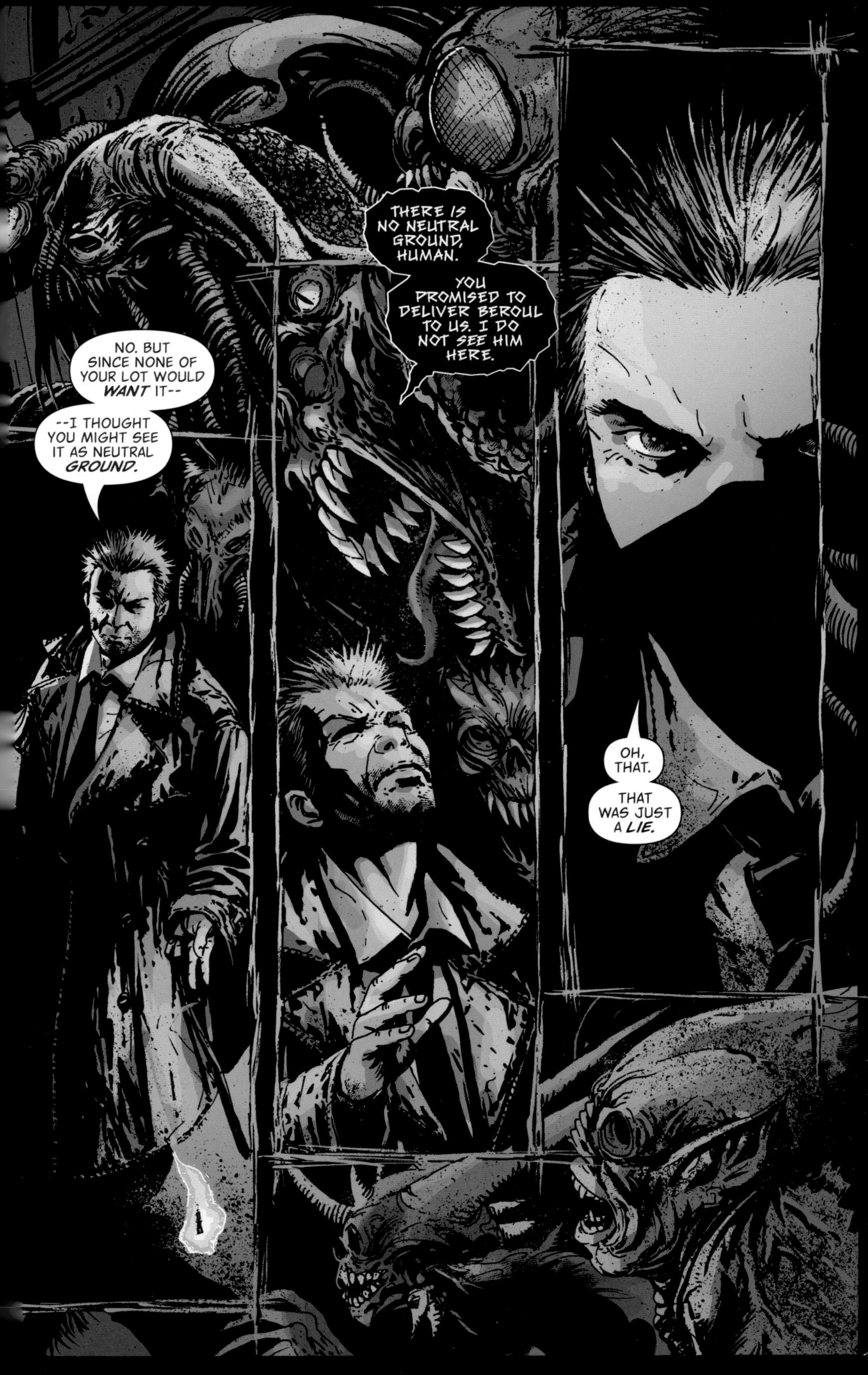

THERE IS NO NEUTRAL GROUND, HUMAN.
YOU PROMISED TO DELIVER BEROUL TO US. I DO NOT SEE HIM HERE.
NO. BUT SINCE NONE OF YOUR LOT WOULD WANT IT--
--I THOUGHT YOU MIGHT SEE IT AS NEUTRAL GROUND.
OH, THAT.
THAT WAS JUST A LIE.

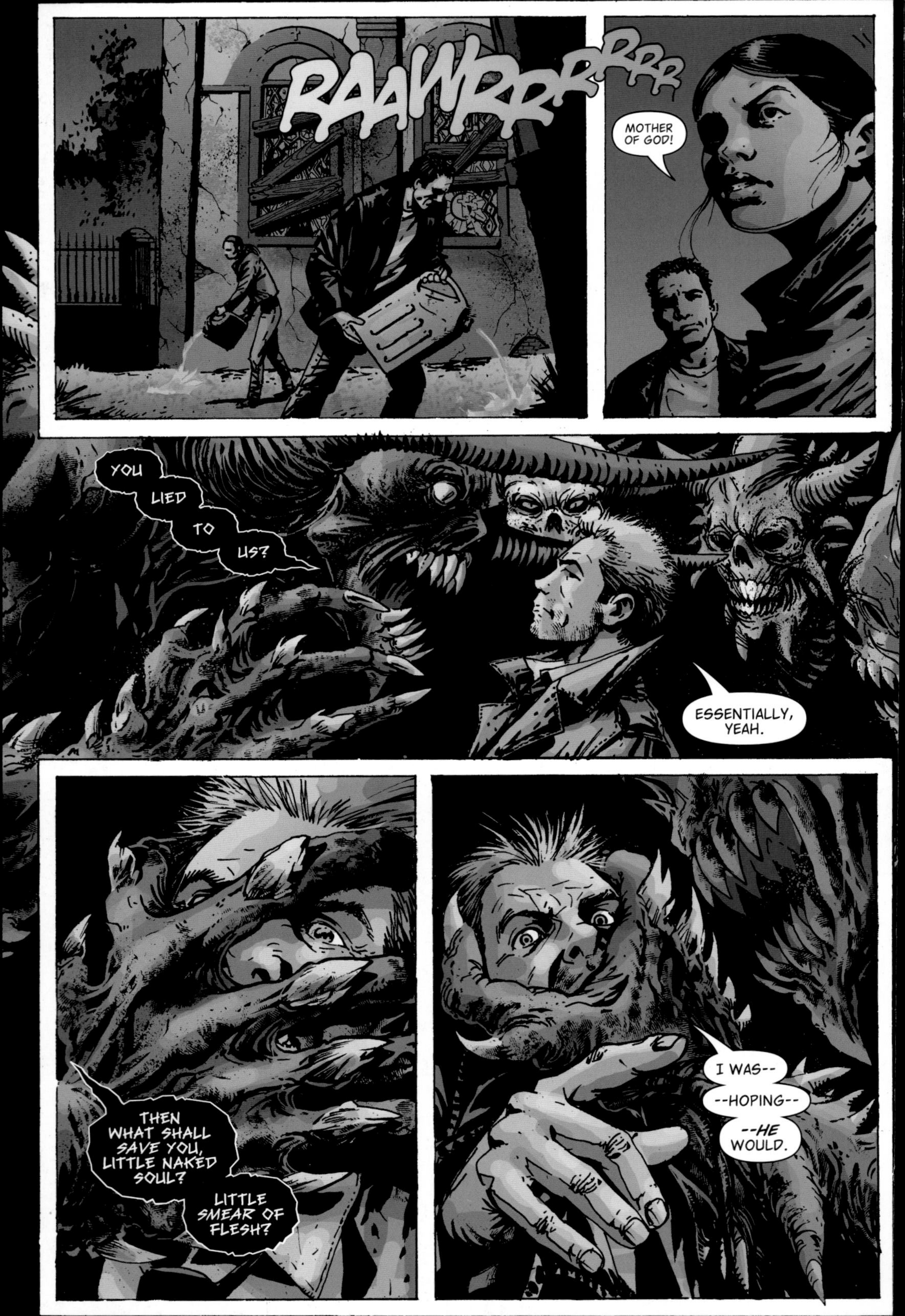
RAAWRRRRRRR
MOTHER OF GOD!
YOU LIED TO US?
ESSENTIALLY, YEAH.
THEN WHAT SHALL SAVE YOU, LITTLE NAKED SOUL?
LITTLE SMEAR OF FLESH?
I WAS--
--HOPING--
--HE WOULD.

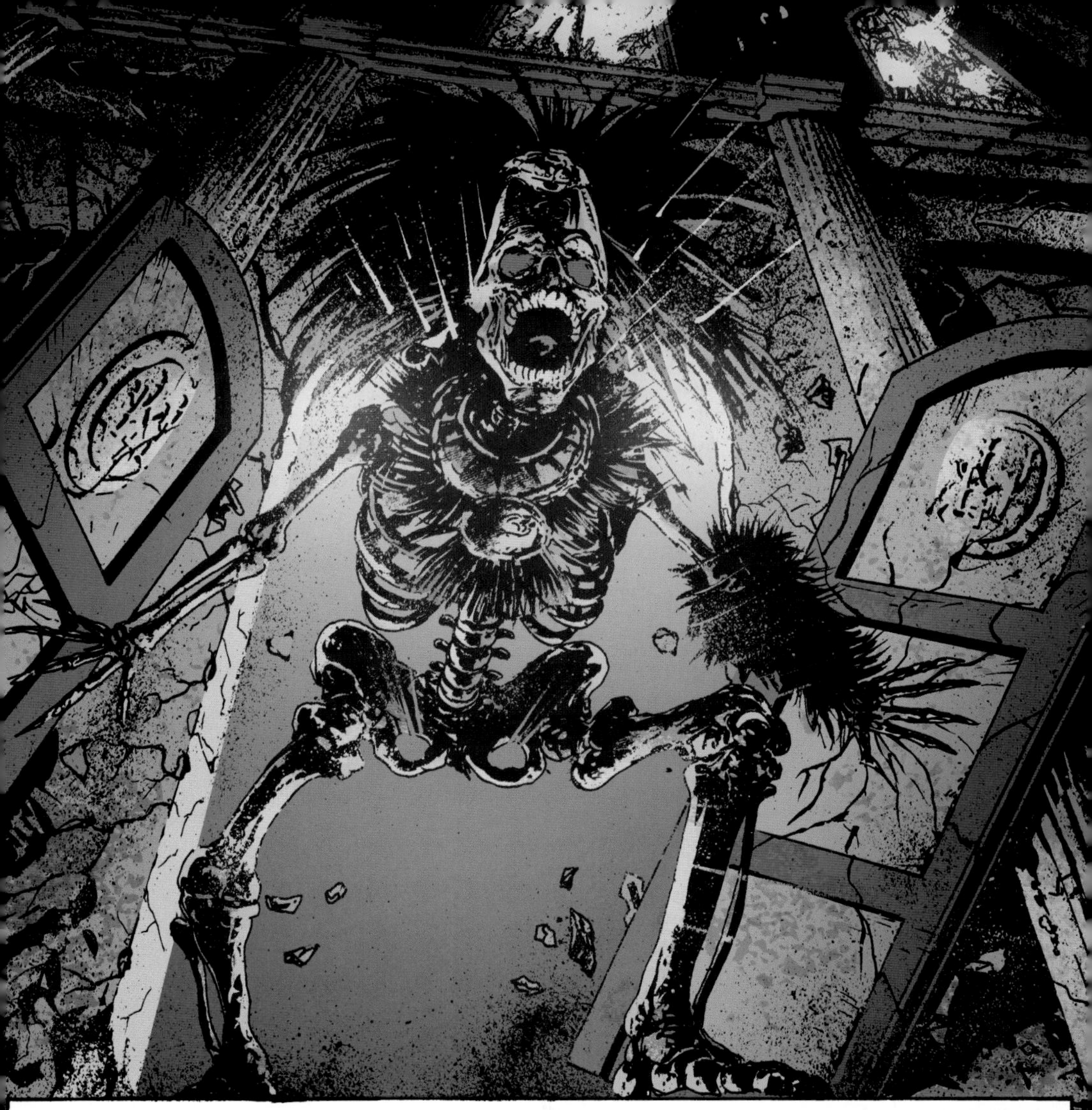

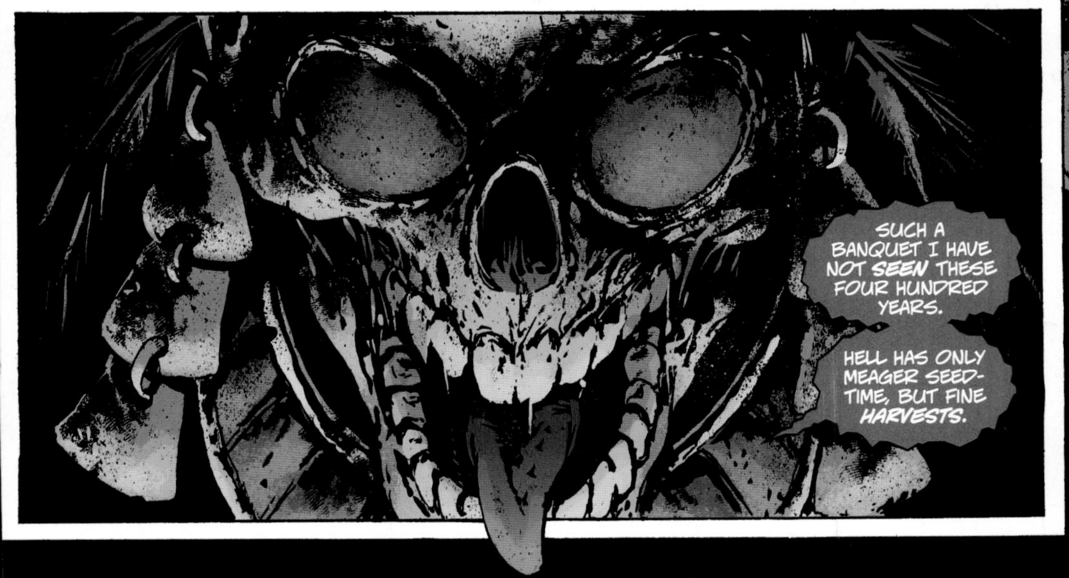
SUCH A BANQUET I HAVE NOT SEEN THESE FOUR HUNDRED YEARS.
HELL HAS ONLY MEAGER SEED-TIME, BUT FINE HARVESTS.

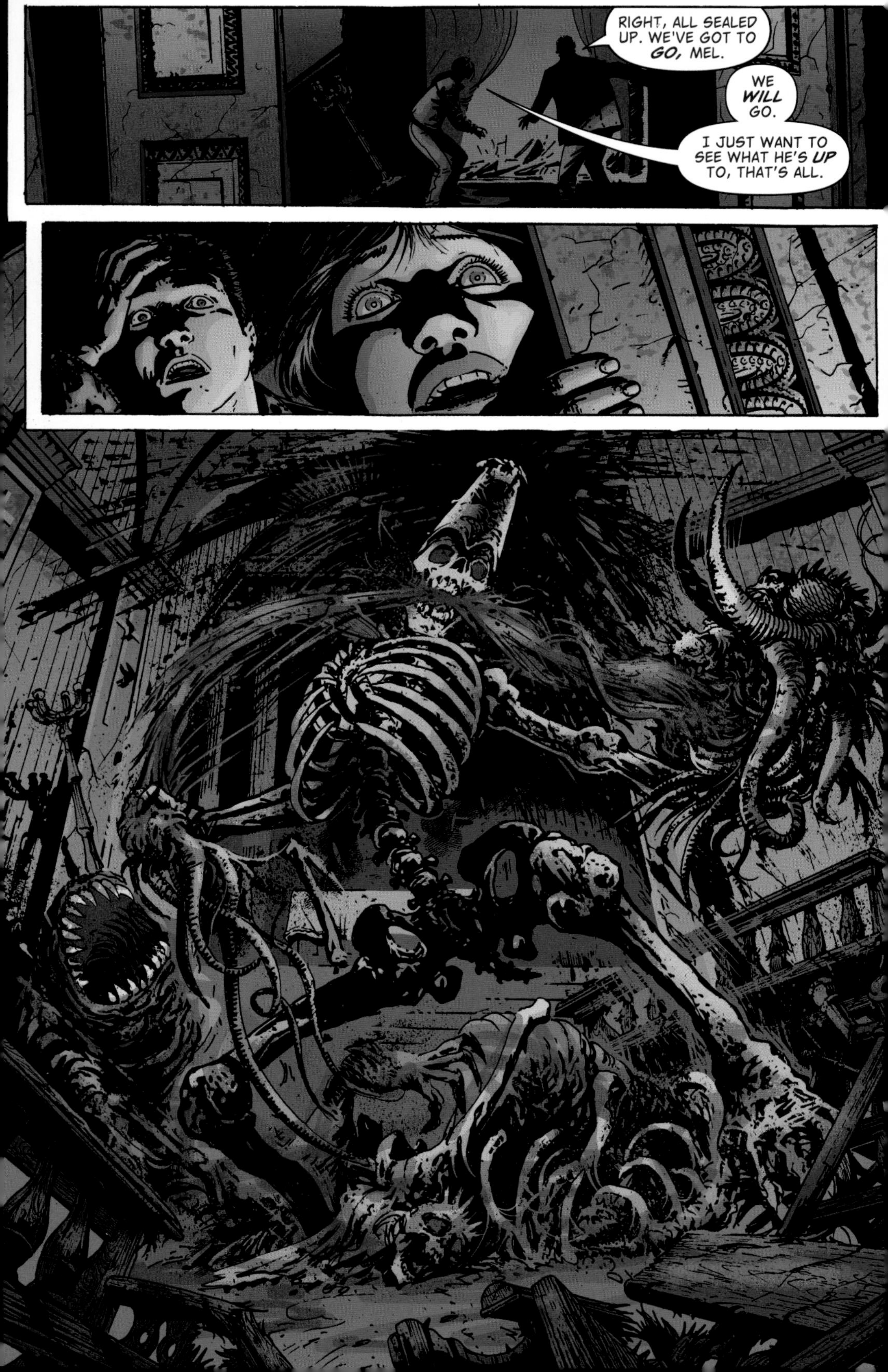
RIGHT, ALL SEALED UP. WE'VE GOT TO GO, MEL.
WE WILL GO.
I JUST WANT TO SEE WHAT HE'S UP TO, THAT'S ALL.

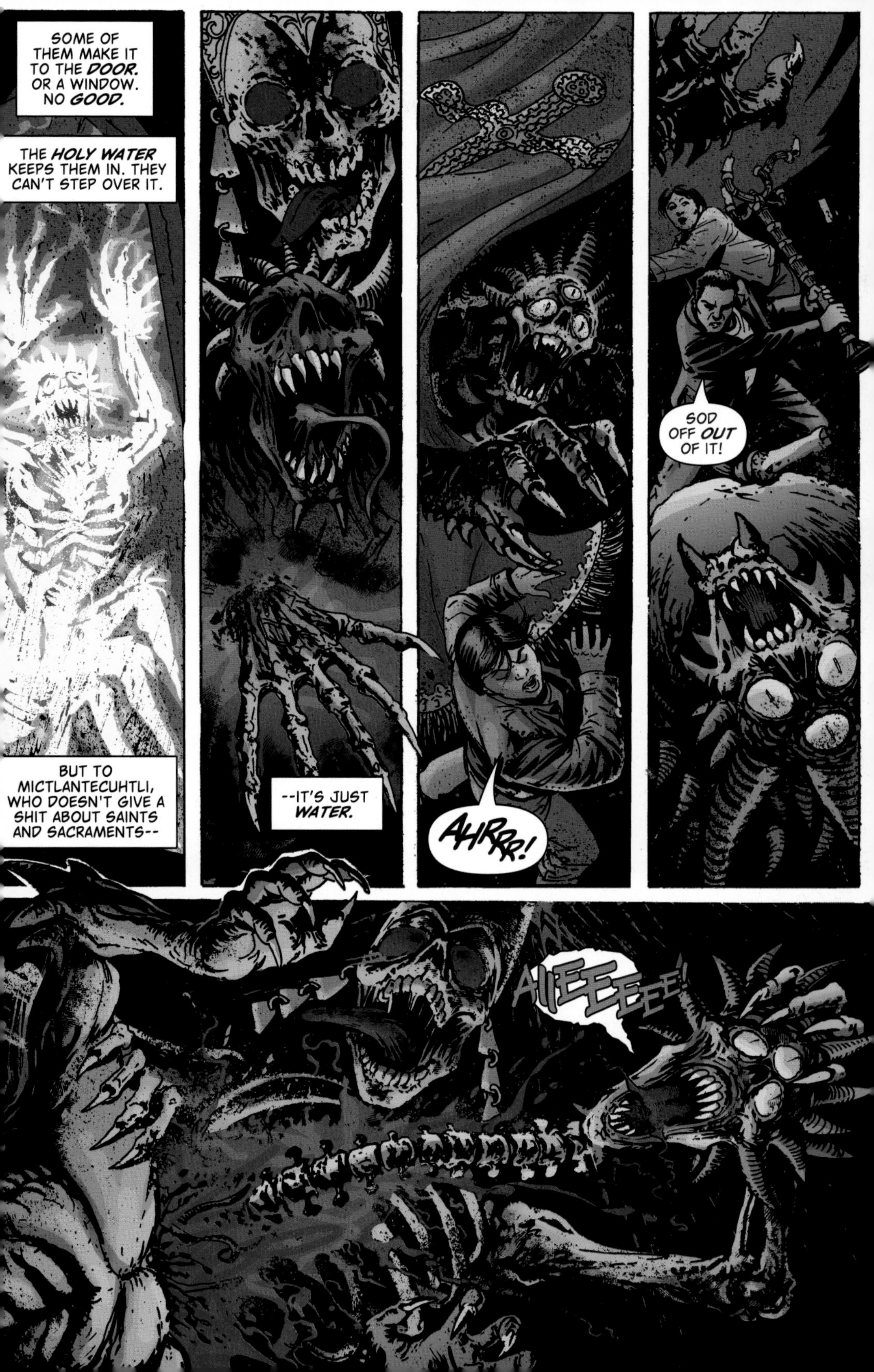
SOME OF THEM MAKE IT TO THE *DOOR.* OR A WINDOW. NO *GOOD.*
THE *HOLY WATER* KEEPS THEM IN. THEY CAN'T STEP OVER IT.
BUT TO MICTLANTECUHTLI, WHO DOESN'T GIVE A SHIT ABOUT SAINTS AND SACRAMENTS--
--IT'S JUST *WATER.*
AHRRR!
SOD OFF *OUT* OF IT!
AIIEEEEEE!

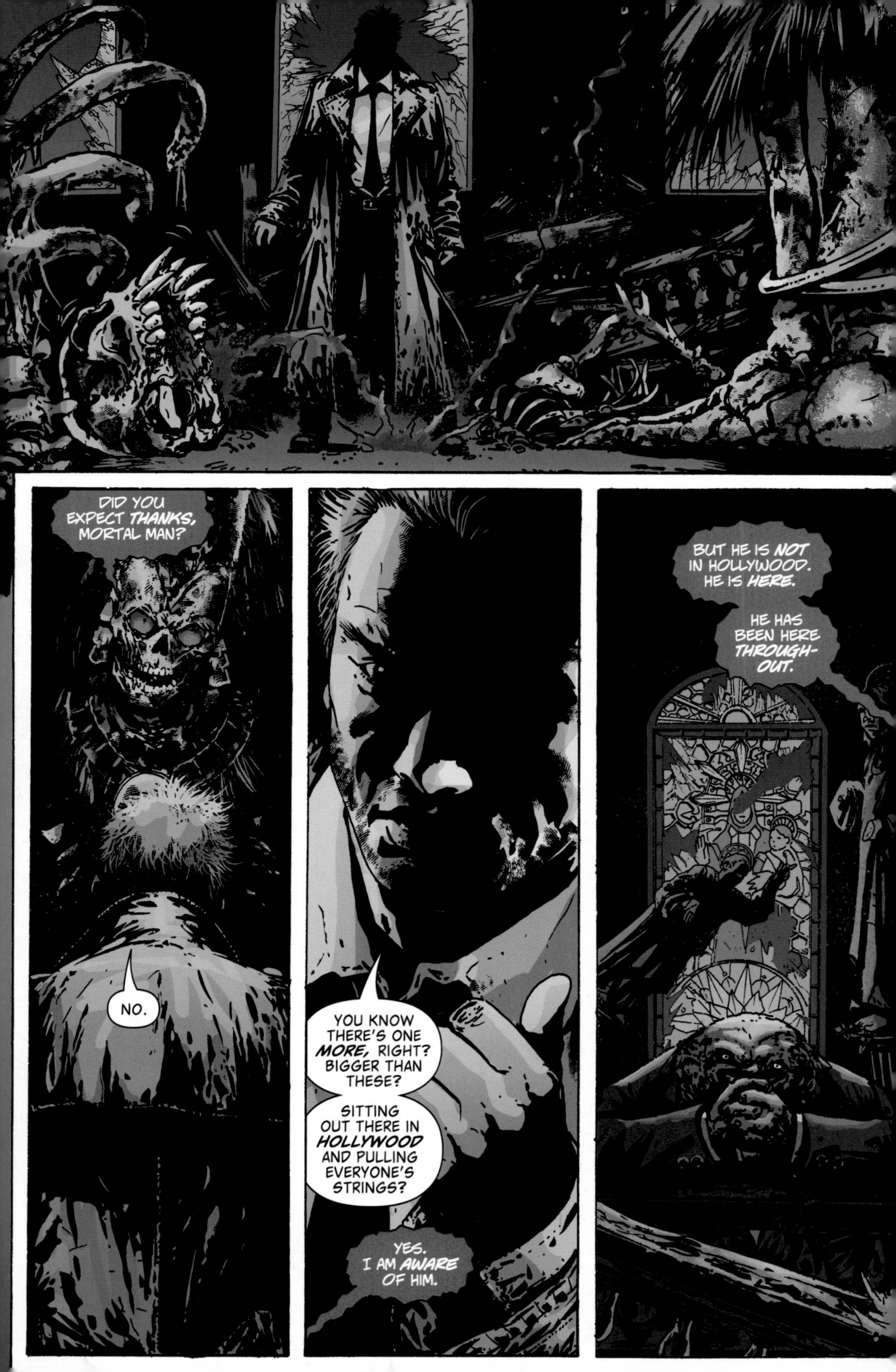
DID YOU EXPECT THANKS, MORTAL MAN?
NO.
YOU KNOW THERE'S ONE MORE, RIGHT? BIGGER THAN THESE?
SITTING OUT THERE IN HOLLYWOOD AND PULLING EVERYONE'S STRINGS?
YES. I AM AWARE OF HIM.
BUT HE IS NOT IN HOLLYWOOD. HE IS HERE.
HE HAS BEEN HERE THROUGH-OUT.

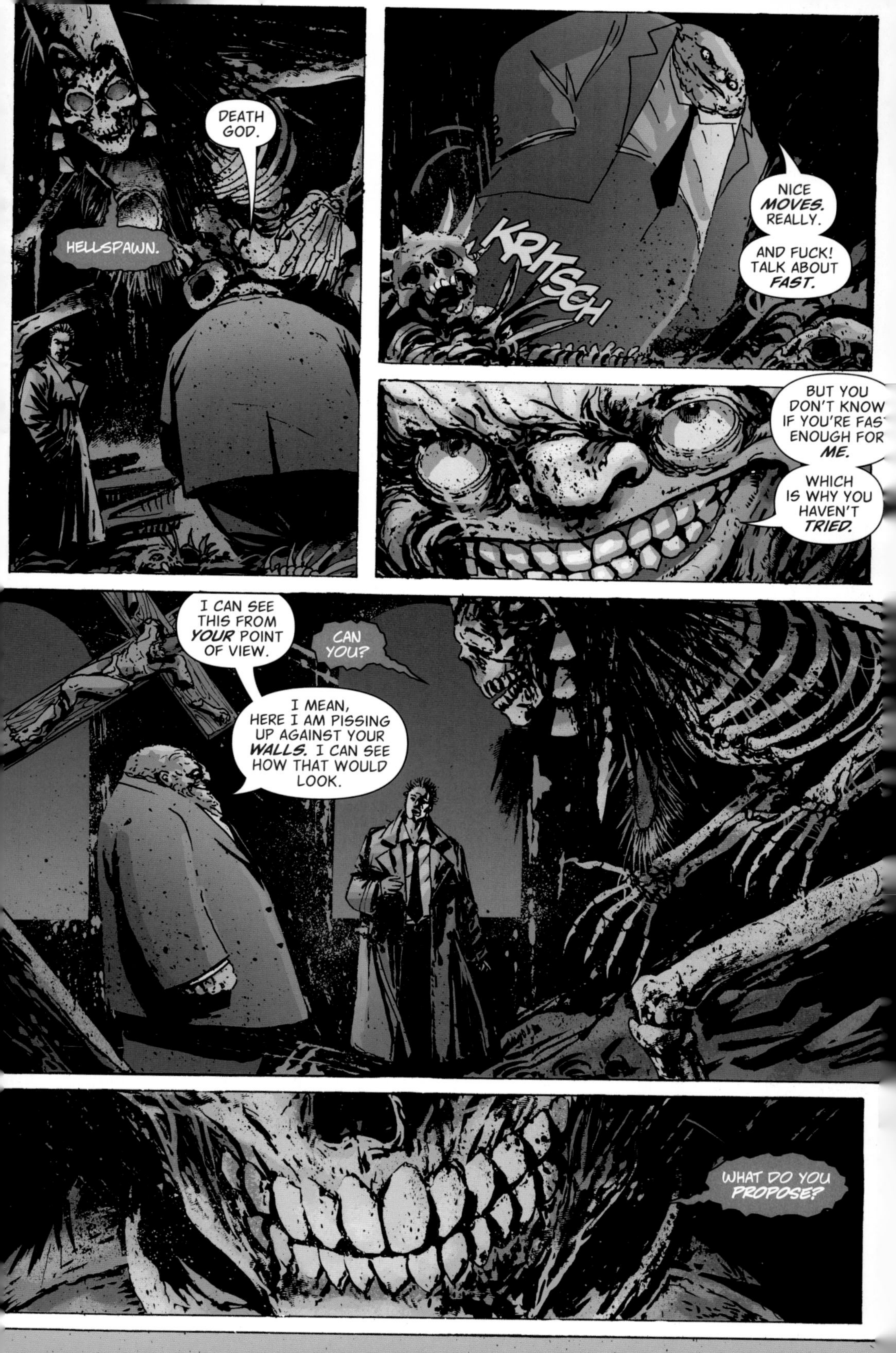
DEATH GOD.
HELLSPAWN.
KRITSCH
NICE MOVES. REALLY.
AND FUCK! TALK ABOUT FAST.
BUT YOU DON'T KNOW IF YOU'RE FAS ENOUGH FOR ME.
WHICH IS WHY YOU HAVEN'T TRIED.
I CAN SEE THIS FROM YOUR POINT OF VIEW.
CAN YOU?
I MEAN, HERE I AM PISSING UP AGAINST YOUR WALLS. I CAN SEE HOW THAT WOULD LOOK.
WHAT DO YOU PROPOSE?

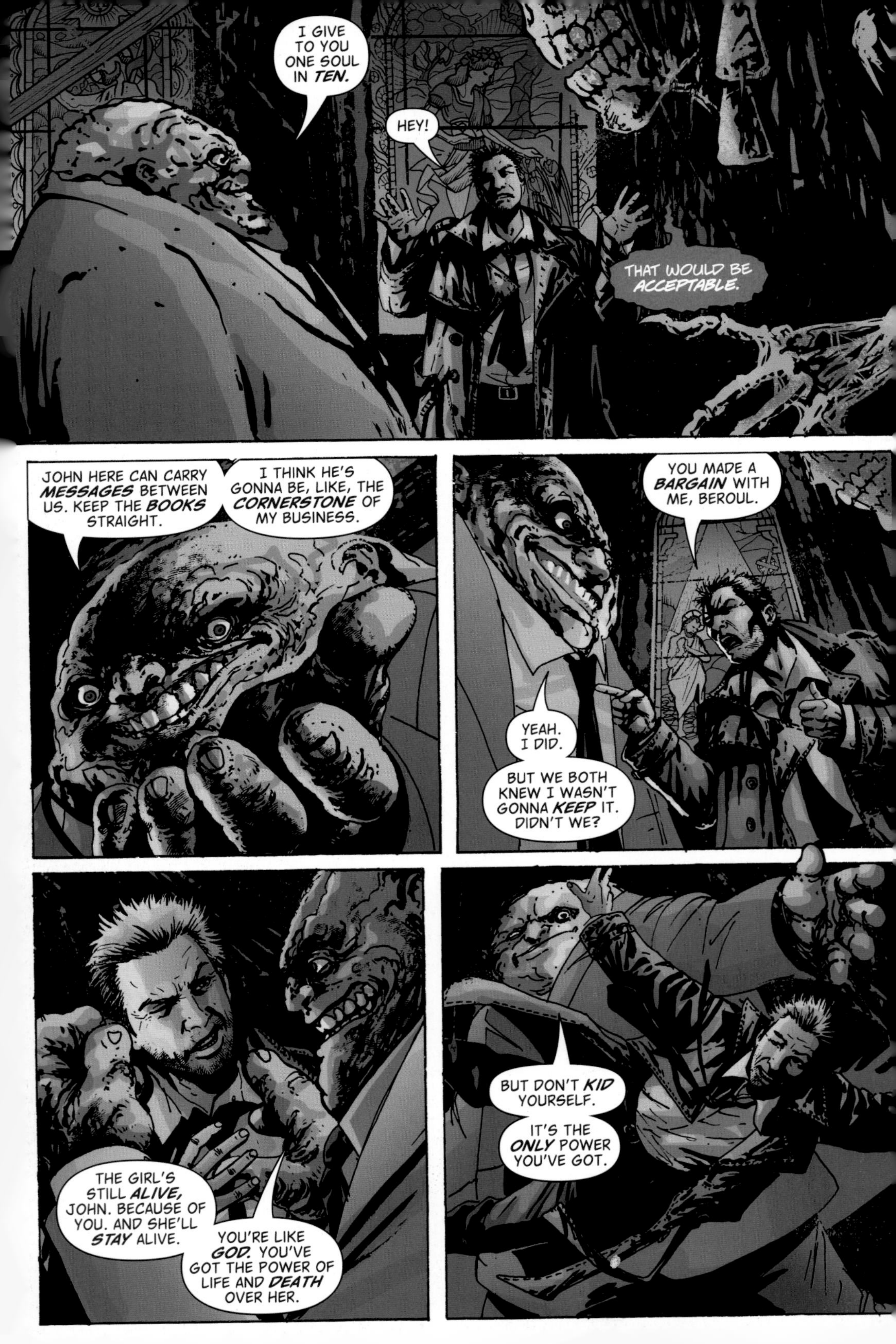
I GIVE TO YOU ONE SOUL IN *TEN.*
HEY!
THAT WOULD BE *ACCEPTABLE.*
JOHN HERE CAN CARRY *MESSAGES* BETWEEN US. KEEP THE *BOOKS* STRAIGHT.
I THINK HE'S GONNA BE, LIKE, THE *CORNERSTONE* OF MY BUSINESS.
YOU MADE A *BARGAIN* WITH ME, BEROUL.
YEAH. I DID.
BUT WE BOTH KNEW I WASN'T GONNA *KEEP* IT. DIDN'T WE?
THE GIRL'S STILL *ALIVE,* JOHN. BECAUSE OF YOU. AND SHE'LL *STAY* ALIVE.
YOU'RE LIKE *GOD.* YOU'VE GOT THE POWER OF LIFE AND *DEATH* OVER HER.
BUT DON'T *KID* YOURSELF.
IT'S THE *ONLY* POWER YOU'VE GOT.

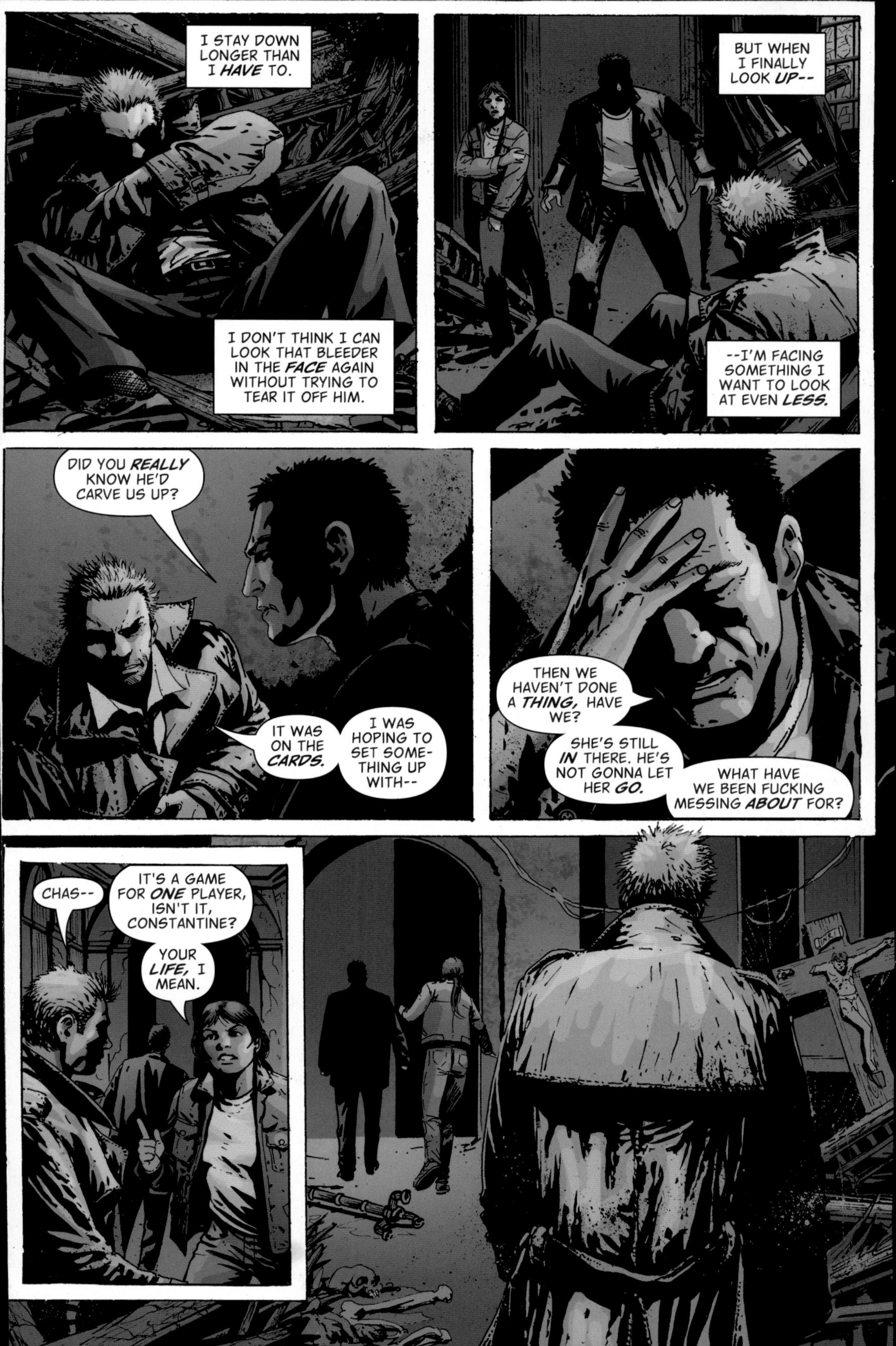

I STAY DOWN LONGER THAN I *HAVE* TO.
I DON'T THINK I CAN LOOK THAT BLEEDER IN THE *FACE* AGAIN WITHOUT TRYING TO TEAR IT OFF HIM.
BUT WHEN I FINALLY LOOK *UP*--
--I'M FACING SOMETHING I WANT TO LOOK AT EVEN *LESS.*
DID YOU *REALLY* KNOW HE'D CARVE US UP?
IT WAS ON THE *CARDS.*
I WAS HOPING TO SET SOME-THING UP WITH--
THEN WE HAVEN'T DONE A *THING,* HAVE WE?
SHE'S STILL *IN* THERE. HE'S NOT GONNA LET HER *GO.*
WHAT HAVE WE BEEN FUCKING MESSING *ABOUT* FOR?
CHAS--
IT'S A GAME FOR *ONE* PLAYER, ISN'T IT, CONSTANTINE?
YOUR *LIFE,* I MEAN.

THE NEXT FEW HOURS RUN TOGETHER INTO A BROWNISH *SLUDGE.*

I WALK BACK UP ALONG *SEPULVEDA,* PAST ABOUT A HUNDRED BARS AND STRIP JOINTS.

END UP *DRINKING* IN ONE OF THEM. NOT SURE HOW.

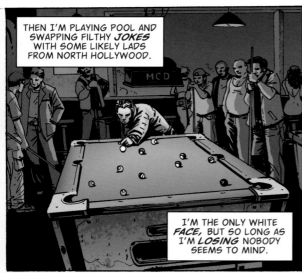

THEN I'M PLAYING POOL AND SWAPPING FILTHY *JOKES* WITH SOME LIKELY LADS FROM NORTH HOLLYWOOD.

I'M THE ONLY WHITE *FACE,* BUT SO LONG AS I'M *LOSING* NOBODY SEEMS TO MIND.

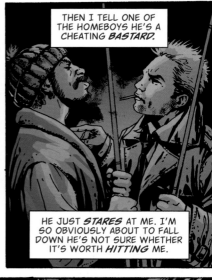

THEN I TELL ONE OF THE HOMEBOYS HE'S A CHEATING *BASTARD.*

HE JUST *STARES* AT ME. I'M SO OBVIOUSLY ABOUT TO FALL DOWN HE'S NOT SURE WHETHER IT'S WORTH *HITTING* ME.

WORKS OUT JUST *FINE.*

I GET TO LAND THE FIRST *PUNCH.*

IT'S THE ONLY ONE I EVEN *REMEMBER.*

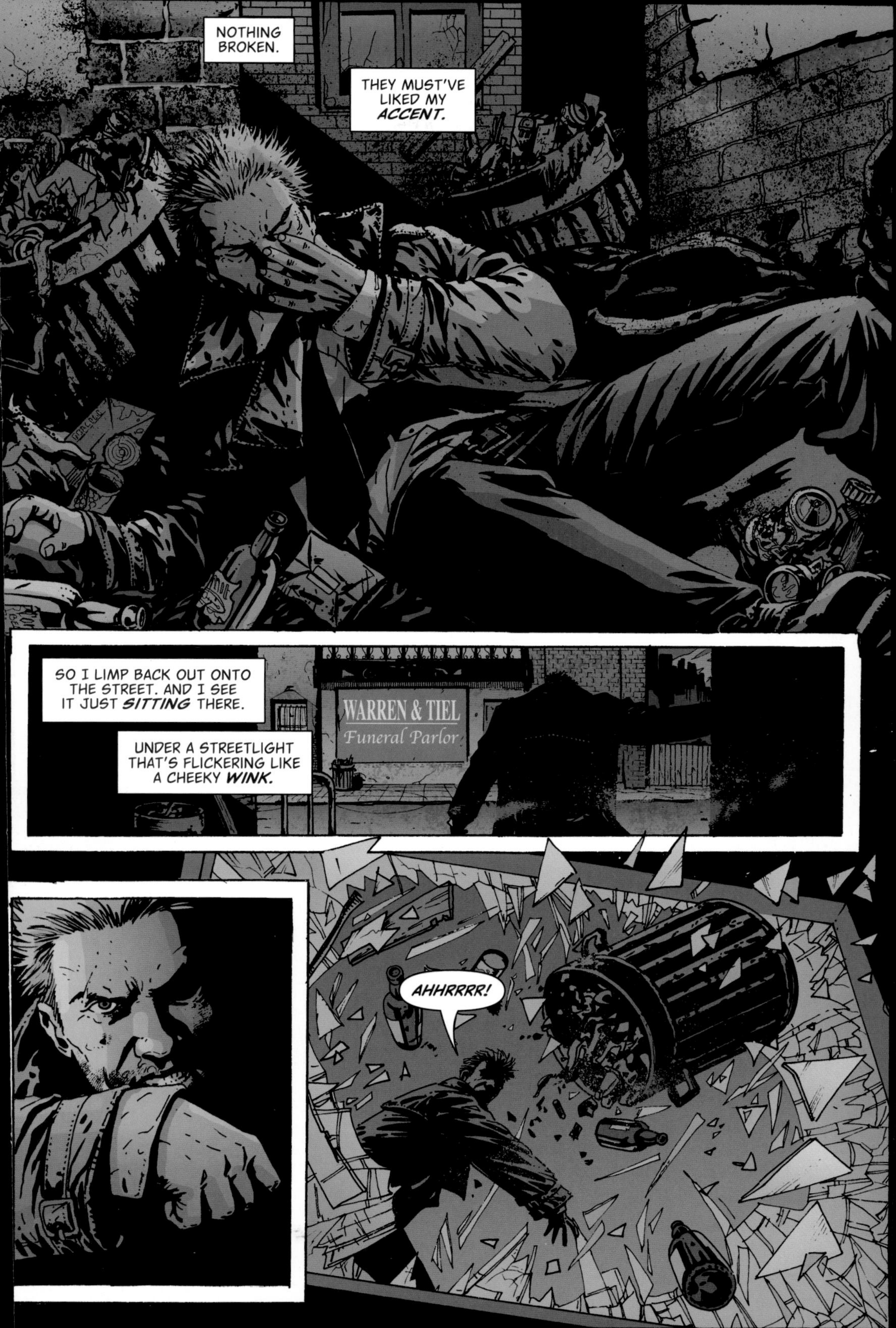
NOTHING BROKEN.
THEY MUST'VE LIKED MY ACCENT.
SO I LIMP BACK OUT ONTO THE STREET. AND I SEE IT JUST SITTING THERE.
WARREN & TIEL
Funeral Parlor
UNDER A STREETLIGHT THAT'S FLICKERING LIKE A CHEEKY WINK.
AHHRRRR!

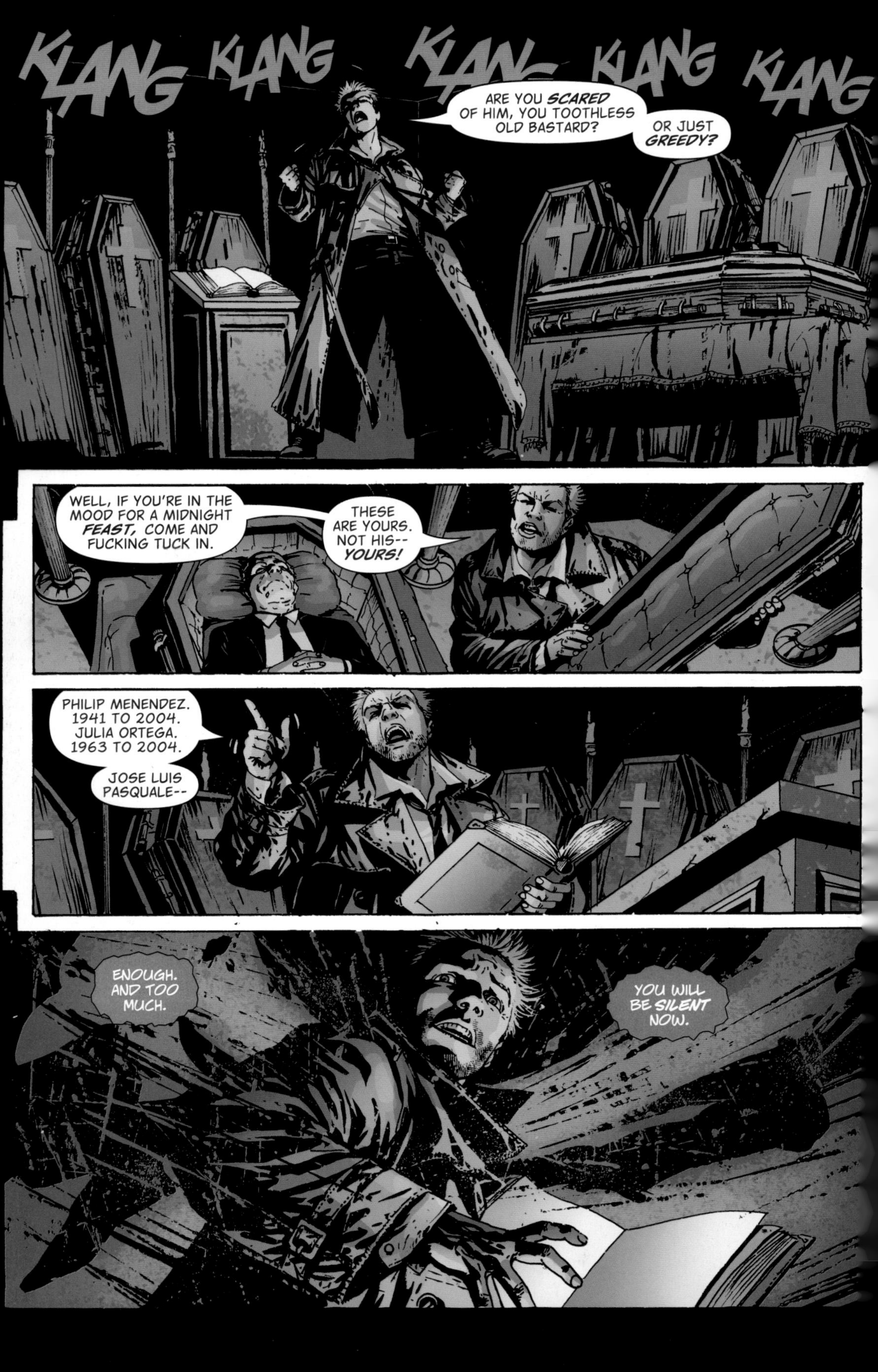
KLANG KLANG KLANG KLANG KLANG
ARE YOU SCARED OF HIM, YOU TOOTHLESS OLD BASTARD?
OR JUST GREEDY?
WELL, IF YOU'RE IN THE MOOD FOR A MIDNIGHT FEAST, COME AND FUCKING TUCK IN.
THESE ARE YOURS. NOT HIS-- YOURS!
PHILIP MENENDEZ. 1941 TO 2004. JULIA ORTEGA. 1963 TO 2004.
JOSE LUIS PASQUALE--
ENOUGH. AND TOO MUCH.
YOU WILL BE SILENT NOW.

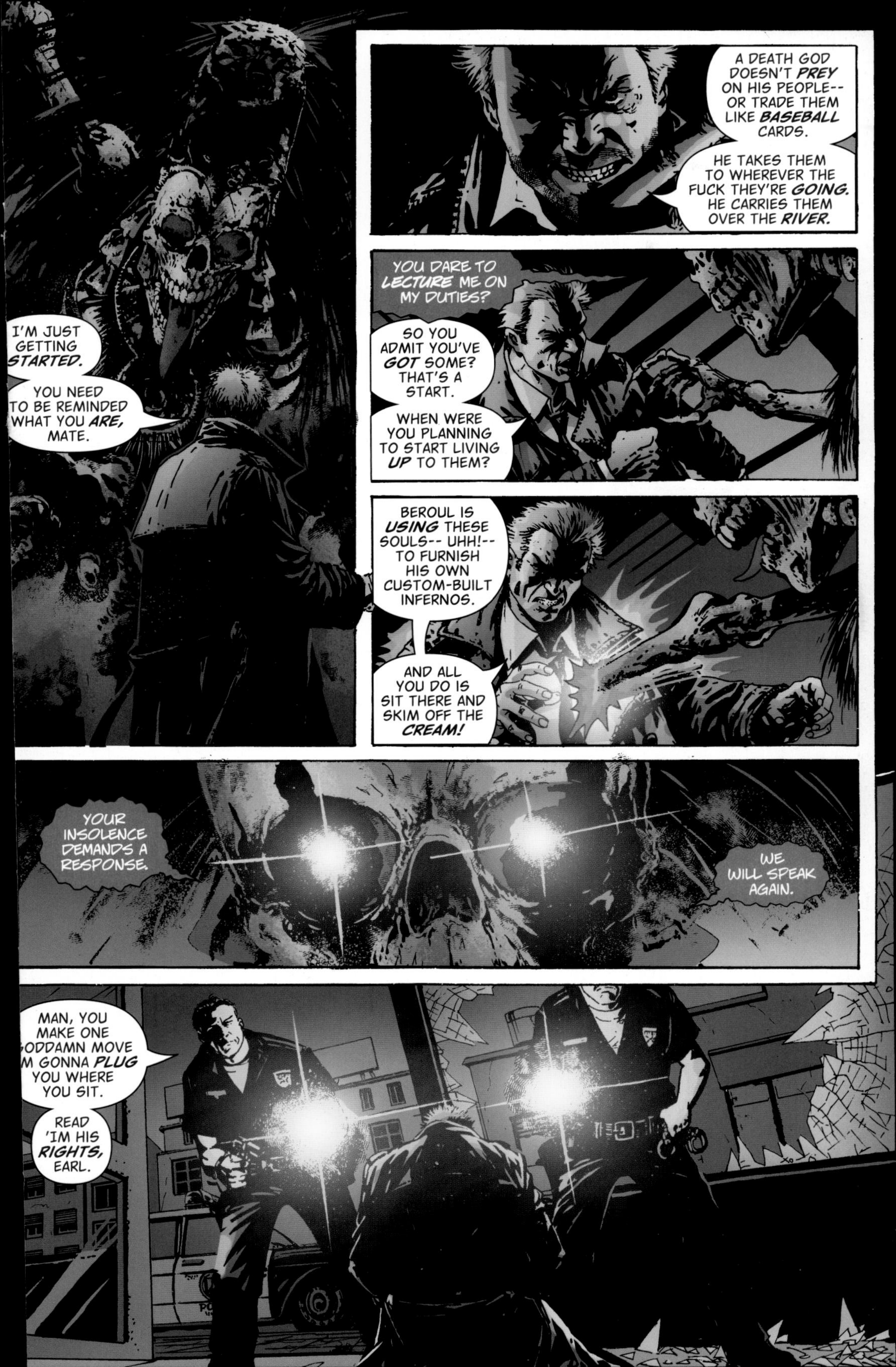
A DEATH GOD DOESN'T PREY ON HIS PEOPLE-- OR TRADE THEM LIKE BASEBALL CARDS.
HE TAKES THEM TO WHEREVER THE FUCK THEY'RE GOING. HE CARRIES THEM OVER THE RIVER.
I'M JUST GETTING STARTED.
YOU NEED TO BE REMINDED WHAT YOU ARE, MATE.
YOU DARE TO LECTURE ME ON MY DUTIES?
SO YOU ADMIT YOU'VE GOT SOME? THAT'S A START.
WHEN WERE YOU PLANNING TO START LIVING UP TO THEM?
BEROUL IS USING THESE SOULS-- UHH!-- TO FURNISH HIS OWN CUSTOM-BUILT INFERNOS.
AND ALL YOU DO IS SIT THERE AND SKIM OFF THE CREAM!
YOUR INSOLENCE DEMANDS A RESPONSE.
WE WILL SPEAK AGAIN.
MAN, YOU MAKE ONE GODDAMN MOVE I'M GONNA PLUG YOU WHERE YOU SIT.
READ 'IM HIS RIGHTS, EARL.

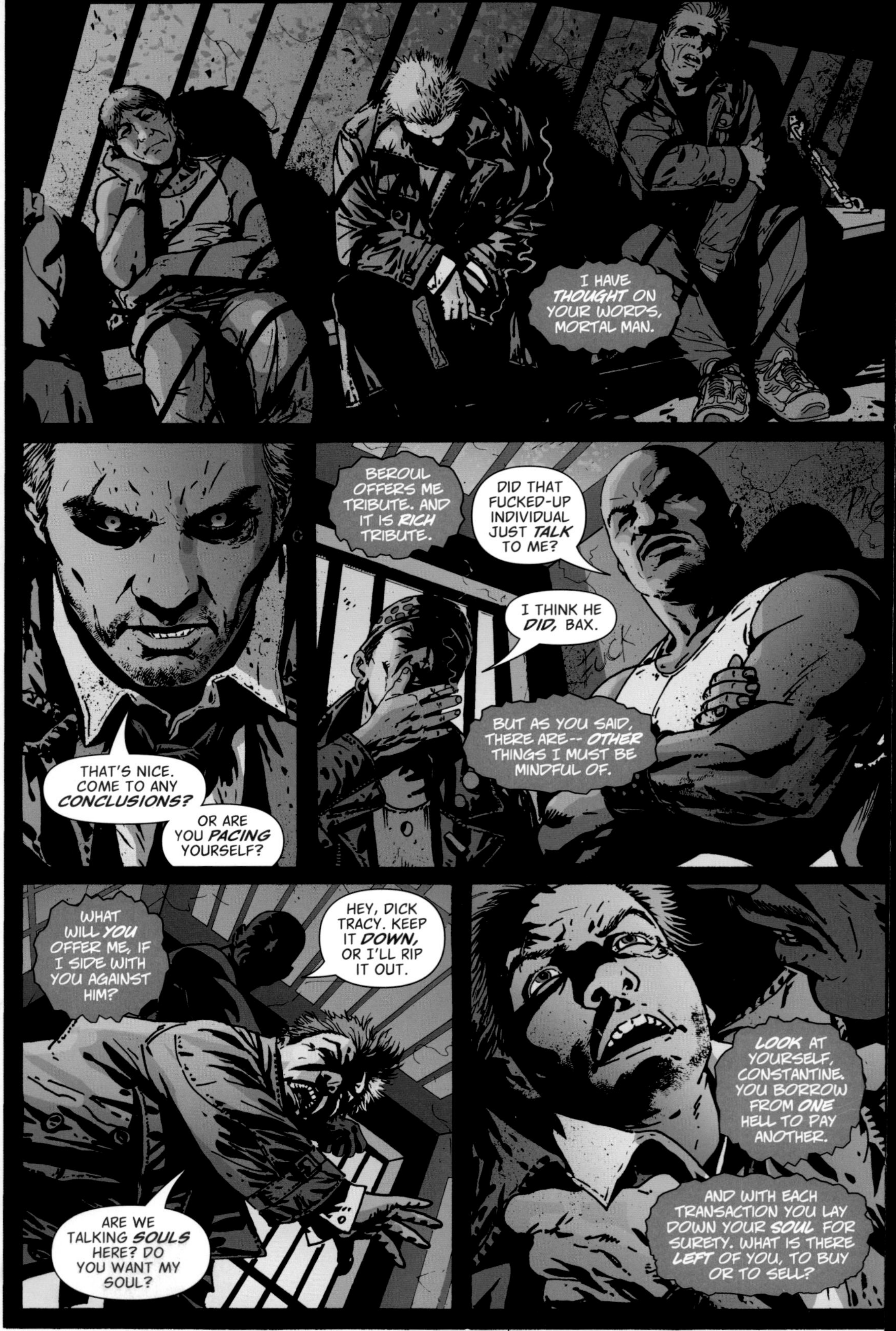
I HAVE THOUGHT ON YOUR WORDS, MORTAL MAN.
BEROUL OFFERS ME TRIBUTE. AND IT IS RICH TRIBUTE.
DID THAT FUCKED-UP INDIVIDUAL JUST TALK TO ME?
I THINK HE DID, BAX.
BUT AS YOU SAID, THERE ARE-- OTHER THINGS I MUST BE MINDFUL OF.
THAT'S NICE. COME TO ANY CONCLUSIONS?
OR ARE YOU PACING YOURSELF?
WHAT WILL YOU OFFER ME, IF I SIDE WITH YOU AGAINST HIM?
HEY, DICK TRACY. KEEP IT DOWN, OR I'LL RIP IT OUT.
ARE WE TALKING SOULS HERE? DO YOU WANT MY SOUL?
LOOK AT YOURSELF, CONSTANTINE. YOU BORROW FROM ONE HELL TO PAY ANOTHER.
AND WITH EACH TRANSACTION YOU LAY DOWN YOUR SOUL FOR SURETY. WHAT IS THERE LEFT OF YOU, TO BUY OR TO SELL?

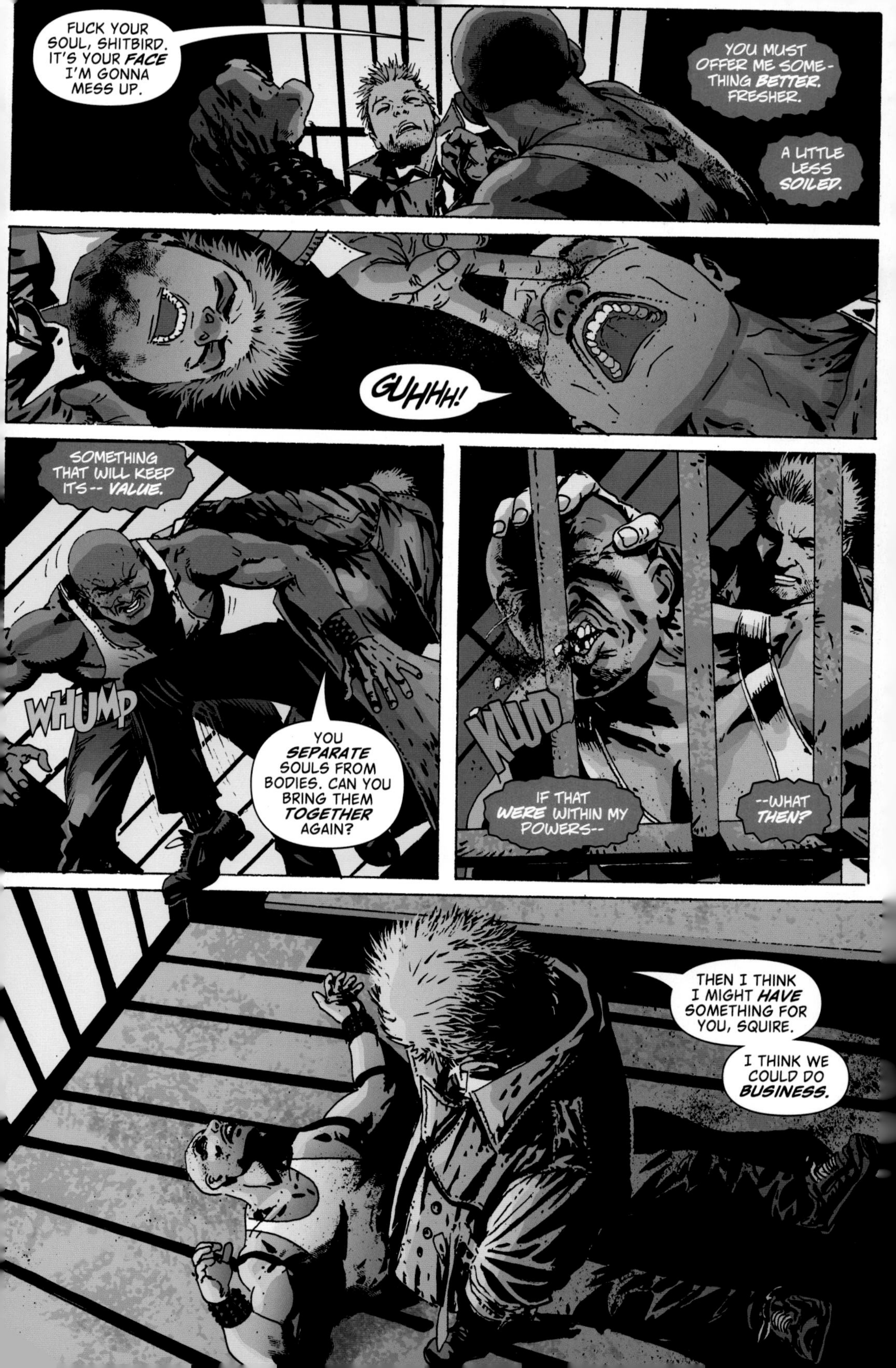
FUCK YOUR SOUL, SHITBIRD. IT'S YOUR FACE I'M GONNA MESS UP.
YOU MUST OFFER ME SOME-THING BETTER. FRESHER.
A LITTLE LESS SOILED.
GUHHH!
SOMETHING THAT WILL KEEP ITS-- VALUE.
WHUMP
YOU SEPARATE SOULS FROM BODIES. CAN YOU BRING THEM TOGETHER AGAIN?
KUD
IF THAT WERE WITHIN MY POWERS--
--WHAT THEN?
THEN I THINK I MIGHT HAVE SOMETHING FOR YOU, SQUIRE.
I THINK WE COULD DO BUSINESS.

CHAPTER FIVE

no second stroke

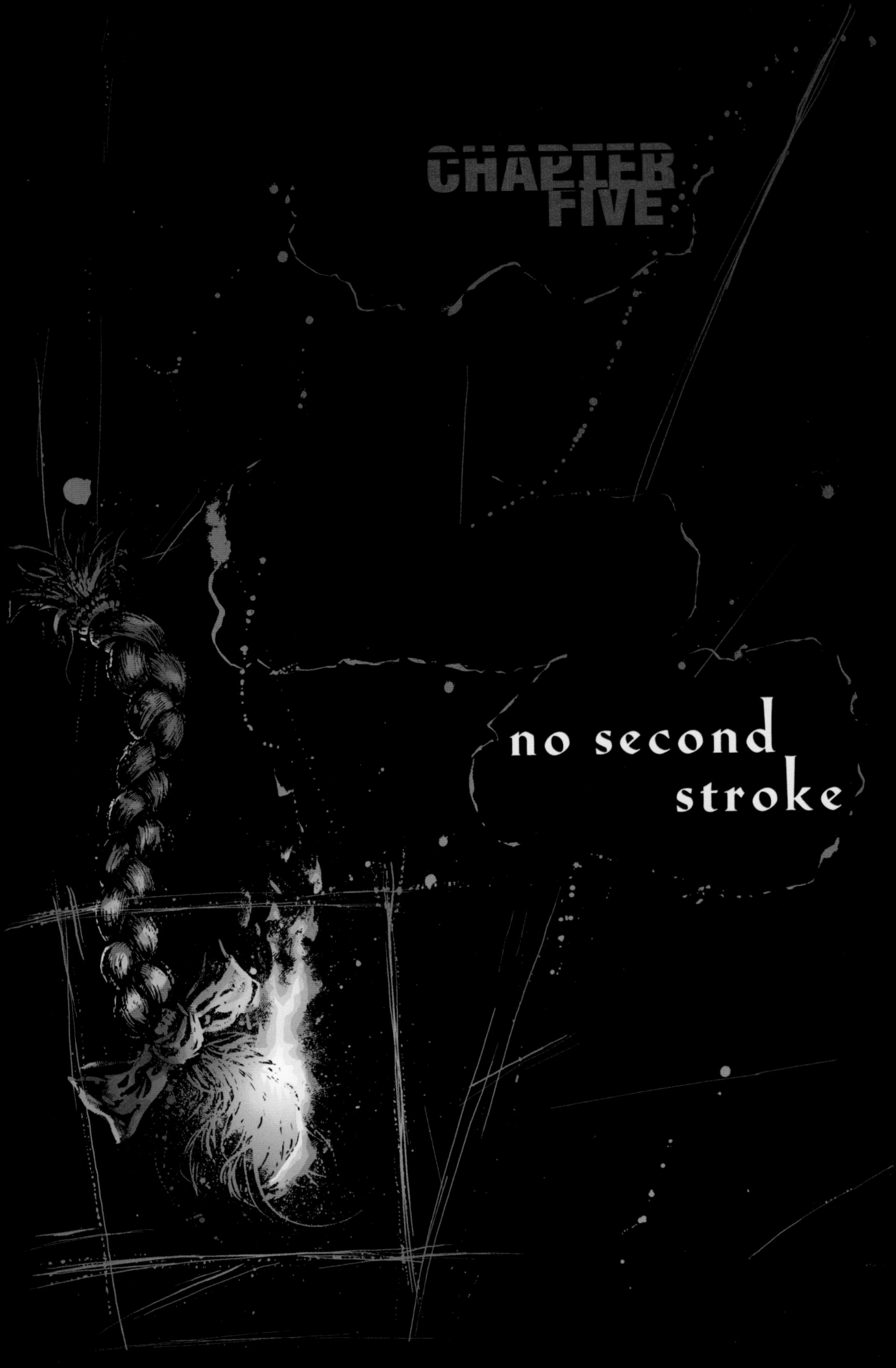

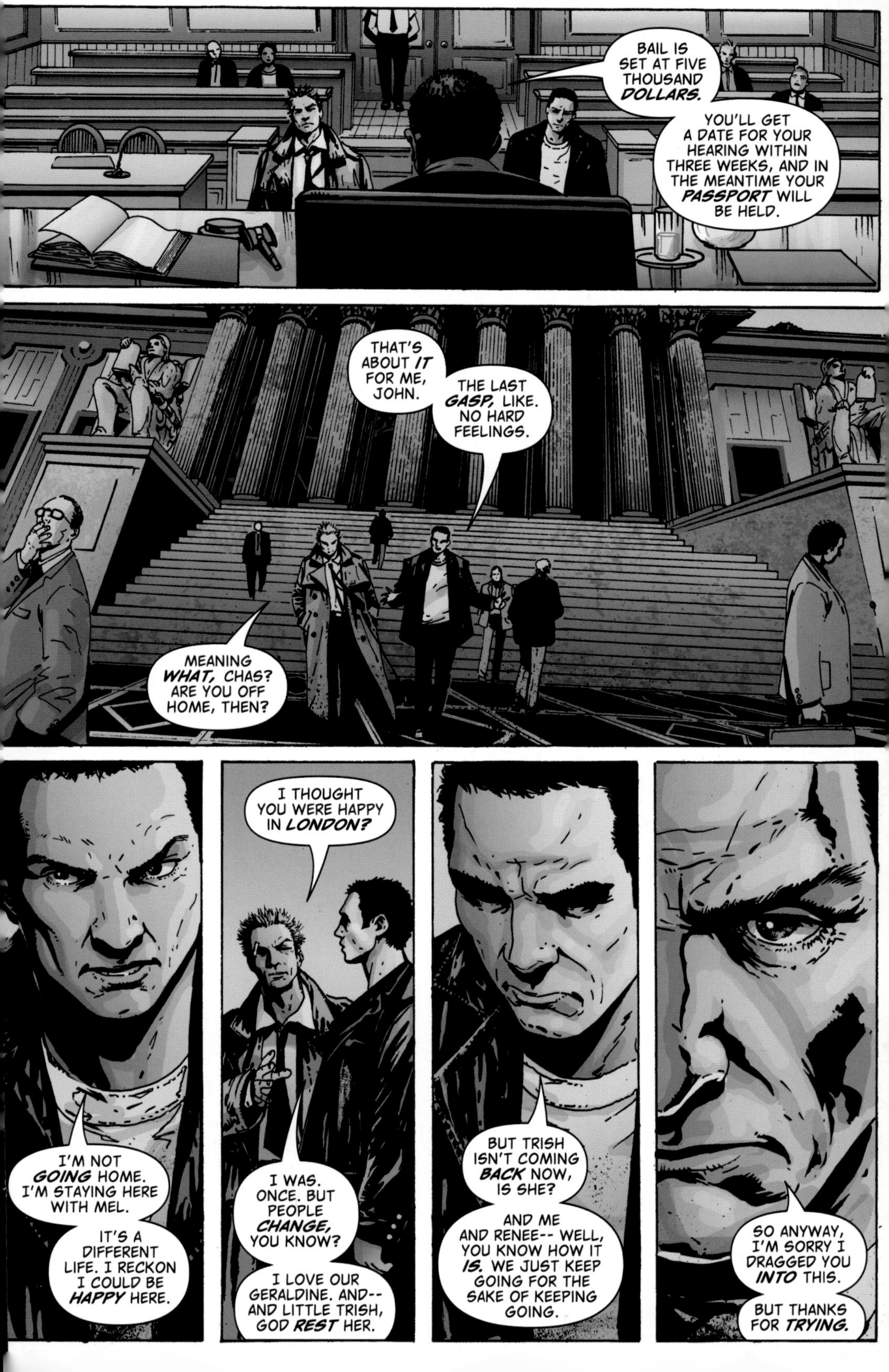
BAIL IS SET AT FIVE THOUSAND *DOLLARS.*
YOU'LL GET A DATE FOR YOUR HEARING WITHIN THREE WEEKS, AND IN THE MEANTIME YOUR *PASSPORT* WILL BE HELD.
THAT'S ABOUT *IT* FOR ME, JOHN.
THE LAST *GASP,* LIKE. NO HARD FEELINGS.
MEANING *WHAT,* CHAS? ARE YOU OFF HOME, THEN?
I'M NOT *GOING* HOME. I'M STAYING HERE WITH MEL.
IT'S A DIFFERENT LIFE. I RECKON I COULD BE *HAPPY* HERE.
I THOUGHT YOU WERE HAPPY IN *LONDON?*
I WAS. ONCE. BUT PEOPLE *CHANGE,* YOU KNOW?
I LOVE OUR GERALDINE. AND-- AND LITTLE TRISH, GOD *REST* HER.
BUT TRISH ISN'T COMING *BACK* NOW, IS SHE?
AND ME AND RENEE-- WELL, YOU KNOW HOW IT *IS.* WE JUST KEEP GOING FOR THE SAKE OF KEEPING GOING.
SO ANYWAY, I'M SORRY I DRAGGED YOU *INTO* THIS.
BUT THANKS FOR *TRYING.*

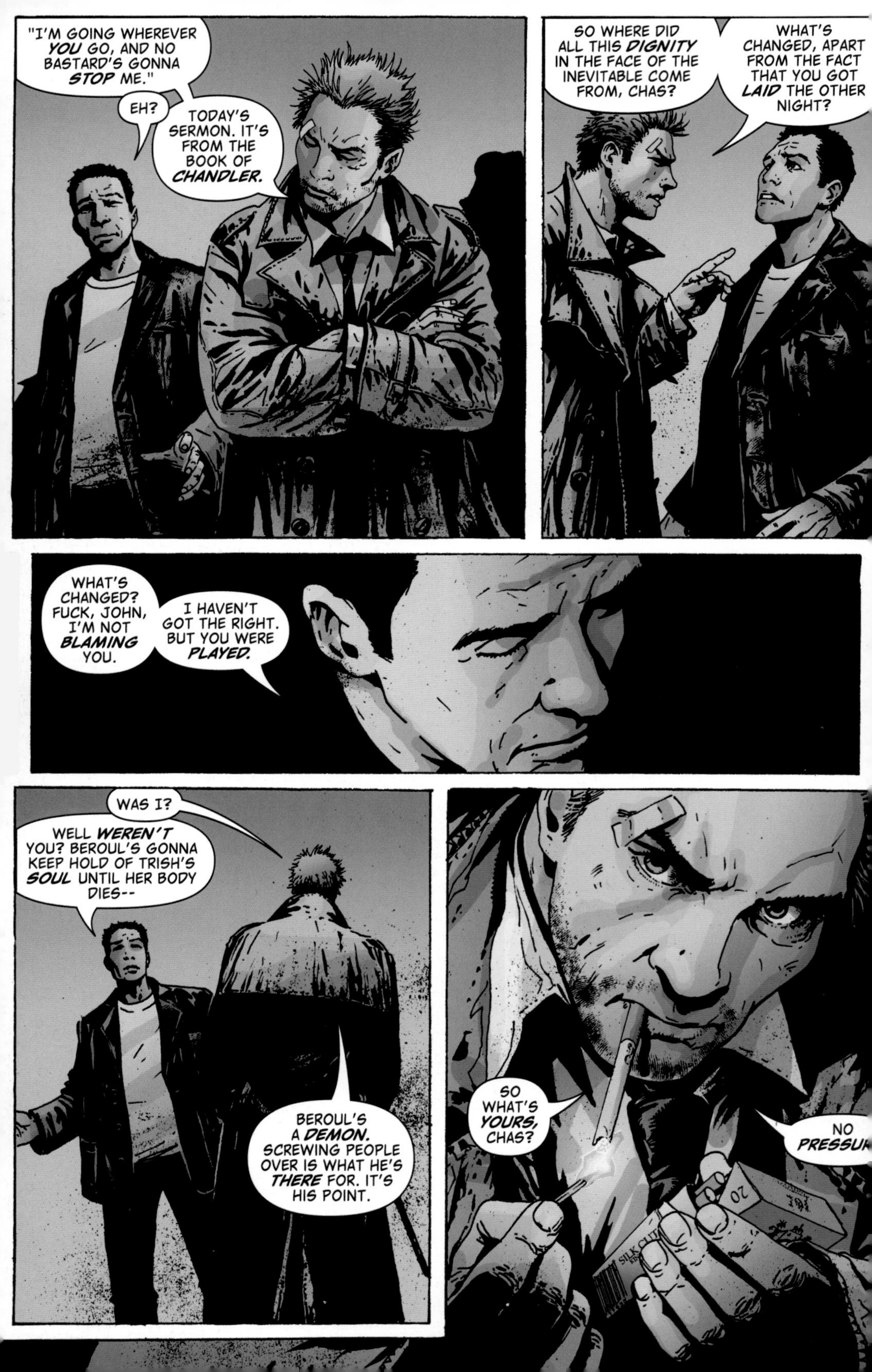
"I'M GOING WHEREVER YOU GO, AND NO BASTARD'S GONNA STOP ME."
EH?
TODAY'S SERMON. IT'S FROM THE BOOK OF CHANDLER.
SO WHERE DID ALL THIS DIGNITY IN THE FACE OF THE INEVITABLE COME FROM, CHAS?
WHAT'S CHANGED, APART FROM THE FACT THAT YOU GOT LAID THE OTHER NIGHT?
WHAT'S CHANGED? FUCK, JOHN, I'M NOT BLAMING YOU.
I HAVEN'T GOT THE RIGHT. BUT YOU WERE PLAYED.
WAS I?
WELL WEREN'T YOU? BEROUL'S GONNA KEEP HOLD OF TRISH'S SOUL UNTIL HER BODY DIES--
BEROUL'S A DEMON. SCREWING PEOPLE OVER IS WHAT HE'S THERE FOR. IT'S HIS POINT.
SO WHAT'S YOURS, CHAS?
NO PRESSU

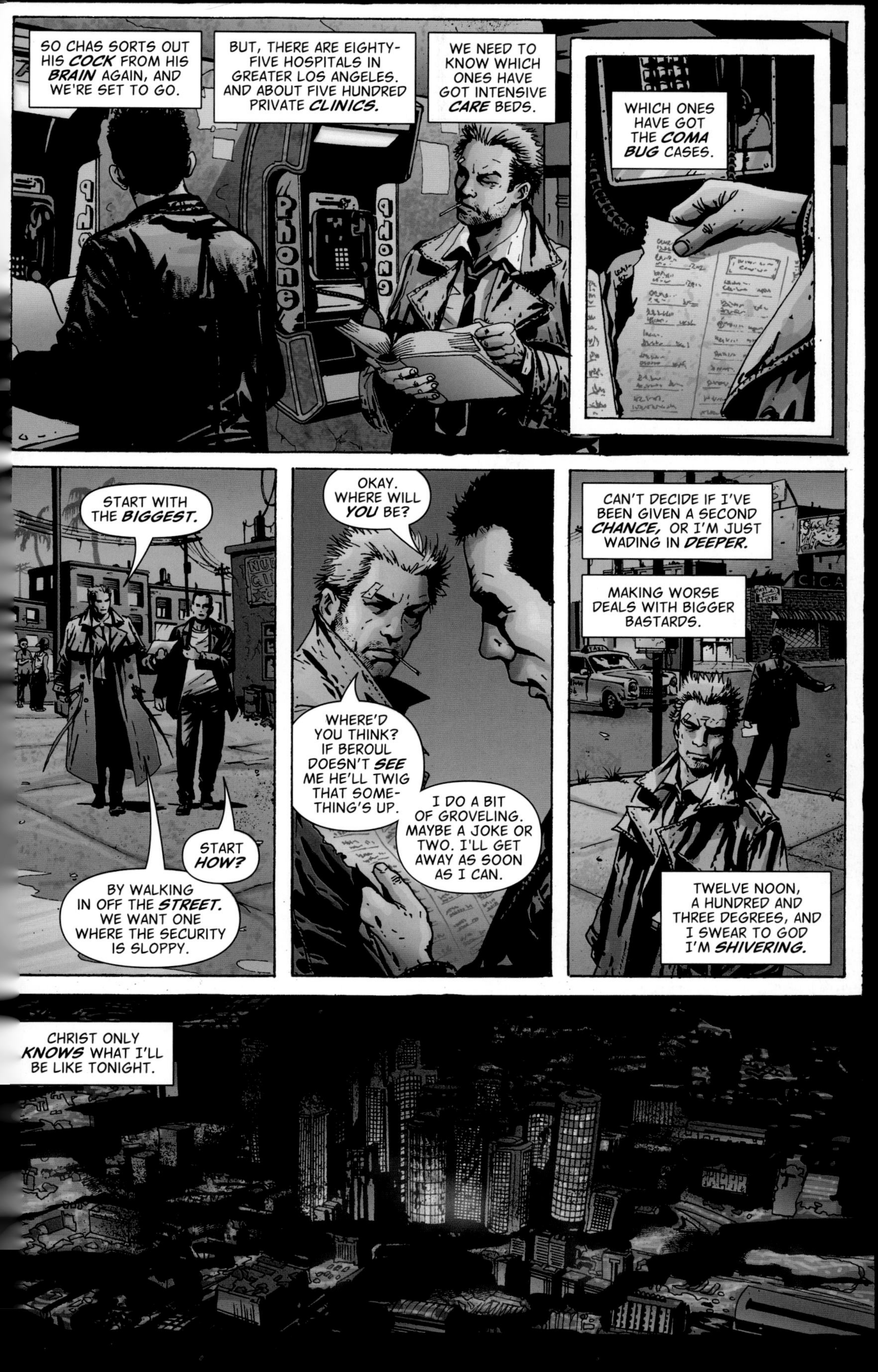

SO CHAS SORTS OUT HIS *COCK* FROM HIS *BRAIN* AGAIN, AND WE'RE SET TO GO.
BUT, THERE ARE EIGHTY-FIVE HOSPITALS IN GREATER LOS ANGELES. AND ABOUT FIVE HUNDRED PRIVATE *CLINICS.*
WE NEED TO KNOW WHICH ONES HAVE GOT INTENSIVE *CARE* BEDS.
WHICH ONES HAVE GOT THE *COMA BUG* CASES.
START WITH THE *BIGGEST.*
START *HOW?*
BY WALKING IN OFF THE *STREET.* WE WANT ONE WHERE THE SECURITY IS SLOPPY.
OKAY. WHERE WILL *YOU* BE?
WHERE'D YOU THINK? IF BEROUL DOESN'T *SEE* ME HE'LL TWIG THAT SOME-THING'S UP.
I DO A BIT OF GROVELING. MAYBE A JOKE OR TWO. I'LL GET AWAY AS SOON AS I CAN.
CAN'T DECIDE IF I'VE BEEN GIVEN A SECOND *CHANCE,* OR I'M JUST WADING IN *DEEPER.*
MAKING WORSE DEALS WITH BIGGER BASTARDS.
TWELVE NOON, A HUNDRED AND THREE DEGREES, AND I SWEAR TO GOD I'M *SHIVERING.*
CHRIST ONLY *KNOWS* WHAT I'LL BE LIKE TONIGHT.

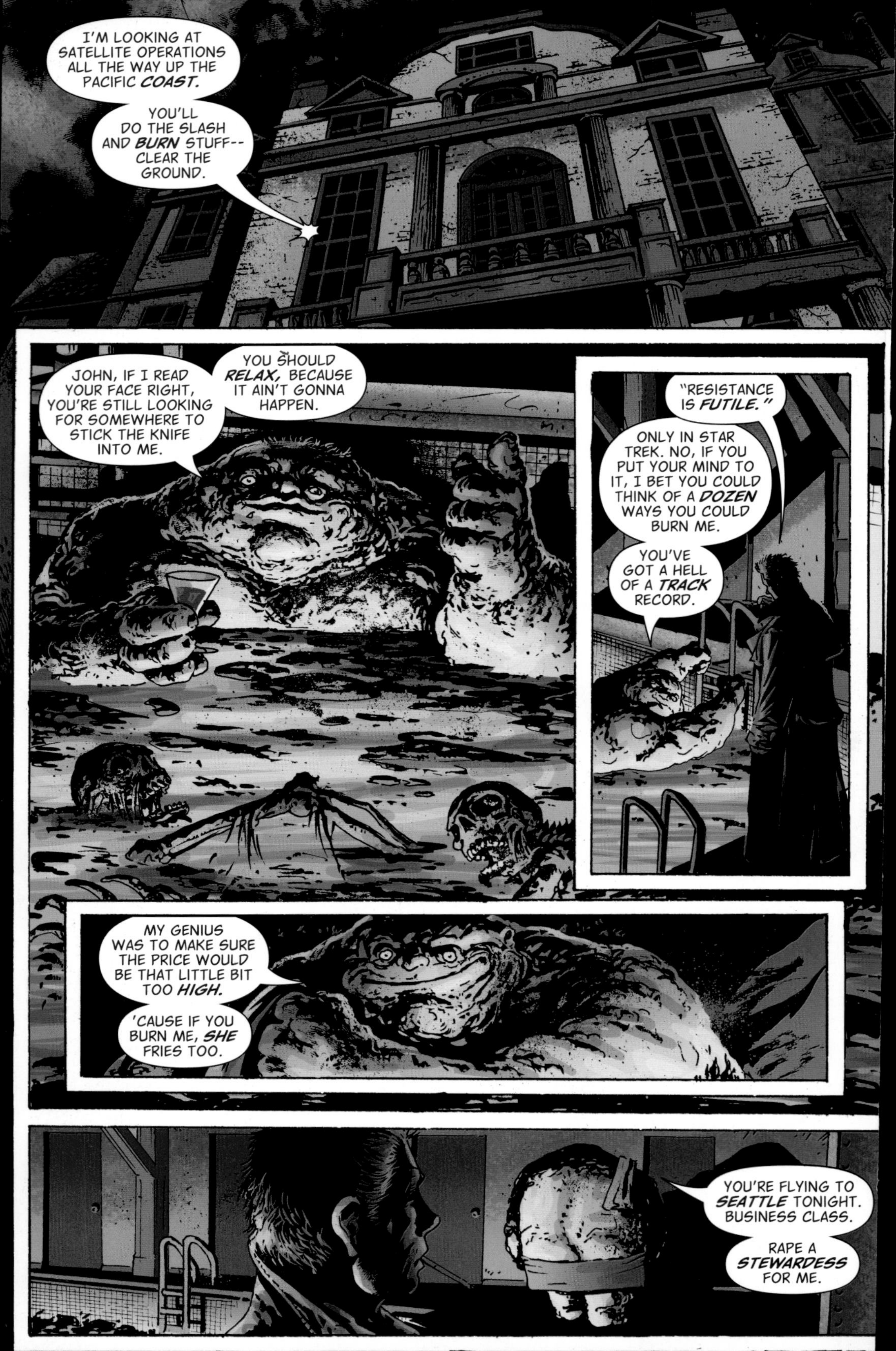
I'M LOOKING AT SATELLITE OPERATIONS ALL THE WAY UP THE PACIFIC COAST.
YOU'LL DO THE SLASH AND BURN STUFF-- CLEAR THE GROUND.
JOHN, IF I READ YOUR FACE RIGHT, YOU'RE STILL LOOKING FOR SOMEWHERE TO STICK THE KNIFE INTO ME.
YOU SHOULD RELAX, BECAUSE IT AIN'T GONNA HAPPEN.
"RESISTANCE IS FUTILE."
ONLY IN STAR TREK. NO, IF YOU PUT YOUR MIND TO IT, I BET YOU COULD THINK OF A DOZEN WAYS YOU COULD BURN ME.
YOU'VE GOT A HELL OF A TRACK RECORD.
MY GENIUS WAS TO MAKE SURE THE PRICE WOULD BE THAT LITTLE BIT TOO HIGH.
'CAUSE IF YOU BURN ME, SHE FRIES TOO.
YOU'RE FLYING TO SEATTLE TONIGHT. BUSINESS CLASS.
RAPE A STEWARDESS FOR ME.

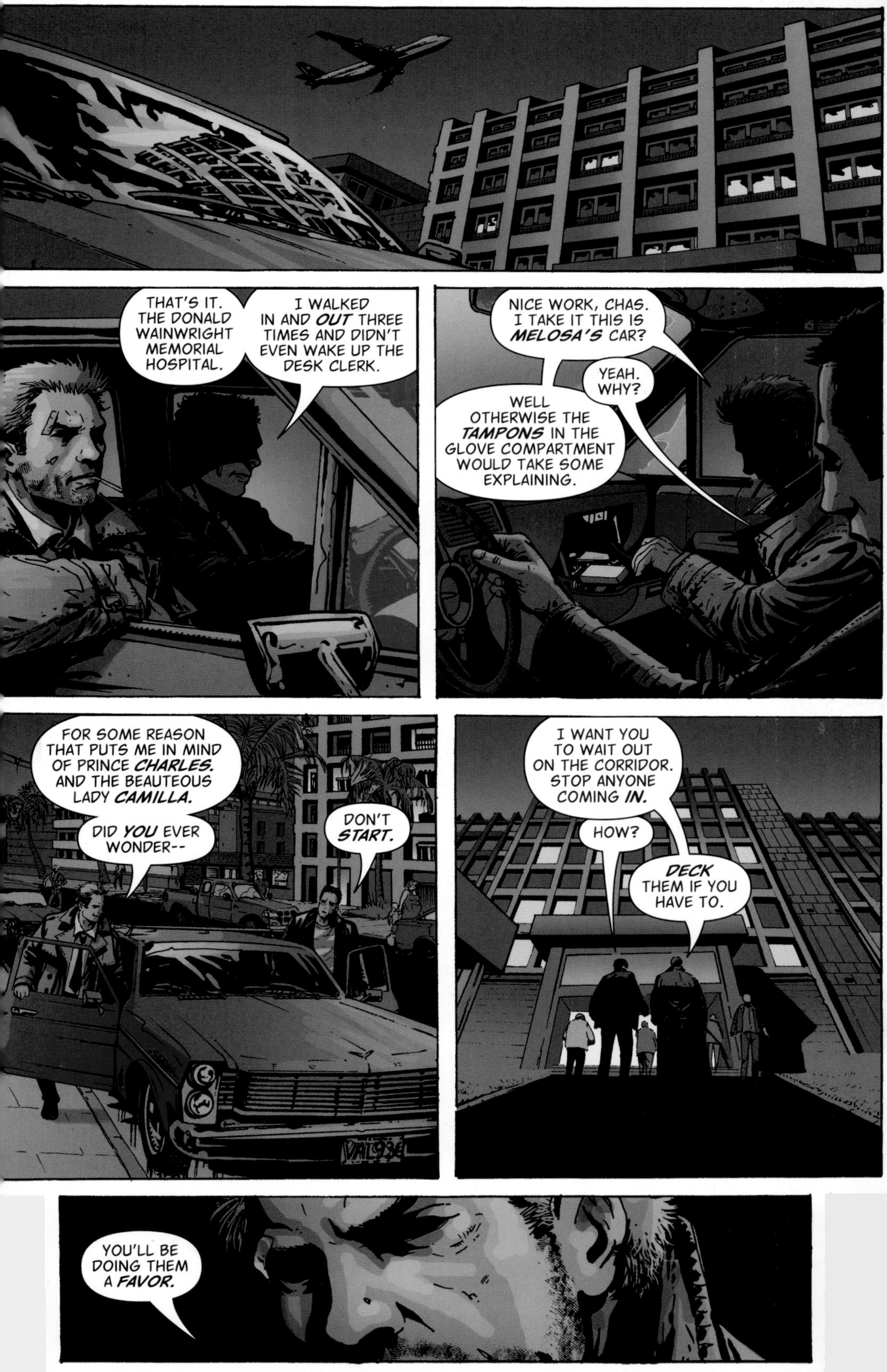
THAT'S IT. THE DONALD WAINWRIGHT MEMORIAL HOSPITAL.
I WALKED IN AND *OUT* THREE TIMES AND DIDN'T EVEN WAKE UP THE DESK CLERK.
NICE WORK, CHAS. I TAKE IT THIS IS *MELOSA'S* CAR?
YEAH. WHY?
WELL OTHERWISE THE *TAMPONS* IN THE GLOVE COMPARTMENT WOULD TAKE SOME EXPLAINING.
FOR SOME REASON THAT PUTS ME IN MIND OF PRINCE *CHARLES.* AND THE BEAUTEOUS LADY *CAMILLA.*
DID *YOU* EVER WONDER--
DON'T *START.*
VAL 93E
I WANT YOU TO WAIT OUT ON THE CORRIDOR. STOP ANYONE COMING *IN.*
HOW?
DECK THEM IF YOU HAVE TO.
YOU'LL BE DOING THEM A *FAVOR.*

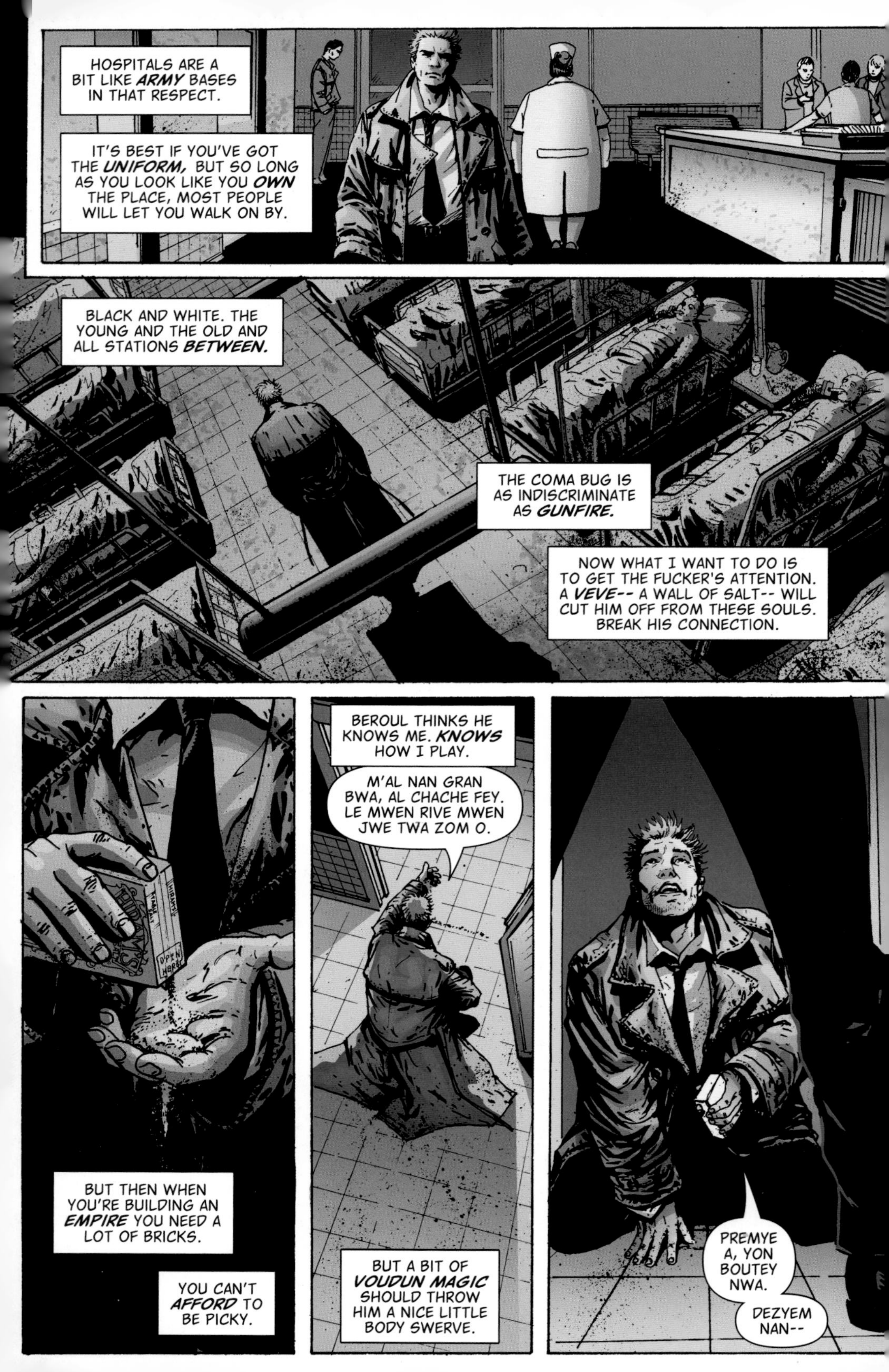

HOSPITALS ARE A BIT LIKE ARMY BASES IN THAT RESPECT.
IT'S BEST IF YOU'VE GOT THE UNIFORM, BUT SO LONG AS YOU LOOK LIKE YOU OWN THE PLACE, MOST PEOPLE WILL LET YOU WALK ON BY.
BLACK AND WHITE. THE YOUNG AND THE OLD AND ALL STATIONS BETWEEN.
THE COMA BUG IS AS INDISCRIMINATE AS GUNFIRE.
NOW WHAT I WANT TO DO IS TO GET THE FUCKER'S ATTENTION. A VEVE-- A WALL OF SALT-- WILL CUT HIM OFF FROM THESE SOULS. BREAK HIS CONNECTION.
BUT THEN WHEN YOU'RE BUILDING AN EMPIRE YOU NEED A LOT OF BRICKS.
YOU CAN'T AFFORD TO BE PICKY.
BEROUL THINKS HE KNOWS ME. KNOWS HOW I PLAY.
M'AL NAN GRAN BWA, AL CHACHE FEY. LE MWEN RIVE MWEN JWE TWA ZOM O.
BUT A BIT OF VOUDUN MAGIC SHOULD THROW HIM A NICE LITTLE BODY SWERVE.
PREMYE A, YON BOUTEY NWA.
DEZYEM NAN--

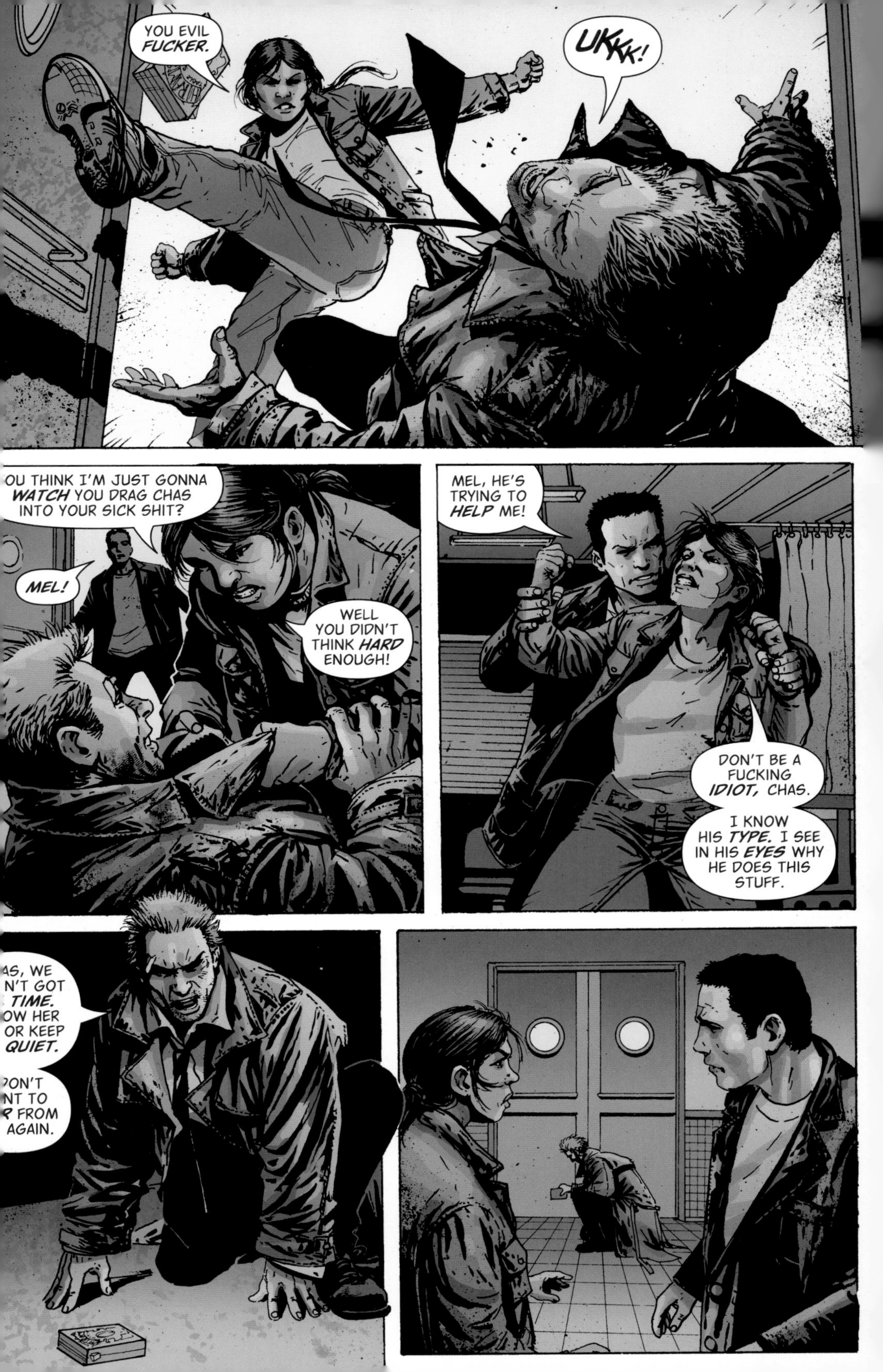

YOU EVIL FUCKER.
UKKK!
OU THINK I'M JUST GONNA WATCH YOU DRAG CHAS INTO YOUR SICK SHIT?
MEL!
WELL YOU DIDN'T THINK HARD ENOUGH!
MEL, HE'S TRYING TO HELP ME!
DON'T BE A FUCKING IDIOT, CHAS.
I KNOW HIS TYPE. I SEE IN HIS EYES WHY HE DOES THIS STUFF.
AS, WE N'T GOT TIME. OW HER OR KEEP QUIET.
DON'T NT TO FROM AGAIN.

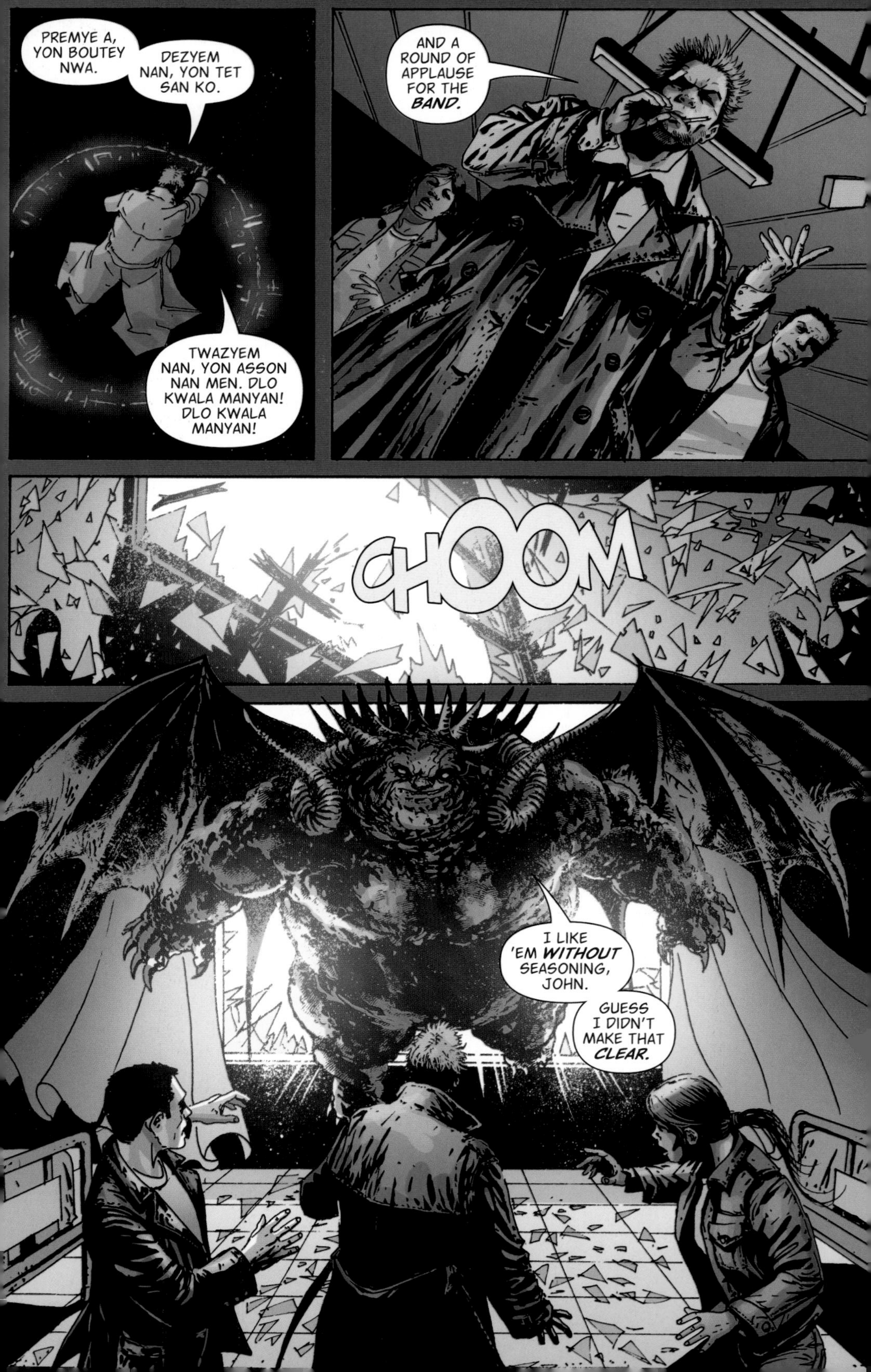
PREMYE A, YON BOUTEY NWA.
DEZYEM NAN, YON TET SAN KO.
TWAZYEM NAN, YON ASSON NAN MEN. DLO KWALA MANYAN! DLO KWALA MANYAN!
AND A ROUND OF APPLAUSE FOR THE BAND.
CHOOM
I LIKE 'EM WITHOUT SEASONING, JOHN.
GUESS I DIDN'T MAKE THAT CLEAR.

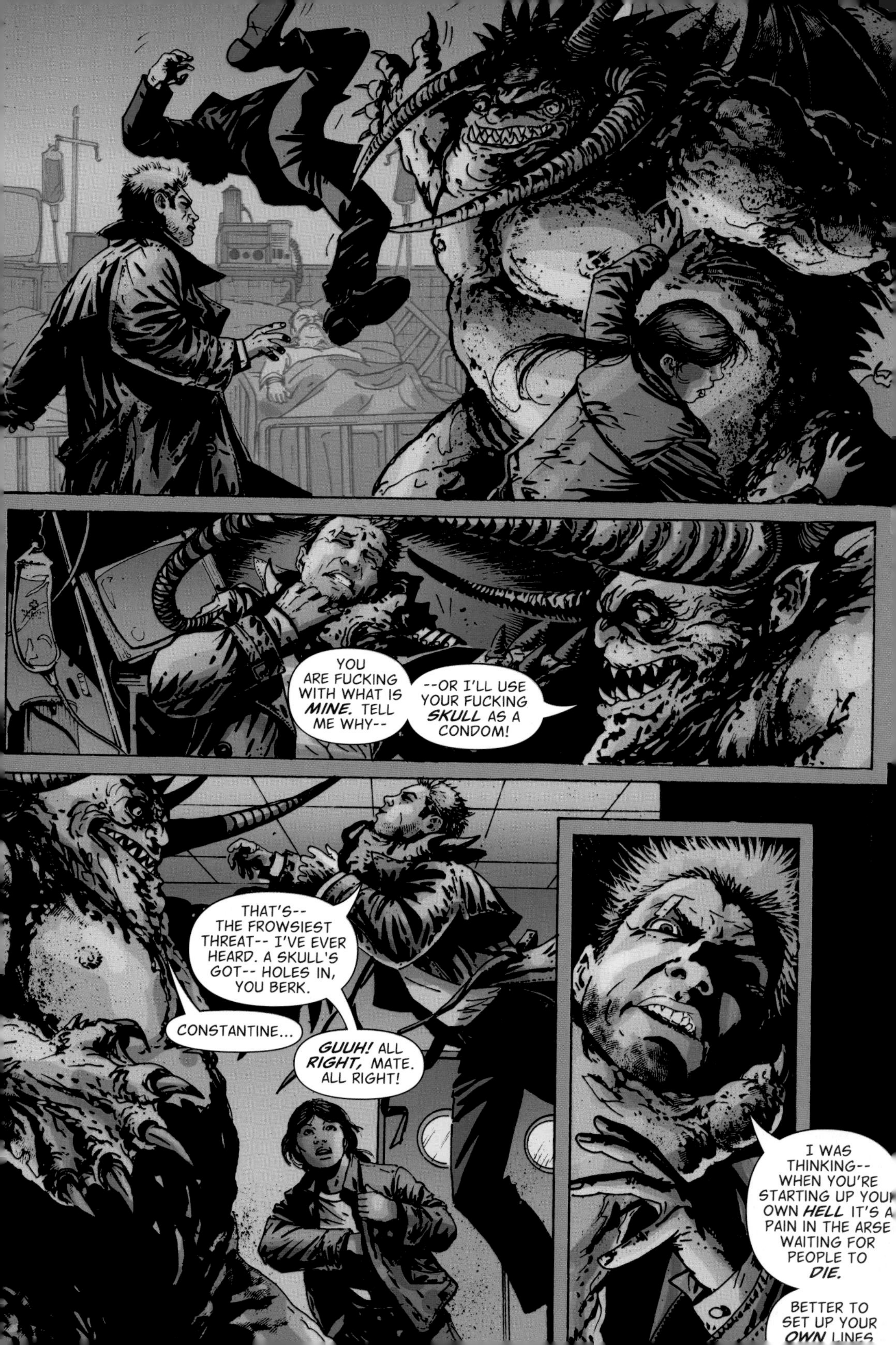
YOU ARE FUCKING WITH WHAT IS MINE. TELL ME WHY--
--OR I'LL USE YOUR FUCKING SKULL AS A CONDOM!
THAT'S-- THE FROWSIEST THREAT-- I'VE EVER HEARD. A SKULL'S GOT-- HOLES IN, YOU BERK.
CONSTANTINE...
GUUH! ALL RIGHT, MATE. ALL RIGHT!
I WAS THINKING-- WHEN YOU'RE STARTING UP YOU OWN HELL IT'S A PAIN IN THE ARSE WAITING FOR PEOPLE TO DIE.
BETTER TO SET UP YOUR OWN LINES

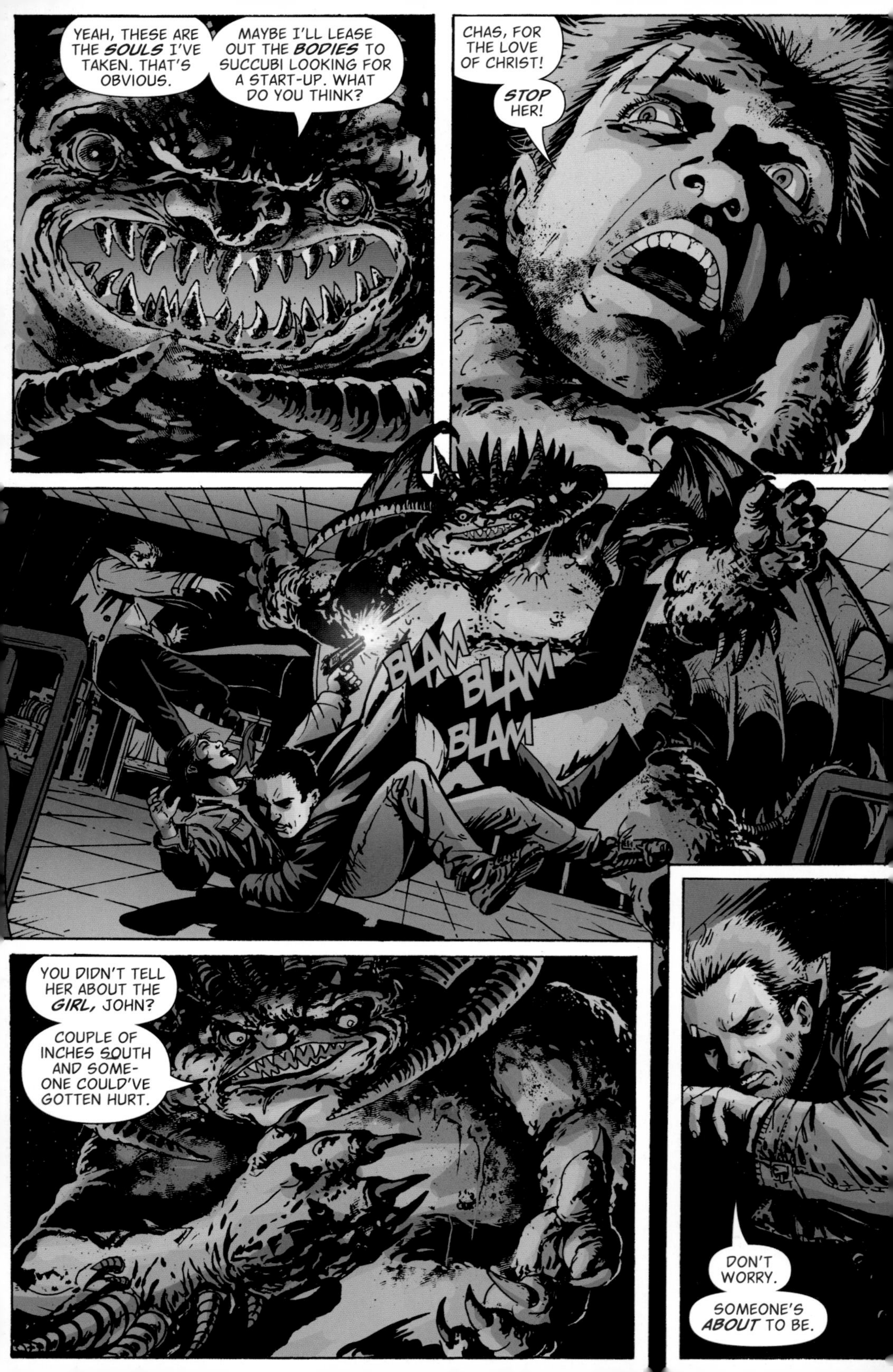
YEAH, THESE ARE THE SOULS I'VE TAKEN. THAT'S OBVIOUS.
MAYBE I'LL LEASE OUT THE BODIES TO SUCCUBI LOOKING FOR A START-UP. WHAT DO YOU THINK?
CHAS, FOR THE LOVE OF CHRIST!
STOP HER!
BLAM
BLAM
BLAM
YOU DIDN'T TELL HER ABOUT THE GIRL, JOHN?
COUPLE OF INCHES SOUTH AND SOME-ONE COULD'VE GOTTEN HURT.
DON'T WORRY.
SOMEONE'S ABOUT TO BE.

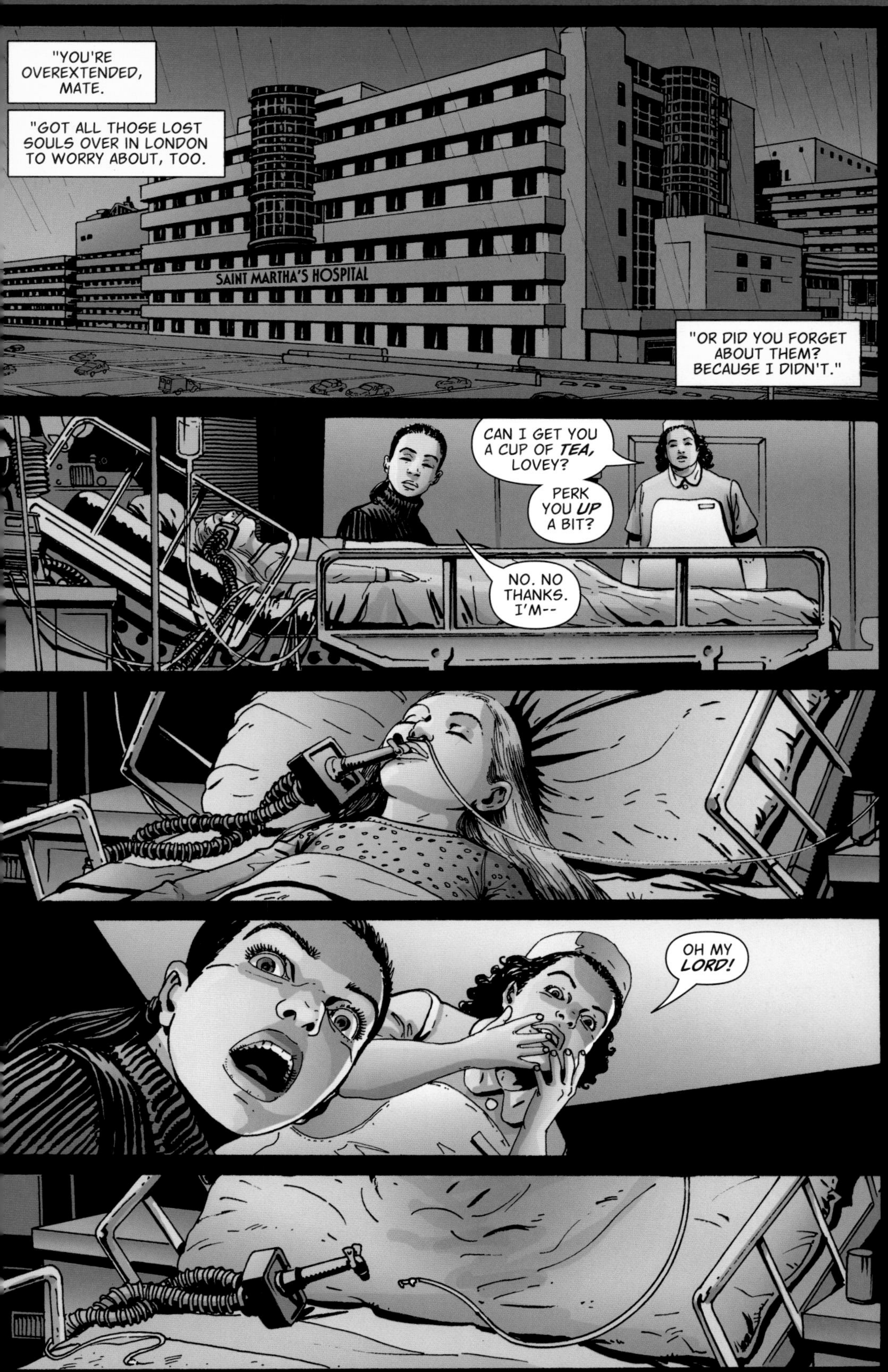
"YOU'RE OVEREXTENDED, MATE.
"GOT ALL THOSE LOST SOULS OVER IN LONDON TO WORRY ABOUT, TOO.
SAINT MARTHA'S HOSPITAL
"OR DID YOU FORGET ABOUT THEM? BECAUSE I DIDN'T."
CAN I GET YOU A CUP OF *TEA,* LOVEY?
PERK YOU *UP* A BIT?
NO. NO THANKS. I'M--
OH MY *LORD!*

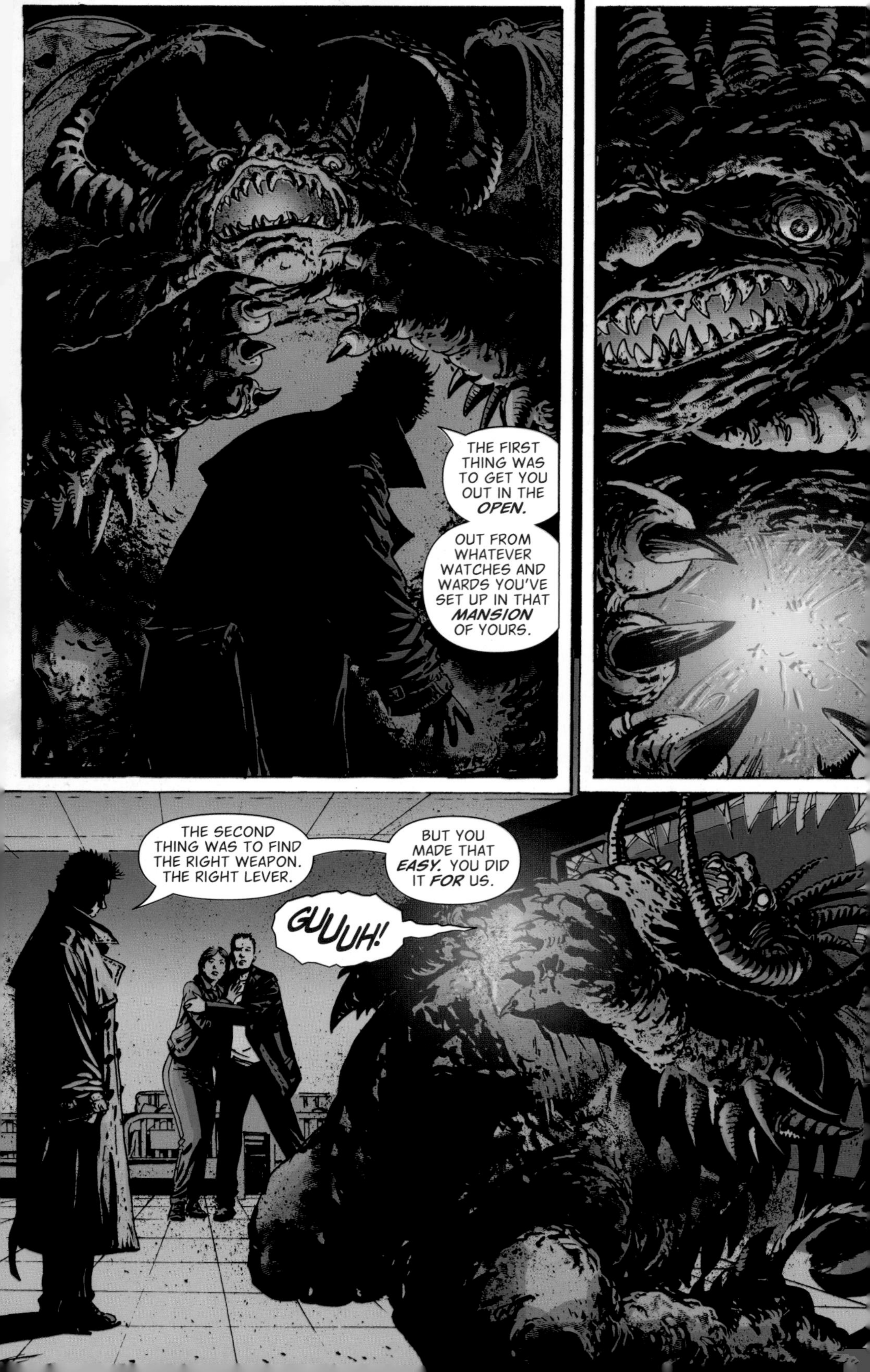
THE FIRST THING WAS TO GET YOU OUT IN THE OPEN.
OUT FROM WHATEVER WATCHES AND WARDS YOU'VE SET UP IN THAT MANSION OF YOURS.
THE SECOND THING WAS TO FIND THE RIGHT WEAPON. THE RIGHT LEVER.
BUT YOU MADE THAT EASY. YOU DID IT FOR US.
GUUUH!

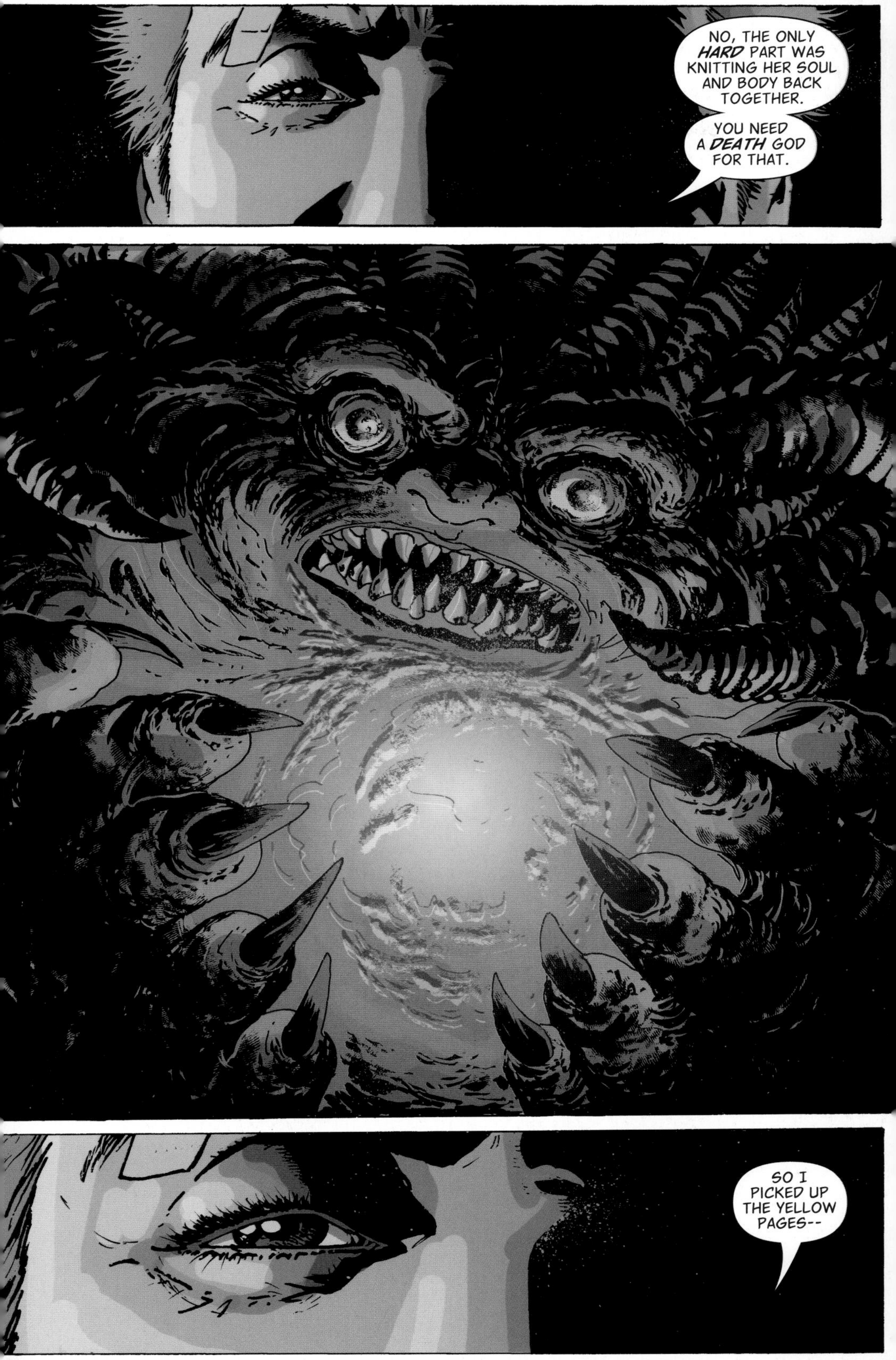
NO, THE ONLY HARD PART WAS KNITTING HER SOUL AND BODY BACK TOGETHER.
YOU NEED A DEATH GOD FOR THAT.
SO I PICKED UP THE YELLOW PAGES--

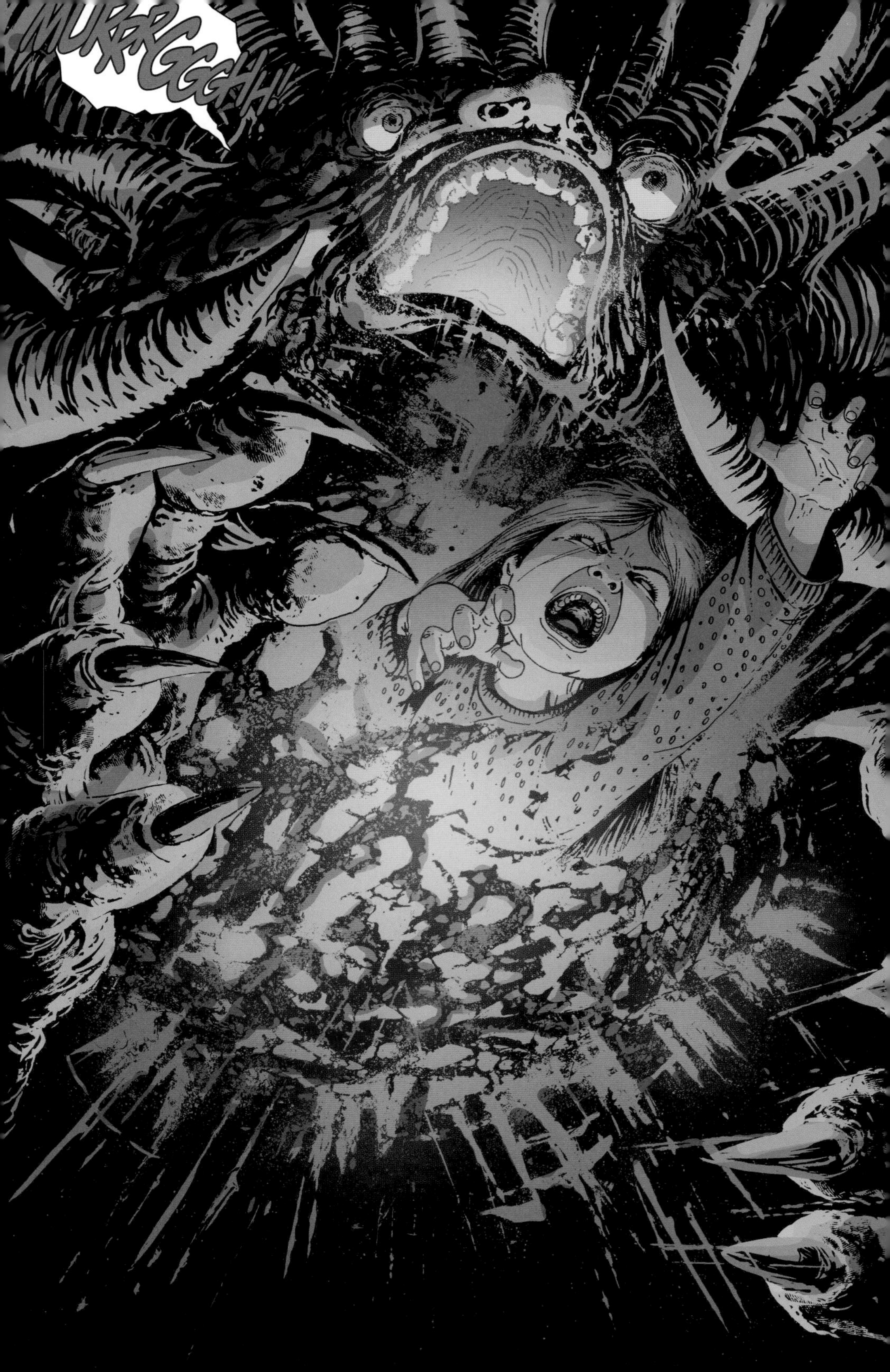
MURRRGGGHH!!

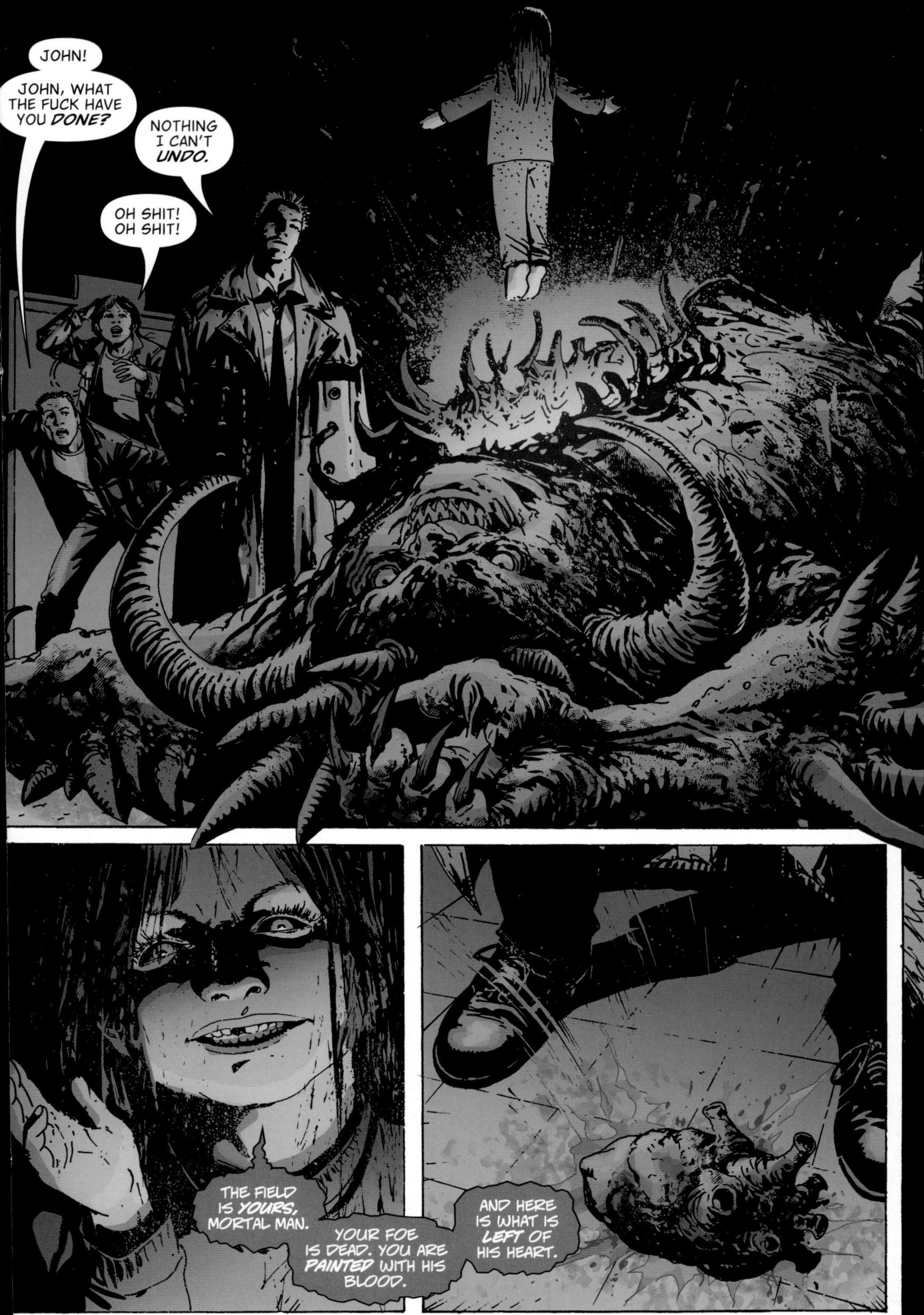
JOHN!
JOHN, WHAT THE FUCK HAVE YOU DONE?
NOTHING I CAN'T UNDO.
OH SHIT! OH SHIT!
THE FIELD IS YOURS, MORTAL MAN.
YOUR FOE IS DEAD. YOU ARE PAINTED WITH HIS BLOOD.
AND HERE IS WHAT IS LEFT OF HIS HEART.

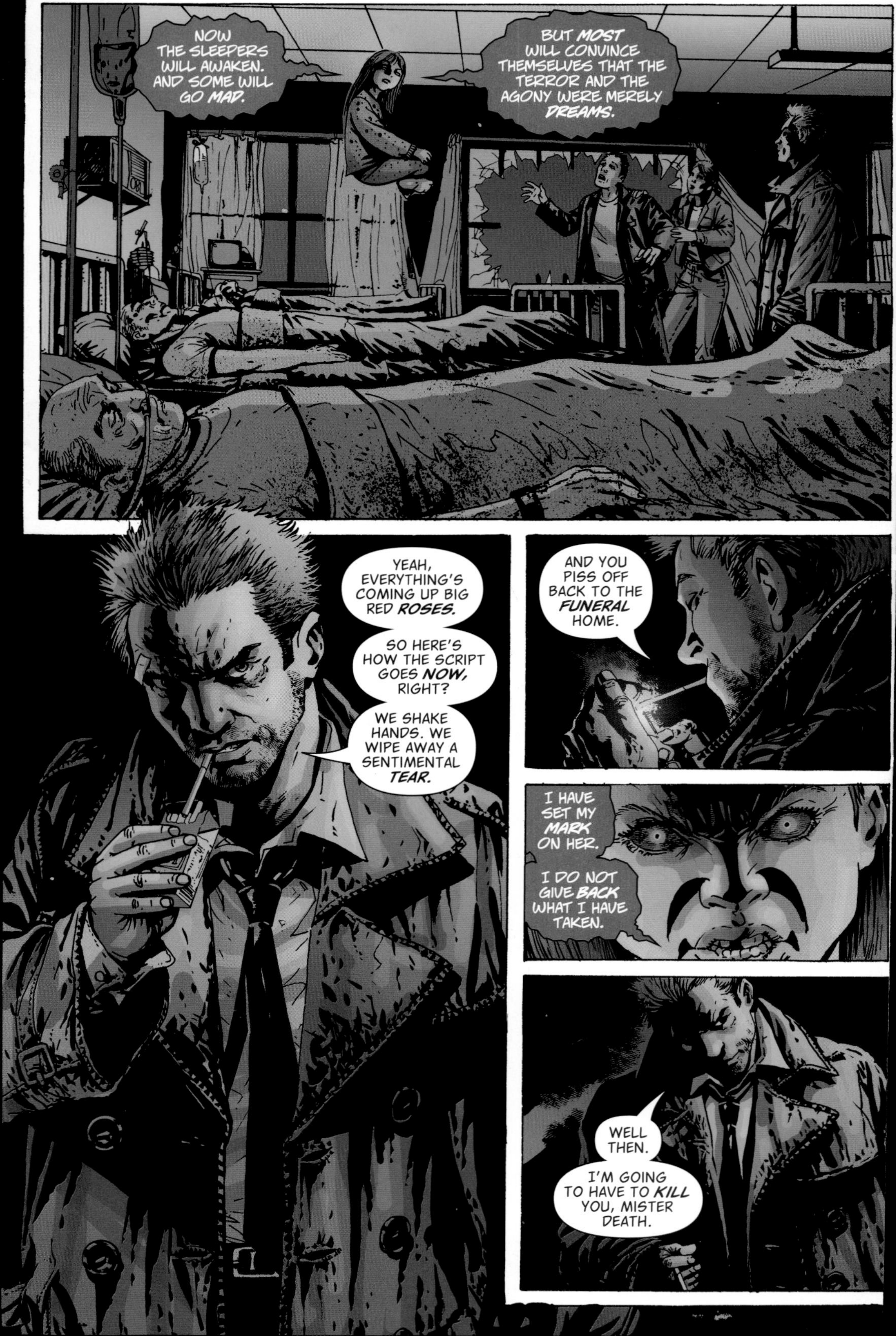
NOW THE SLEEPERS WILL AWAKEN. AND SOME WILL GO MAD.
BUT MOST WILL CONVINCE THEMSELVES THAT THE TERROR AND THE AGONY WERE MERELY DREAMS.
YEAH, EVERYTHING'S COMING UP BIG RED ROSES.
SO HERE'S HOW THE SCRIPT GOES NOW, RIGHT?
WE SHAKE HANDS. WE WIPE AWAY A SENTIMENTAL TEAR.
AND YOU PISS OFF BACK TO THE FUNERAL HOME.
I HAVE SET MY MARK ON HER.
I DO NOT GIVE BACK WHAT I HAVE TAKEN.
WELL THEN.
I'M GOING TO HAVE TO KILL YOU, MISTER DEATH.

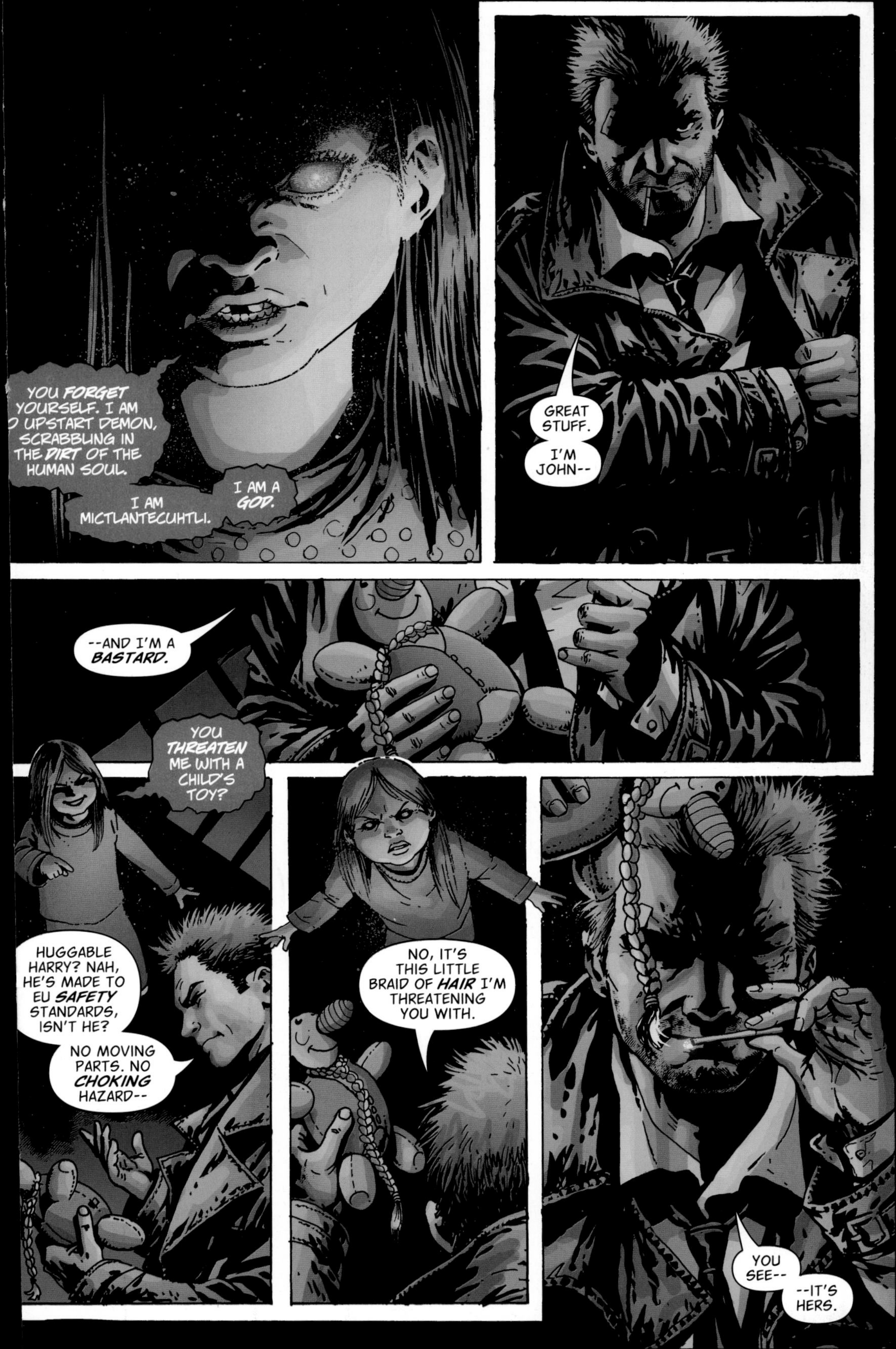
YOU FORGET YOURSELF. I AM NO UPSTART DEMON, SCRABBLING IN THE DIRT OF THE HUMAN SOUL.
I AM MICTLANTECUHTLI.
I AM A GOD.
GREAT STUFF.
I'M JOHN--
--AND I'M A BASTARD.
YOU THREATEN ME WITH A CHILD'S TOY?
HUGGABLE HARRY? NAH, HE'S MADE TO EU SAFETY STANDARDS, ISN'T HE?
NO MOVING PARTS. NO CHOKING HAZARD--
NO, IT'S THIS LITTLE BRAID OF HAIR I'M THREATENING YOU WITH.
YOU SEE--
--IT'S HERS.

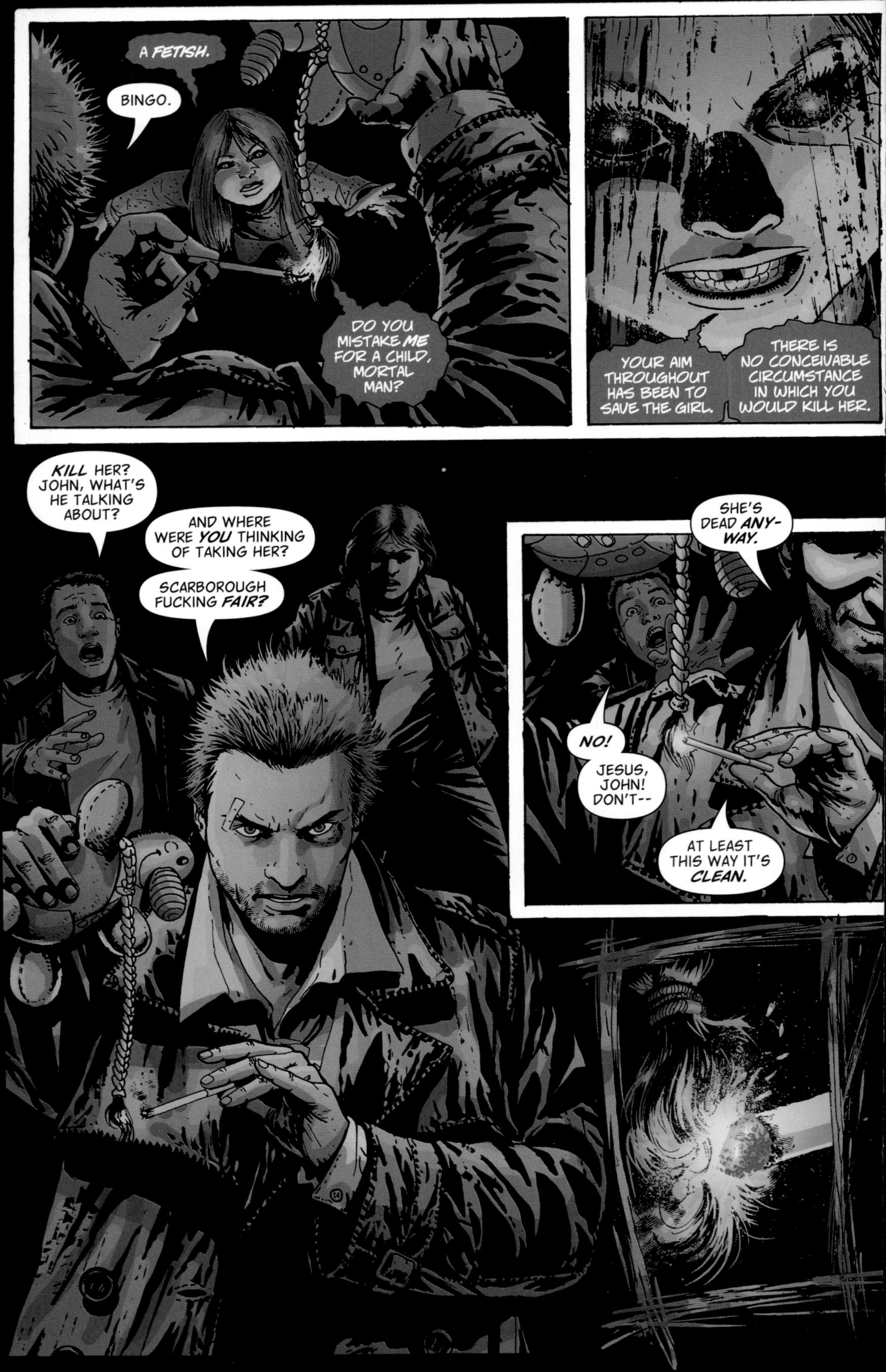
A FETISH.
BINGO.
DO YOU MISTAKE ME FOR A CHILD, MORTAL MAN?
YOUR AIM THROUGHOUT HAS BEEN TO SAVE THE GIRL.
THERE IS NO CONCEIVABLE CIRCUMSTANCE IN WHICH YOU WOULD KILL HER.
KILL HER? JOHN, WHAT'S HE TALKING ABOUT?
AND WHERE WERE YOU THINKING OF TAKING HER?
SCARBOROUGH FUCKING FAIR?
SHE'S DEAD ANY-WAY.
NO!
JESUS, JOHN! DON'T--
AT LEAST THIS WAY IT'S CLEAN.

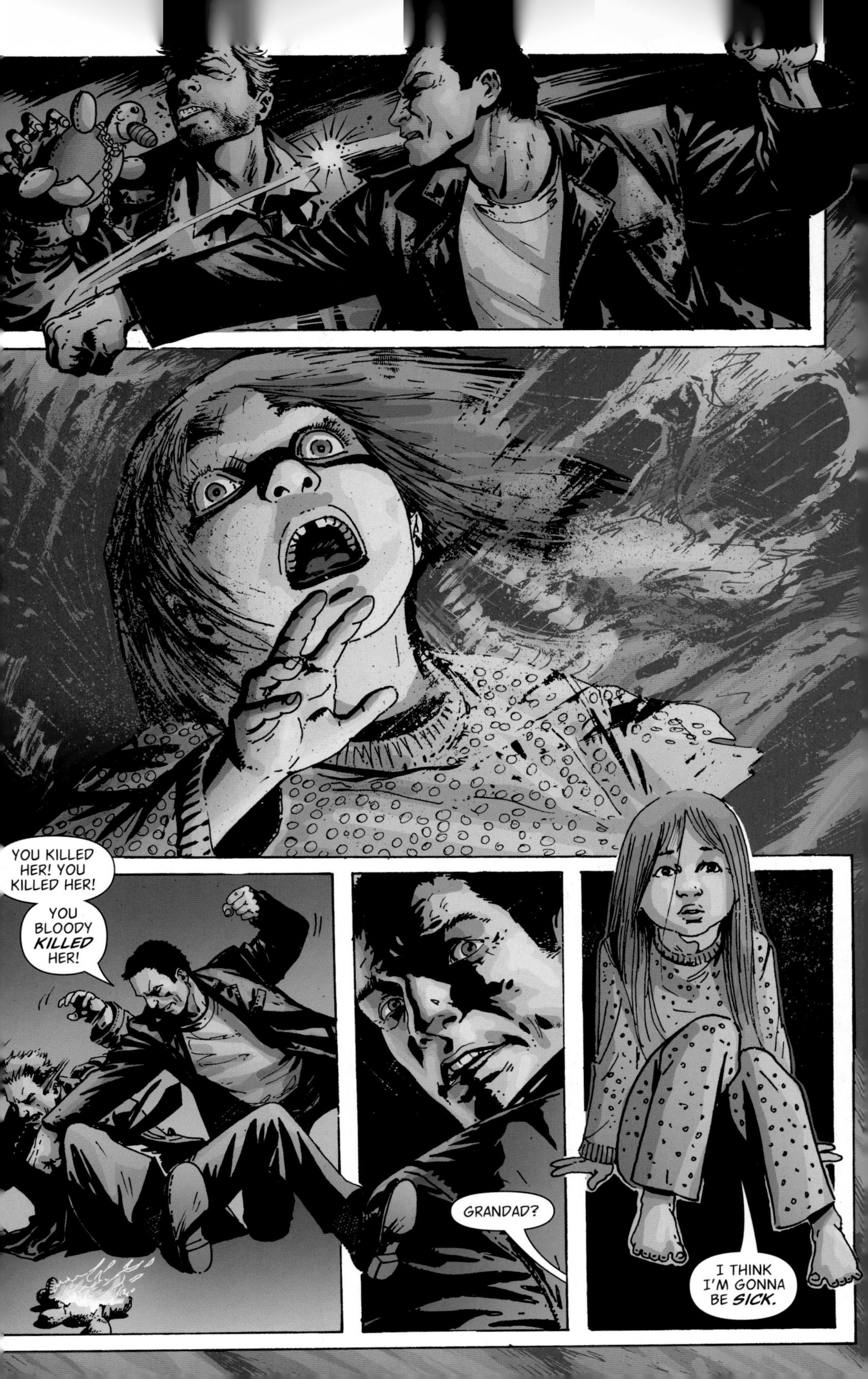
YOU KILLED HER! YOU KILLED HER!
YOU BLOODY KILLED HER!
GRANDAD?
I THINK I'M GONNA BE SICK.

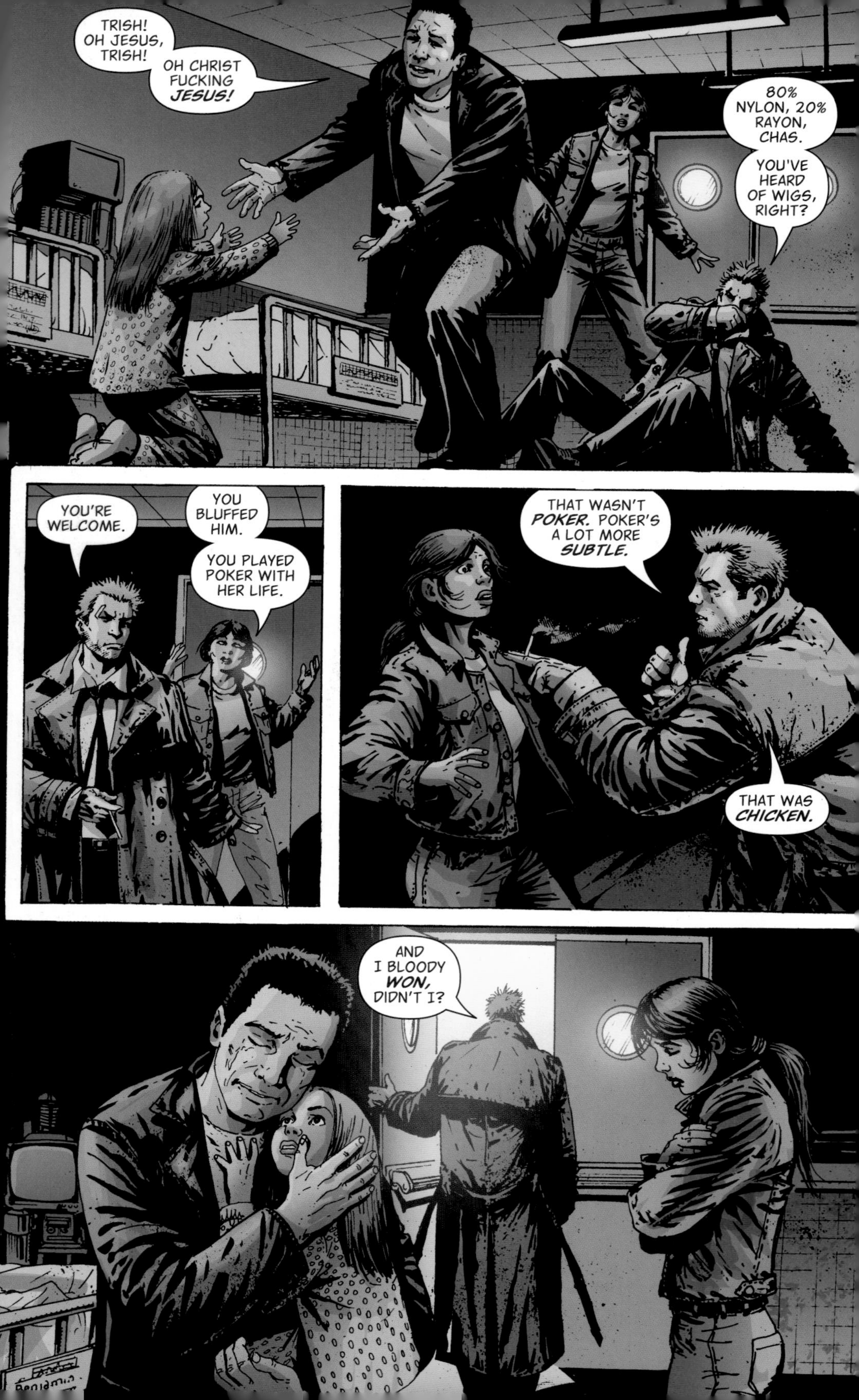
TRISH! OH JESUS, TRISH!
OH CHRIST FUCKING JESUS!
80% NYLON, 20% RAYON, CHAS.
YOU'VE HEARD OF WIGS, RIGHT?
YOU'RE WELCOME.
YOU BLUFFED HIM.
YOU PLAYED POKER WITH HER LIFE.
THAT WASN'T POKER. POKER'S A LOT MORE SUBTLE.
THAT WAS CHICKEN.
AND I BLOODY WON, DIDN'T I?

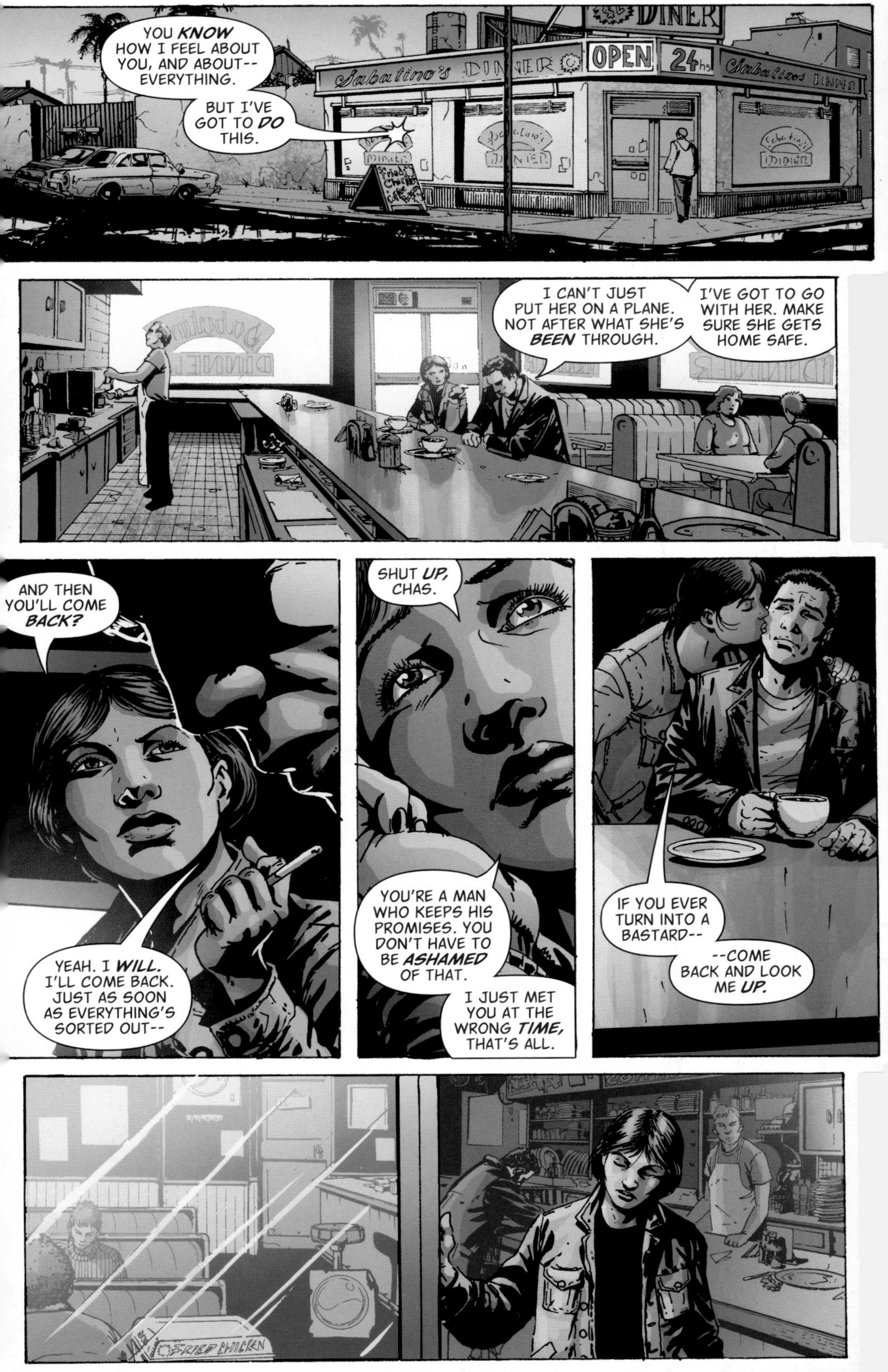
DINER
OPEN
24hs
Sabatino's DINNER
YOU KNOW HOW I FEEL ABOUT YOU, AND ABOUT-- EVERYTHING.
BUT I'VE GOT TO DO THIS.
I CAN'T JUST PUT HER ON A PLANE. NOT AFTER WHAT SHE'S BEEN THROUGH.
I'VE GOT TO GO WITH HER. MAKE SURE SHE GETS HOME SAFE.
AND THEN YOU'LL COME BACK?
YEAH. I WILL. I'LL COME BACK. JUST AS SOON AS EVERYTHING'S SORTED OUT--
SHUT UP, CHAS.
YOU'RE A MAN WHO KEEPS HIS PROMISES. YOU DON'T HAVE TO BE ASHAMED OF THAT.
I JUST MET YOU AT THE WRONG TIME, THAT'S ALL.
IF YOU EVER TURN INTO A BASTARD--
--COME BACK AND LOOK ME UP.

YOU'RE TRYING TO *HUSTLE* ME.

DIDN'T ANYONE EVER TELL YOU HOW *DANGEROUS* THAT IS?

HAVE YOU GOT MRS. *BRICK* THE BUILDER'S WIFE?

REDHEAD WITH AN ARSE LIKE AN AIRCRAFT CARRIER? SORRY, CAN'T *HELP* YOU.

COME ON, TRI! WE'VE G TO GC

BEFORE UNCLE JOHN YOU GAMBI FOR *MON*

WHAT'S HER MARKER *WORTH* TO YOU? I'VE GOT A POCKETFUL OF THEM.

ARE YOU *SURE* ABOUT GIVING TRISH YOUR TICKET?

I MOVE IN MYSTERIOUS WAYS, CHAS. I'LL *WALK* HOME.

BUT I'VE GOT A *BEER* TO FINISH FIRST.

YOU STOOD *BY* ME, MATE. YOU DID ME *PROUD.*

YEAH, BUT I ONLY DID IT TO PISS *RENEE* OFF, SO IT COUNTS AS A SIN.

DON'T FORGET YOUR *SICK* BAGS, CHAS.

HAPPY FAMILIES. WHAT'S *THAT* ALL ABOUT, EH?

A BLOO

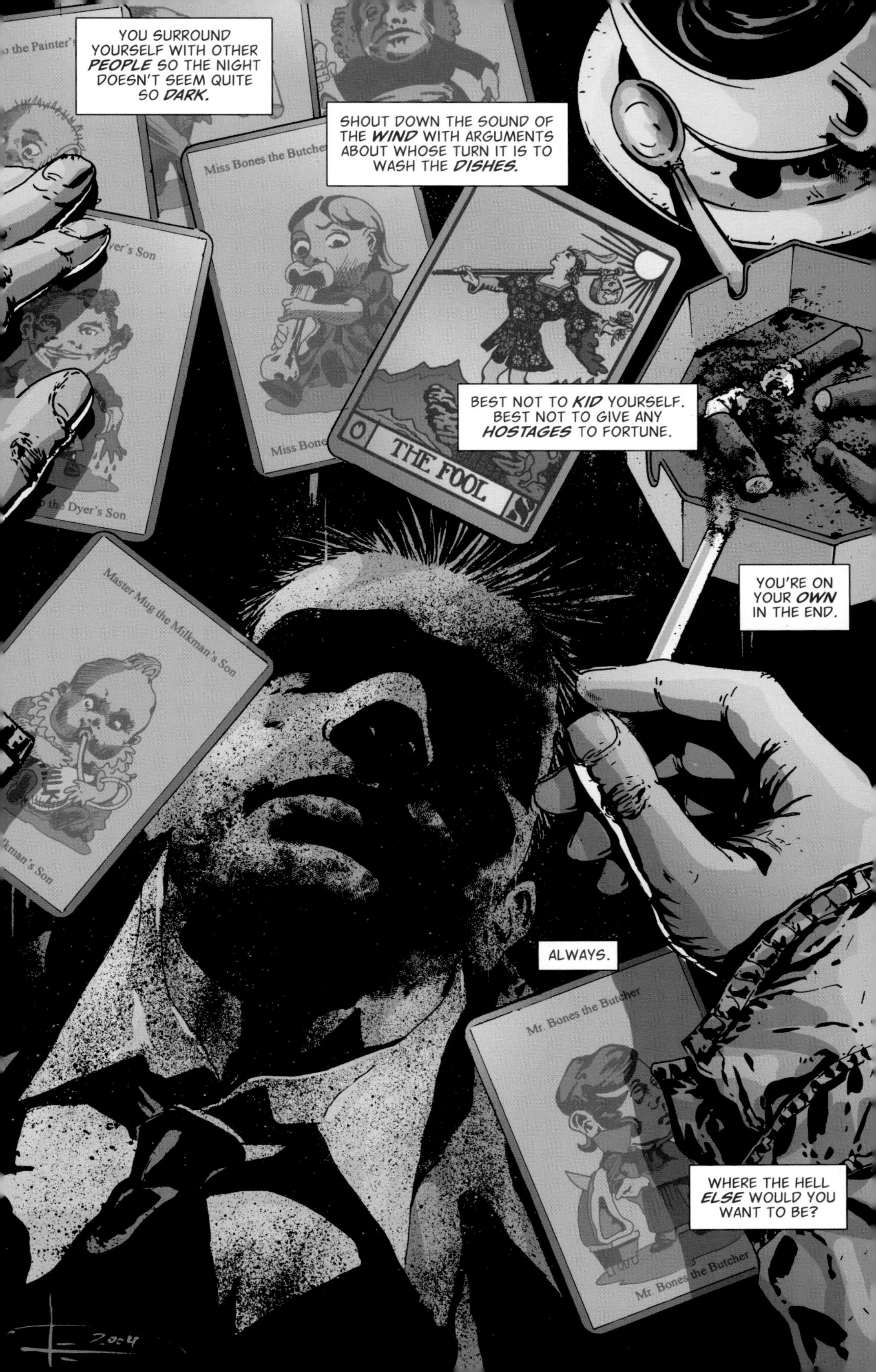
YOU SURROUND YOURSELF WITH OTHER *PEOPLE* SO THE NIGHT DOESN'T SEEM QUITE SO *DARK.*
SHOUT DOWN THE SOUND OF THE *WIND* WITH ARGUMENTS ABOUT WHOSE TURN IT IS TO WASH THE *DISHES.*
Miss Bones the Butcher
THE FOOL
BEST NOT TO *KID* YOURSELF. BEST NOT TO GIVE ANY *HOSTAGES* TO FORTUNE.
Master Mug the Milkman's Son
YOU'RE ON YOUR *OWN* IN THE END.
ALWAYS.
Mr. Bones the Butcher
WHERE THE HELL *ELSE* WOULD YOU WANT TO BE?
Mr. Bones the Butcher

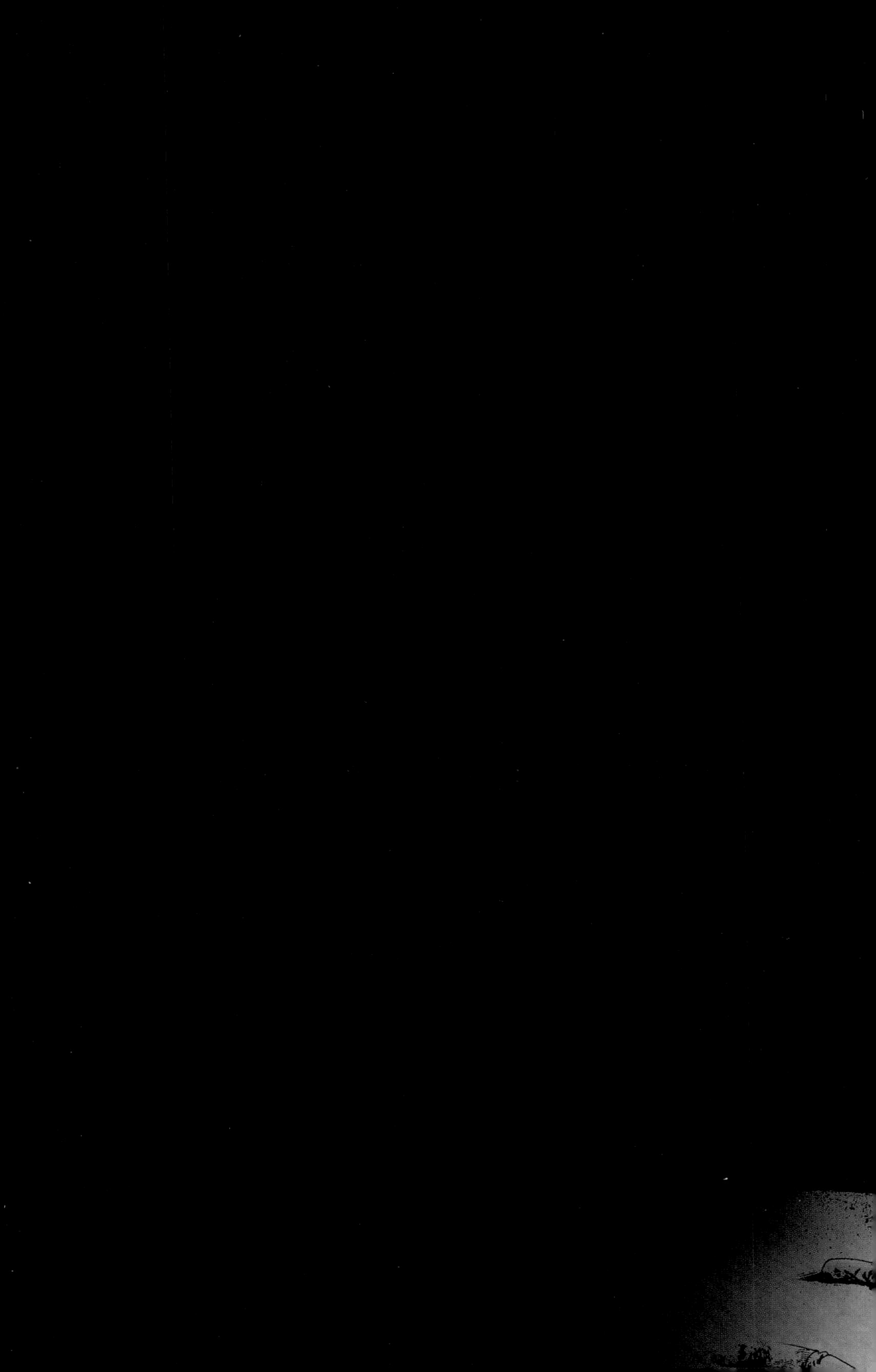

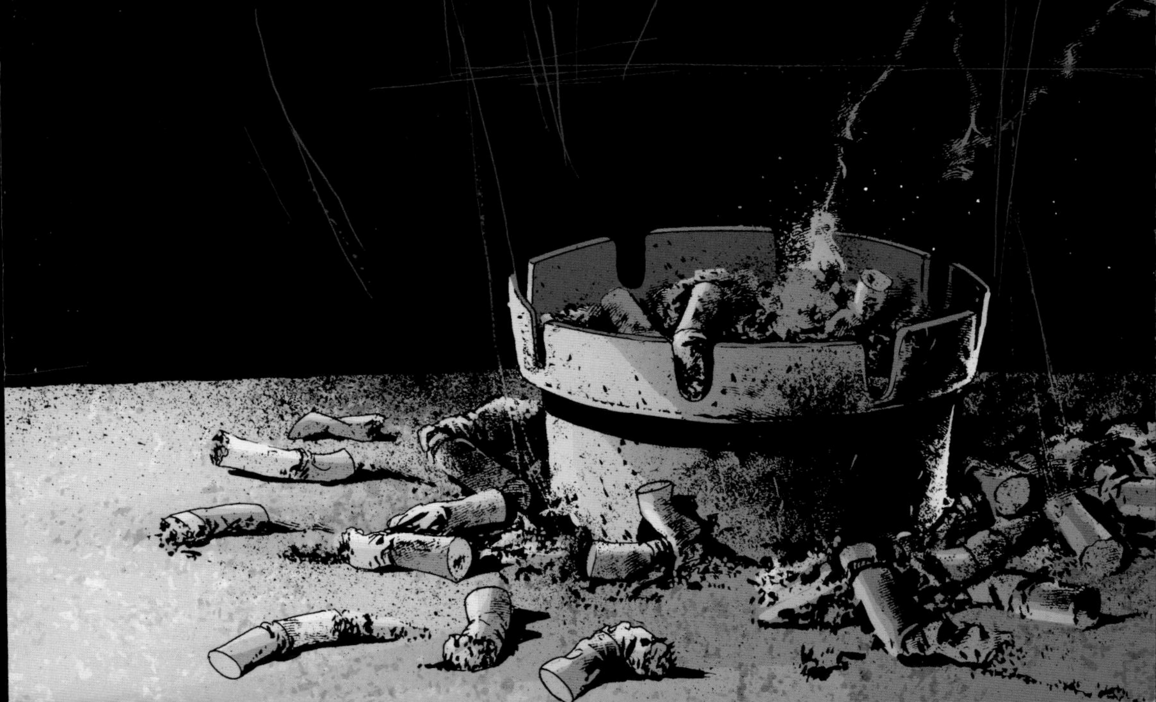

MIKE CAREY lives in London with his family which now includes a cat—a fact which puzzles him because he doesn't have the faintest idea where she came from. He's been writing comics for 15 years, starting with the UK anthology title *Toxic!*, now deceased. In fact, he worked for quite a few companies that have died since. Pretty suspicious, when you think about it.

His credits include LUCIFER, HELLBLAZER and MY FAITH IN FRANKIE for DC/Vertigo comics, and *Inferno* from Titan books. He looks fairly normal, up to a point. Just don't remove the bracelet from his left arm, or walk widdershins around him under a full moon.

Or buy him a drink.

LEONARDO MANCO was born in the coastal city of Mar del Plata, Argentina, in 1971, and now resides in Buenos Aires. He started his career when he was 19 years old, and in 1991 made his stateside debut at Marvel Comics with *Hellstorm: Prince of Lies*. He has since then continued working for the American market, pencilling and inking such titles as *Blaze o. Glory, Apache Skies, Doom, Nick Fury/Captain Americ* for Marvel, and BATMAN, which opened the doors of DC Comics for him.

Manco recently became the ongoing monthly artist or HELLBLAZER for DC/Vertigo, which he states is "one of my greatest artistic passions." Another of his passions is watching his son, Augusto, grow, and take him for rides on endless highways to visit strange and exciting places. The problem is his son is able to retu to reality, but Leo… well, he can't.

ZYLONOL STUDIO was formed in 1996 by Lee Loughridge. Based in Savannah, Georgia, Zylonol has work on hundreds of titles over the past 10 years. Current titles include DC/Vertigo's HELLBLAZER, Y: THE LAST MAN HUMAN TARGET, ANGELTOWN and THE LOSERS.